RELIGIOUS EXPERIENCE
IN
EARLIEST CHRISTIANITY

RELIGIOUS EXPERIENCE IN EARLIEST CHRISTIANITY

*A Missing Dimension
in New Testament Studies*

Luke Timothy Johnson

Fortress Press   Minneapolis

To Joy

RELIGIOUS EXPERIENCE IN EARLIEST CHRISTIANITY
A Missing Dimension In New Testament Studies

Copyright © 1998 Augsburg Fortress. All rights reserved. Except for brief quotations in critical articles or reviews, no part of this book may be reproduced in any manner without prior written permission from the publisher. Write: Permissions, Augsburg Fortress, Box 1209, Minneapolis, MN 55440.

Cover design by Mike Mihelich.
Cover illustration, *La Cène,* courtesy of the Musée d'Unterlinden, Colmar, France.

Library of Congress Cataloging-in-Publication Data
ISBN 0-8006-3129-3

The paper used in this publication meets the minimum requirements of American National Standard for Information Sciences — Permanence of Paper for Printed Library Materials, ANSI Z329.48-1984.

Manufactured in the U.S.A.   AF 1-3129

02   01   00   99   98   1   2   3   4   5   6   7   8   9   10

CONTENTS

PREFACE

This short book began as the 1997 Stone Lectures at Princeton Theological Seminary and develops a straightforward sort of argument. Beginning with the observation that the dominant paradigms for studying early Christianity tend to miss its specifically religious character, I argue the need for a phenomenological approach to religious experience in early Christianity and then, in three case studies, try to show how it might be done. The Epilogue draws together the explicit and implicit lines of the argument.

This is neither history in the strict sense of the term, nor is it theology. That's the whole point: we need a new way of looking in order to see what we can't otherwise see. If I have succeeded at least in whetting an appetite for getting at what these chapters try to get at, I am content, for what they try to get at is important.

I am grateful to President Thomas Gillespie for the invitation to lecture at Princeton, and to the entire Princeton Theological Seminary community for the welcome it accorded me and these presentations. As customary, one of these lectures, "Glossolalia and the Embarrassments of Experience," has been published in *The Princeton Seminary Bulletin*. Mary Foskett played an important role in the early stages of preparation of these lectures as conversation partner and researcher. In the latter phases, David Charnon gave invaluable assistance as researcher (especially in the Philo material) and as critical reader. Others who helped by reading or being (more or less willing) conversation partners are Carl Holladay, Steve Kraftchick, David Moessner, and Todd Penner. They did the best they could and bear no blame for the remaining deficiencies in plan or execution.

ABBREVIATIONS

ANRW   W. Haase and H. Temporini, eds., *Aufstieg und Niedergang der römischen Welt* (Berlin/New York: de Gruyter, 1972–)

BETL   Bibliotheca ephemeridum theologicarum lovaniensium

EPRO   Études préliminaires aux religions orientales dans l'empire Romain

FRLANT   Forschungen zur Religion und Literatur des Alten und Neuen Testaments

GBS   Guides to Biblical Scholarship

JSNTSup   Journal for the Study of the New Testament Supplement Series

JSOTS   Journal for the Study of the Old Testament Supplement Series

NovTestSup   Novum Testamentum Supplements

SANT   Studien zum Alten und Neuen Testament

SBLDS   Society of Biblical Literature Dissertation Series

TDNT   G. Kittel and G. Friedrich, eds., *Theological Dictionary of the New Testament*

ZNW   *Zeitschrift für die neutestamentliche Wissenschaft und die Kunde der älteren Kirche*

WHAT'S MISSING FROM CHRISTIAN ORIGINS

The back of a typical Catholic church in America suggests a different religious world than does the front. In the sanctuary everything is orderly and correct. From the altar and the pulpit formulas from books or discourses based on those books are spoken. Both furniture and iconography reflect institutional power and its celestial counterpart: the choirs of saints and angels are placed below the throne of the pantocrator depicted on the ceiling of the apse, just as the bishop's cathedra, priest's presiding chair, and stools of the lesser ministers express a more obvious arrangement of power.

In the vestibule of the church, however, another religious world thrives. Here is the parish book of needs, with its astonishing catalogue of pains and anxieties and desires, spelled out for all the world to peruse. Here is the bulletin board with its brochures and announcements democratically stuck any which way, announcing Mary's appearance at this farmer's property, and charismatic prayer at this parishioner's house; novenas said to St. Jude, and pilgrimages to nearby shrines; healing services at the convent, and meetings gathered in the name of various saints, with no distinction between them on the basis of celestial rank or even historical existence.

At the front of the church, religion is much concerned with correctness: of doctrine, morality, authority, procedure. Back in the vestibule, religion is much more about the experience of transforming power in any available form. The issue is not whether St. Philomena lived but whether prayer to her cures cancer, not whether Mary's latest declarations in the presence of a harried housewife square with papal decrees but whether pilgrimage to the place of Mary's appearance might transform this family.

The genius of Catholicism has been its ability to hold these two worlds of religion — the world of formal discourse and the world of informal power — together in some sort of creative tension. Academic study of the religion called Christianity has been far less successful at holding the two worlds together. Compared to the volume of scholarship devoted to Christian theology and institutional development, attention to Christian religious experience lags far behind.[1]

One reason why scholarship has privileged formal religion is that religious studies originated among scholars comfortable in the world of clerical religion, not least because it is centered in legitimized texts and predictable routines.

1. The study of popular Christianity has significantly been advanced in recent years. Among outstanding examples, see (for the ancient period) P. Brown, "The Rise and Function of the Holy Man in Late Antiquity," in *Society and the Holy in Late Antiquity* (Berkeley: University of California Press, 1981) 103–52; idem, *The Body and Society: Men, Women, and Sexual Renunciation in Early Christianity* (New York: Columbia University Press, 1988); idem, *The Cult of the Saints: Its Rise and Function in Latin Christianity* (Chicago: University of Chicago Press). For the Medieval period, see C. W. Bynum, *Holy Feast and Holy Fast: The Religious Significance of Food to Medieval Women* (Berkeley: University of California Press, 1987); idem, *Jesus as Mother: Studies in the Spirituality of the High Middle Ages* (Berkeley: University of California Press, 1982); idem, *The Resurrection of the Body in Western Christianity, 200–1336* (Lectures on the History of Religions 15; New York: Columbia University Press, 1995). For the contemporary period, see M. J. Weaver, *New Catholic Women: A Contemporary Challenge to Traditional Religious Authority* (New York: Harper and Row, 1986); R. Orsi, *The Madonna of 115th Street* (New Haven: Yale University Press, 1985); idem, *Thank You, St. Jude: Women's Devotion to the Patron Saint of Hopeless Causes* (New Haven: Yale University Press, 1996); C. McDannell, *Material Christianity: Religion and Popular Culture in America* (New Haven: Yale University Press, 1995).

The fortuitous fit between texts that scholars could control and the claim of those texts to represent "true religion" — as distinguished from the messily demotic and oral world of "popular religion" — helped fix attention on formal scripture, doctrine, morality, and institution as the appropriate defining elements in Christianity. The academic study of Christianity has also been subtly influenced by the distinctively Protestant conviction that the world of saints and appearances and relics and pilgrimages and ecstasy and healing is not "authentic" religion, certainly not "authentically Christian," and should therefore be relegated to a separate category called "popular religion," deserving of dismissal rather than serious study. Authentic Christianity, in this perspective, is a matter of theological principles and actions based on them. It is certainly not a matter of negotiating spiritual powers. Thinking of religion in terms of power sounds like magic or paganism or, to draw the obvious if not always explicitly expressed conclusion, Roman Catholicism.[2]

The dual bias in favor of the textually defined and the theologically correct has profoundly affected the academic study of earliest Christianity, with the dual result that the beginnings of Christianity remain religiously *terra incognita* and that much of what the earliest Christian texts talked about is simply ignored. On one side, then, we possess marvelously intricate and methodologically sophisticated scholarship about early Christianity, a veritable mountain of learning about every word of the New Testament and its milieu, every literary seam, every possible source, every discernible pulse of

2. For analysis of this tendency, see Jonathan Z. Smith, *Drudgery Divine: On the Comparison of Early Christianities and the Religions of Late Antiquity* (The Jordan Lectures in Comparative Religion 14; Chicago: University of Chicago Press, 1990) 1–35; idem, "The Temple and the Magician," in *Map Is Not Territory: Studies in the History of Religions* (Studies in Judaism in Later Antiquity, ed. J. Neusner, vol. 23; Leiden: E. J. Brill, 1978) 188; and idem, "Earth and Gods," in *Map Is Not Territory*, 107–8.

historical development. On the other side, we are virtually ignorant concerning a remarkable range of statements in the
New Testament that appear to be of first importance to the
writers, that seem to express fundamental convictions, that
demand some kind of account, but that all of our learning
does not touch. This range of statements has to do with religious experience and power. Our inability to deal with this
register of language, I suggest, has complex causes within
scholarship, including a bias in favor of theology against religion, and the lack of an epistemology specifically calibrated
to the religious dimensions of human existence.

My task in this first chapter is to indicate some elements
of this register of language and the ways in which scholarship
has missed (widely or narrowly) accounting for it. In the next
chapter I suggest a mode of knowing that might enable us, if
not to understand, at least to apprehend and appreciate the
realities of which such language speaks. The next three chapters will then take up analysis of specific religious phenomena
in the New Testament.

The Language of Religious Experience

The New Testament writings contain an impressive amount
of experiential language. By "experiential," I mean language
that does not serve primarily to state propositions about reality (whether with reference to God or to humans) so much
as to express, refer to, and argue from human experiences.
Indeed, the New Testament is remarkable among ancient religious texts for its high proportion of first-order discourse
about experience. Let me acknowledge immediately how difficult it is to define or analyze "human experience." Some of
the problems facing any such endeavor will be touched on
in the next chapter. But such conceptual difficulties should
not lead us to ignore the plain fact that it takes considerable effort to read through the pages of the New Testament

without encountering statements and claims about what the
writers and readers were either experiencing or had already
experienced.

We might expect to find such statements to be made by
Paul about himself, since he has the reputation of being a
mystic and a certifiable "religious type."[3] But Paul includes his
readers as well as himself in such claims to experience.[4] Nor
are such statements restricted to Paul's letters. They occur
in other New Testament epistolary,[5] visionary,[6] and narrative
writings.[7] It is literally impossible to read the New Testament
at any length without encountering claims that something
is happening to these people, and it is happening *now*.[8]
Claims to experience, in other words, are not based simply
on records of what happened to others in the past or on fond

3. Among other passages, see 1 Cor 9:1-2; 14:18; 15:8; 2 Cor 1:3, 22;
3:18; 4:6; 5:14; 12:1-4, 7, 12; Gal 1:12, 16; 2:2, 20; 4:19; 6:14, 17; Phil 3:8,
12; Col 1:24; 1 Tim 1:12-16; 2 Tim 1:11; Eph 3:3. For Paul as a "religious
personality," see the diverse appreciations by L. Baeck, "Paul's Romanticism,"
in *The Writings of Saint Paul*, ed. Wayne A. Meeks (New York: W. W. Norton, 1972) 334–49; A. Deissmann, *Paul: A Study in Social and Religious History*,
trans. W. E. Wilson (2nd ed., 1927; New York: Harper and Row, 1957) 135–83;
A. Schweitzer, *The Mysticism of Paul the Apostle*, trans. W. Montgomery (1931;
New York: Seabury, 1968) 1–25; A. F. Segal, *Paul the Convert* (New Haven: Yale
University Press, 1990) 34–71.

4. See, e.g., Rom 5:5; 6:11, 22; 8:15; 1 Cor 3:16; 5:4; 12:3, 4-11, 27-31;
14:5-32; 2 Cor 3:18; 4:12; 12:12; 13:3, 5; Gal 3:2-5; 4:6-7, 9; 5:1, 25; Phil 2:1;
1 Thess 1:5-6; 5:19; 1 Tim 1:18; 4:14; 2 Tim 1:6-7; Tit 3:4-6.

5. See, e.g., Heb 2:2-4; 12, 18-24; 1 Pet 1:8, 18-21, 23; 2:3, 10, 24; 3:21;
4:10, 13; 2 Pet 1:16-18; 1 John 1:1-4; 2:20, 27; 4:13, 19.

6. All of Revelation is the report of visionary experience, so the language
of "seeing" and "hearing" runs throughout the composition, as, e.g., in 1:9-20;
4:1-2; 5:1, 11; etc.

7. See above all the experiences reported in the Acts of the Apostles, e.g.,
1:9-10; 2:1-4; 4:23-31; 5:12-16, 19; 7:55-60; 8:26, 39; 9:1-9, 10-16, 40-41; 10:1-15,
41, 44; 12:7-11, 23; 13:1-2, 9-12; 14:3, 8-11; 16:9-10, 18; 19:11; 20:7-12.

8. The sense of present experience can be gained by examination of the
New Testament's use of "now" (*nyn*) in many critical formulations (e.g., Rom
3:21, 26; 5:1, 11; 6:22; 7:6; 8:1; 16:26; 2 Cor 6:2; Gal 4:9; Eph 2:2; 3:5; Heb
9:26; 1 John 3:2; 1 Pet 1:12; 2:20; 3:21; 2 Tim 1:10; Col 1:22, 26).

hopes for what the future might hold, but on the witness of present participants.[9]

The experiences articulated by these texts, furthermore, are not mainly about quotidian matters of upkeep and maintenance, routine engagements with domestic and social realities.[10] The New Testament shows scant interest in domestic economy, city politics, or imperial stability.[11] The experiences expressed by these texts involve *power*[12] but a power of a peculiar sort. It has nothing to do with rank or status derived from a place within society's disposition of military, social, or economic resources.[13] The power is not simply physical, although it involves bodies.[14] It is not simply mental, although

9. See the use of *martyrein* in 1 Cor 15:15; 2 Cor 8:3; Gal 4:15; 1 John 1:2; 4:14; Rev 2:18; Eph 4:7, and *martys* in Acts 1:28; 2:32; 10:41; 13:31; 2 Cor 1:23; 1 Pet 5:1; 1 Thess 2:10.

10. Among the few items of what Paul calls *ta biotika* (1 Cor 6:3-4) that receive significant attention are matters of diet (Acts 11:1-4; 15:1-29; Rom 14:1-23; Gal 2:12-14; 1 Cor 8-10; Col 3:21; 1 Tim 4:3-5; Heb 13:9; Rev 2:14-15), care of widows and other poor (Acts 6:1-7; Heb 13:2-3; 1 Tim 5:3-16; 1 Cor 16:1-4; 2 Cor 8-9; Rom 15:25-32; Gal 2:10), and hospitality (Rom 16:1-2; 1 Cor 16:10; Phil 2:25-30; Col 4:7-10; Phm 22; Heb 13:1-2; 2 John 10; 3 John 5-7).

11. Household matters are discussed in 1 Cor 7:1-40; 1 Thess 4:3-6; Col 3:18-4:1; Eph 5:21-6:9; 1 Tim 5:3-16; 6:1-2; Tit 2:1-3:2; Heb 13:4; the only reference to the affairs of the *polis* comes in Paul's offhanded mention of Erastus as *oikonomos tēs poleōs* in Rom 16:23; submission to the rulers of the *oikoumenē* is advocated in Rom 13:1-7; 1 Pet 3:17-20; 1 Tim 2:1-3; Tit 3:1.

12. A range of terms with their cognates are used by the New Testament writings: *exousia*, with its connotations of freedom and authority (e.g., John 1:12; 1 Cor 6:12; 8:9; 9:4; 2 Cor 10:8; 13:10; 2 Thess 3:9; Heb 13:10; Rev 2:26); *energeia*, with its suggestions of efficacy and energy (e.g., 1 Cor 12:6, 11; 1 Thess 2:13; Phm 6; Gal 3:5; 5:6; Col 1:29; Eph 3:20-21); and most frequently, *dynamis* (Rom 1:16; 15:13, 19; 1 Cor 1:18; 6:14; 12:3; 12:28; 14:31; 15:50; 2 Cor 1:4; 6:7; 8:3; 10:4; 12:9-10; 13:4, 9; Gal 3:5; Eph 3:20; 6:10; Phil 3:10, 21; 4:13; Col 1:29; 1 Thess 1:5; 2 Thess 2:11; 1 Tim 1:7; 2:1; 4:17; 1 Tim 1:12; Heb 2:4; James 1:21; 2:14; 4:12; 1 Pet 1:5; 2 Pet 1:16).

13. See the discussion of "The Social Level of Pauline Churches," in W. A. Meeks, *The First Urban Christians: The Social World of the Apostle Paul* (New Haven: Yale University Press, 1983) 51-73; nn. 214–20.

14. See, e.g., Acts 2:1-4; 3:12-16; 4:7-12, 33; 5:1-16; 8:18-19; 13:10-11; Rom

it affects emotional and cognitive capacities.[15] It is not simply individual, although it is personal.[16] Neither is it exclusively social, although it has social consequences.[17]

Perhaps most significantly, the texts do not speak of this power as something generated by or originating with those experiencing it even though those experiencing it provide the vehicle for its expression. It is a power that comes from outside those touched by it and is transmitted to them from another, to whom it properly belongs.[18] The power transmitted to them reaches external expression in various "wonders and signs," including healings and exorcisms and gifts of ecstatic speech.[19] But it is also said to be at work in the internal transformation of human freedom.[20]

The only term adequate to define the extraordinary

6:12-14; 1 Cor 5:3-5; 6:14-20; 11:29-30; 15:35-56; 2 Cor 4:10-12; Phil 3:20-21; James 5:14-16.

15. See, e.g., Rom 12:2; 1 Cor 2:16; 14:14-19; 2 Cor 4:16-18; 5:16; Eph 4:17-24; Phil 2:1-5; Col 3:2-11; 2 Tim 1:7; 2 Pet 1:3-9.

16. For power at work in individual persons, see, e.g., Acts 6:8; 8:19; 19:11; Gal 2:8; Col 1:29; 1 Cor 4:19; 16:9; 12:3-15; 2 Cor 8:3; 12:9; 13:10; Phil 4:13; Phm 6; 1 Tim 1:12; 2 Tim 2:1; 3:15; 4:17; Heb 1:3;

17. For power at work among groups, see, e.g., Acts 1:8; Rom 1:16; 16:25; Gal 3:5; 1 Thess 1:5; 2:13; 2 Thess 3:9; 1 Cor 1:18; 6:14; 8:9; 9:4-6; 14:31; 2 Cor 13:4; Eph 3:20; 6:10; James 1:21; 2 Pet 1:3, 16.

18. See, e.g., Acts 2:33; 3:12-16; Rom 1:4; 16:25; 1 Cor 1:24; 5:4; 12:3; 2 Cor 1:4; 6:7; 12:9; 13:4; Eph 3:16, 20; Phil 3:10, 21; Heb 5:7; James 4:12; Jude 24; 2 Tim 1:7; 1 Pet 1:5; 2 Pet 1:16.

19. For "signs and wonders" as demonstration of power, see Acts 2:19, 22, 43; 4:16, 22, 30; 5:12; 6:8; 8:6, 13; 14:3; 15:18; Rom 15:19; 2 Cor 12:12; Heb 2:4. For "powerful deeds" in the same connection, see Acts 2:22; 3:12; 4:7, 33; 6:8; 8:13; 10:38; 19:11; Rom 15:19; 1 Cor 2:4-5; 12:10, 28-29; 2 Cor 12:12; Gal 3:5; 1 Thess 1:5; Heb 2:4. For healings as demonstration of power, see Acts 3:1-9; 5:15-16; 8:7; 9:32, 41; 14:8-10; 19:11; 20:7-12; 1 Cor 12:9, 28; James 5:13-18. For exorcisms, see Acts 5:16; 8:2; 13:6-11; 16:16-18; 19:11-16. And for ecstatic speech, see Acts 2:1-4; 4:31; 10:46; 19:6; 21:11; Rom 12:6; 1 Cor 12:10; 14:1-39; 1 Thess 5:19.

20. See Gal 3:5; Rom 12:2; 1 Cor 2:16; 2 Cor 3:18; Eph 4:23; Col 3:10; 1 Pet 1:22.

combination of characteristics ascribed to such power is *transcendent*. But that term must be understood in its full richness, not as a "going beyond" that involves distance alone but also as a "going beyond" that enables the most intense intimacy and communication.[21] In this sense, transcendence is a function of *spirit*. This is another term that can lead us disastrously astray if understood in the contemporary etiolated manner as a dubious property of mental activity, rather than as a symbol for precisely the "going beyond in order to be within" transformative energy-field spoken of in these texts.[22]

Language about the spirit (*to pneuma*) and more specifically the Holy Spirit (*to pneuma to hagion*) in the texts of the New Testament has specific reference to this complex experiential field in which power is transmitted and exchanged. The *pneuma* is, precisely, active power.[23] The *pneuma* comes to humans from another.[24] It indwells them,[25] moves them,[26] transforms and gives them life.[27] It is poured out upon them[28]

21. See now W. C. Placher, *The Domestication of Transcendence: How Modern Thinking about God Went Wrong* (Louisville: Westminster John Knox Press, 1995); and my review, "Explaining God Away," *Commonweal* 123/22 (1996) 18–20.

22. The general framework for my language about spirit and transcendence can be found in L. B. Puntel, "Spirit" and K. Lehmann, "Transcendence," in K. Rahner, ed. *Encyclopedia of Theology: The Concise Sacramentum Mundi* (New York: Seabury Press, 1975) 1619–23 and 1734–42.

23. For sentences in which power and spirit are brought together, see Luke 24:49; Acts 1:8; 8:18-19; 10:38; Rom 1:4; 8:26; 15:13, 19; 1 Cor 2:4; 5:3-4; 12:11; 2 Cor 4:13; Gal 3:1-5; Eph 2:2; 3:16; 6:18-20; 1 Thess 1:5; Heb 2:4.

24. See John 20:22; Acts 1:8; 2:33, 38; 8:15-19; Rom 8:15; 1 Cor 2:12-14; 2 Cor 5:5; 1 John 3:24; 4:13.

25. See Rom 8:9, 111; 1 Cor 3:16; 6:19; 2 Tim 1:14; James 4:5.

26. See Acts 8:39; 13:11; 15:29; 16:6-7; 19:1; 29:22; Rom 8:14; Gal 5:16, 18; 2 Pet 1:21.

27. For transforming, see Rom 12:2; 2 Cor 3:18; Eph 4:23; Tit 3:5; for giving life, see Rom 8:2, 10, 11; 1 Cor 15:45; 2 Cor 3:6; Gal 5:25; 6:8; 1 Pet 3:18; 4:6; Rev 11:11.

28. Acts 2:17-18; 10:41; Tit 3:6.

and poured into them.[29] It is drunk,[30] and it fills humans.[31] So pervasive is such language that the unsettling consequences of taking it literally rather than metaphorically seldom occur to the reader. But calling something a symbol means to take it at least as much literally as metaphorically, for a symbol in the proper sense participates in that which it signifies.[32] In this sense, the symbol "Holy Spirit" serves as the linguistic expression of the experience of power.

The world evoked by the texts of the New Testament is literally a spirit-filled world. There the visibly human activities of eating and sleeping and mating and working and traveling and assembling are intersected by (and themselves intersect) the invisible yet equally real domain of spirits. There live not only the spirit called "holy" but also those spirits called variously demons,[33] unclean spirits,[34] Satan[35] or the devil, whose own power is sufficient to be taken with deadly seriousness.[36] The writings of the New Testament do not evoke this powerful spirit world as imaginary or possible or under construction

29. Rom 5:5.

30. 1 Cor 12:13

31. See Acts 2:4; 4:8, 31; 6:3, 5; 7:55; 9:17, 31; 11:24; 13:9, 52; Eph 5:18.

32. See K. Rahner, "Theology of the Symbol," in *Theological Investigations* IV, trans. K. Smyth (New York: Seabury Press, 1974) 221–52.

33. Outside the Gospels, see 1 Cor 10:20-21; 1 Tim 4:1; James 2:19; Rev 9:20; 16:14.

34. See Mark 1:23-27; 9:27; Matt 10:1; 12:43; Luke 4:36; Acts 5:16; 8:7; Rev 16:13.

35. Outside the Gospels, see Acts 5:3; 26:18; Rom 16:20; 1 Cor 5:5; 7:5; 2 Cor 2:11; 11:14; 12:7; 1 Thess 2:18; 2 Thess 2:9; 1 Tim 1:10; 5:15; Rev 2:9-24; 12:9; 20:2, 7.

36. E.g., "that through death he might destroy him who has the power of death, that is, the devil, and deliver all those who through fear of death were subject to lifelong bondage" (Heb 2:14-15; see also Matt 4:11; 13:39; 25:41; John 6:70; 8:44; 13:2; Acts 10:38; 13:10; Eph 4:27; 6:11; 1 Tim 3:6, 7, 11; 2 Tim 2:16; James 4:7; 1 Pet 5:8; 1 John 3:8-10; Jude 9; Rev 2:10; 12:9, 12; 20:2, 10. For the way such spiritual forces play an important role in a specific writing, see S. R. Garrett, *The Demise of the Devil: Magic and the Demonic in Luke's Writings* (Minneapolis: Fortress, 1989).

but as one in which the writers and readers of this literature actually exist.[37] The interactions and exchanges of the human characters all have a kind of liminal character, as though the realm of human power were a beach over which there constantly washed as well the even greater power of spirits.

As a result, the New Testament is filled with statements of the most shocking character. Only the habituation caused by two millennia of domesticated reading buffers us from intimations of incest,[38] cannibalism,[39] ritual mutilation,[40] magic,[41] and necromancy,[42] not to mention conditions of delusional paranoia.[43] A sample from a longer list: "The world or life

37. Of particular interest is Paul's language about "powers, principalities, and rulers" (see 1 Cor 2:6, 8; 1:21; Eph 2:2; 1 Cor 15:24; Col 1:16). See H. Schlier, *Powers and Principalities in the New Testament* (New York: Herder and Herder, 1961); the way in which such "transcendental" language intersects social and institutional realities is studied by W. Wink, *Naming the Powers: the Language of Power in the New Testament* (Philadelphia: Fortress, 1984); idem, *Unmasking the Powers: the Invisible Forces that Determine Human Existence* (Philadelphia: Fortress, 1986); idem, *Engaging the Powers: Discernment and Resistance in a World of Domination* (Minneapolis: Fortress, 1992).

38. As in "kissing the brethren" (Rom 16:16; 1 Cor 16:20; 2 Cor 13:12; 1 Thess 5:26; 1 Pet 5:14; for this charge against the Christians, see Minucius Felix, *Octavius*, 8–9.

39. See 1 Cor 11:23-26 and above all John 6:48-58; for a thorough examination, see A. McGowan, "Eating People: Accusations of Cannibalism against Christians in the Second Century," *Journal of Early Christian Studies* 2 (1994) 413–42.

40. In Galatians, we find talk of forced circumcision (2:3), voluntary circumcision (5:2-4), castration (5:12) and other physical markings (*stigmata*, 6:17).

41. See Acts 5:12-16, 19; 13:8-11; 19:11-20; 1 Cor 5:3-4.

42. If necromancy is the invocation of the power of the dead to influence the living (see 1 Sam 28:8-19), then it is hard to avoid the impression that much of the language about the resurrection power of Jesus would fit within this category (see, e.g., Luke 9:7-9; Acts 3:12-16; Gal 2:20-21; 2 Cor 4:10-12; 13:4-5.

43. Because of the remarkable success of Christianity as a movement that eventually became the religion of the Roman Empire, it is easy to miss the outrageousness of the statements claiming, within only a few years of the death

or death or the present or the future, all are yours; and you are Christ's; and Christ is God's" (1 Cor 3:22), and "Do you not know that the saints will judge the world? Do you not know that we are to judge angels?" (1 Cor 6:2-3). "You are to deliver this man to Satan for the destruction of his flesh, that his spirit may be saved in the day of the Lord Jesus" (1 Cor 5:5; see 1 Tim 1:20). "Anyone who eats and drinks without discerning the body eats and drinks judgment upon himself. That is why many of you are weak and ill, and some have died" (1 Cor 11:29). "If, therefore, the whole church assembles and all speak in tongues and outsiders or unbelievers enter, will they not say that you are mad?" (1 Cor 14:23). "Henceforth let no man trouble me: for I bear on my body the marks of Jesus" (Gal 6:17). "This is why the Gospel was preached to the dead, that though judged in the flesh like men, they might live in the Spirit like God" (1 Pet 4:6). "Do you not know that all of us who have been baptized into Christ were baptized into his death?" (Rom 6:3). "So we wanted to come to you ... but Satan hindered us" (1 Thess 2:18). And, perhaps least intelligible of all, Paul's matter-of-fact question, "Otherwise, what do people mean by being baptized on behalf of the dead? If the dead are not raised at all, why are people baptized on their behalf?" (1 Cor 15:29).

Humans touched by and touching transcendent power, exchanges between the dead and the living, behavior at meals involving life and death consequences, journeys enabled or impeded by spiritual forces, human speech being also spirit-speech: This is language of a very specific character, namely,

---

of its founder, a worldwide mission (Acts 1:8) that would make disciples of all nations (Matt 28:19), not to mention its present ascendancy over the world (1 Cor 3:22; 6:23; 1 John 5:4-5), and its role as the future of the world (2 Cor 5:19; Rom 8:20-22; 11:15; Eph 3:9-10; Rev 11:15; 22:4-5). One of the benefits of the discovery of the writings from Qumran is that they remind us of how bizarre such claims appear when the cult in question simply disappears from history.

the language of religious experience. It occurs everywhere in the earliest Christian writings and points to realities and convictions of fundamental importance to both writers and readers of these writings. Yet precisely this register of language is least recognized or appreciated by the academic study of early Christianity.

What Escapes the Scan of Scholars

The academic study of earliest Christianity has been dominated for over a hundred years by what is usually referred to as the historical-critical method,[44] although, as I have argued elsewhere, it is more properly called a historical model.[45] There are two reasons why this model has paid little attention to the specifically religious language of the New Testament. First, history necessarily focuses on definable events in time and space that can be placed in some sort of chronological sequence. Given the fragmentary character of the literature from the period of Christian nascence, the selection of hard historical data is necessarily limited. As a result, the history of early Christianity has tended to be a history primarily of theological ideas or social institutions and one in which developmental theories have had do much of the heavy lifting to

44. This is so much the case that the history of biblical interpretation often becomes simply the history of historical-critical scholarship; see, e.g., W. G. Kümmel, *The New Testament: The History of the Investigation of Its Problems,* trans. S. Macl. Gilmour and H. C. Kee (Nashville: Abingdon, 1972); S. Neill, *The Interpretation of the New Testament, 1861-1961* (London: Oxford University Press, 1964); W. Baird, *History of New Testament Research,* vol. 1: *From Deism to Tübingen* (Minneapolis: Fortress Press, 1992).

45. See L. T. Johnson, *The Writings of the New Testament: An Interpretation* (Philadelphia: Fortress Press, 1986) 8–11; and idem, *The Real Jesus: The Misguided Quest for the Historical Jesus and the Truth of the Traditional Gospels* (San Francisco: Harper San Francisco, 1996) 67–76, 81–104.

compensate for the lack of real evidence.[46] Within an enterprise thus understood and thus constrained, the language of religious experience appears as overly subjective and elusive to serve the cause of historical reconstruction.

It has also been too embarrassing. The supposedly scientific histories of early Christianity from F. C. Baur onward were scarcely neutral. They were themselves essentially theological projects, driven by specifically Protestant preoccupations. The incessant quest for the "origins" of Christianity was in no small part the search for the essential form of Christianity that was of enduring ("eternal") worth, covered over, perhaps, by the tendencies of ecclesiastical manipulation, but recoverable in principle both by Reformation and by critical scholarship itself.[47] Given this agenda (always present though not often explicit),[48] the raw language of religious experience appears as deeply problematic.

If the original essence of Christianity was the simple moral teaching of Jesus or the simple theological principle of justification by grace, the register of language I have here catalogued seems as alien as the encroachments of law and organization from the side of Judaism or the influence of

46. See the extensive discussion in L. T. Johnson, *The Letter of James* (Anchor Bible 37A; New York: Doubleday, 1995) 89–123.

47. F. C. Baur declared, "Christianity is on the one hand the great spiritual power which determines all the belief and thought of the present age, the absolute principle on which the self-consciousness of the spirit is supported and maintained, so that, unless it were essentially Christian, it would have no stability or firmness in itself at all. On the other hand, *the essential nature of Christianity is a purely historical question,* whose solution lies only *in that Past in which Christianity itself had its origin;* it is a problem which can only be solved by that critical attitude of thought which the consciousness of the present age assumes towards the Past" (emphasis added). See *Paul, the Apostle of Jesus Christ, His Life and Work, His Epistles and His Doctrine: A Contribution to the Critical History of Primitive Christianity,* (1st ed. 1845, 2nd ed. by E. Zeller, trans. A. Menzies, 2 vols.; London: Williams and Norgate, 1875) 2.

48. Paul Wernle states in the Preface to *The Beginnings of Christianity* 2 vols., trans. G. A. Bienemann (London: Williams and Norgate, 1903), "An age of

ritual and sacrament from the side of paganism, both elements thought to distort the pure essence of the gospel and
make the development of Christianity in the direction of
Catholicism one of decline.[49]

A great — but only partial — exception within the historical paradigm was the *religionsgeschichtliche Schule,* which
briefly flourished in Germany (mainly at the University of
Göttingen) in the late nineteenth and early twentieth centuries.[50] This history-of-religions approach had the merit of
recognizing that the New Testament was not first of all a

transition such as ours needs above all else a constant recurrence of the
Gospel of Jesus for guidance. But it is well known that the Gospel does not lie
everywhere on the surface, even of the New Testament, in its primitive simplic-
ity, but has in many instances been covered up or transformed" (1:ix-x). See
also the discussion of Christianity as a form of ethics in C. Von Weizsaecker,
The Apostolic Age of the Christian Church 2 vols. (London: Williams and Norgate, 1907–12) 2:338–97; or the conclusion to A. C. McGiffert's, *A History of
Christianity in the Apostolic Age* (New York: Charles Scribner's Sons, 1897): the
later part of the New Testament showed "the subjection of the spirit to law
and of the individual to the institution, and thus foreshadowed the rise of
Catholicism" (672).

49. The theological tendentiousness of A. Harnack's attempt to extract
the "kernel" of essential Christianity from its historical "husk" by means of
historical method (in his 1900 monograph *Das Wesen des Christentums* [Leip-
zig], translated by T. B. Sanders as *What Is Christianity?* [London: Williams
and Norgate, 1901]) was brilliantly dissected by A. Loisy in *The Gospel and
the Church,* trans. C. Home (London: Isbister and Company, 1903). The same
basic premise, however, has remained powerfully alive until very recently, even
among scholars whose "scientific" credentials are highly respected. See, e.g.,
the remarkable declaration by Hans Von Campenhausen at the very start of
his *Ecclesiastical Authority and Spiritual Power in the Church of the First Three Centuries,* trans. J. Baker (Stanford: Stanford University Press, 1969) 3: "In the
course of these three centuries the ideal to which Christianity had originally
been committed was impaired in various ways: not only do we find rigidities
of attitude, curtailment of aspiration, distortion of insight, but also in every
department — an indisputable trivialization."

50. For a useful summation of the movement, see H. Boers, "Die religionsgeschichtliche Schule," in *Essays on New Testament Interpretation* (articles from
the forthcoming *Dictionary of Biblical Interpretation,* ed. John Hayes, published
separately by Abingdon Press, 1995) 18–24; also, W. G. Kümmel, *The New*

compilation of theological propositions but rather the expression of religious experience and conviction.[51] Wilhelm Bousset, for example, declares of the Christian cult at Antioch, "Here we have to do not at all with a notion, an idea which is thought up and then propagated by one individual, but rather with something that lies much deeper, with a conviction which stems from the immediacy of the religious feeling."[52] Hermann Gunkel likewise explicitly recognized the necessity for the historian's entering empathetically into the experiences being described:

> Now I believe I have a better and more discerning knowledge of the subject...and I see that these things take on life...only when we are able to live the pneumatic's inner states after him....Whoever happens to write on this theme in the future...must first somehow put himself in a position to share the feeling of the pneumatic.[53]

Testament, 206–25, 245–80; and H. Räisänen, *Beyond New Testament Theology* (London: SCM Press, 1990) 13–31.

51. Of pivotal importance for the development of this movement was W. Wrede's programmatic statement, *Über Aufgabe und Methode der sogennanten Neutestamentlichen Theologie* (Göttingen: Vandenhoeck & Ruprecht, 1897) 7–80; reprinted in G. Strecker, *Das Problem der Theologie des Neuen Testaments* (Darmstadt: Wissenschaftliche Buchgesellschaft, 1975) 81–154. Wrede brings the study of early Christianity more decisively within historical methodology by abandoning the artificial frame of the canon, and by focusing on the religious realities to which the texts bear witness, rather than the dogmatic concepts. It is nevertheless instructive to see that in Wrede's separate study of Paul, despite some attention to Paul's vision of Christ and his "religious character" (pp. 6–30), his main focus is on Paul's theology, characterized this way: "The religion of the apostle is theological through and through; his theology is his religion," *Paul,* trans. E. Lummis (Boston: American Unitarian Association, 1908) 76.

52. W. Bousset, *Kyrios Christos: A History of the Belief in Christ from the Beginnings of Christianity to Irenaeus* (1913), trans. of the fifth German edition by J. Steely (Nashville: Abingdon Press, 1970) 136.

53. H. Gunkel, *The Influence of the Holy Spirit: A View of the Apostolic Age and the Teaching of the Apostle Paul: A Biblical-Theological Study,* trans. R. A. Harrisville and P. A. Quanbeck II (1888; Philadelphia: Fortress, 1979) 3.

The goal for these researchers was less the description of specific religious forms than the depiction of a religious sensibility that need not be even specifically Christian. Richard Reitzenstein stated, "What we are focusing our attention upon in fact is not this religion, but the religiousness, the piety, of an entire period or stage in the development."[54] Such an interest enabled a positive appreciation of Paul's visions as specifically religious experiences[55] and a capacity to locate Paul as a specific sort of religious person, the pneumatic.[56] Most of all, these scholars understood that Paul's language had an expressive and not merely a cognitive character. As Gunkel observes:

> It is tempting to conceive of the Spirit in Paul as a "concept" that merely needs defining in order to be mastered. But to this concept belong very concrete views and deep inner experiences in which we must imitate the Apostle in order to understand his dogmatic statements.[57]

The history-of-religions school, furthermore, clearly saw how much of this language concerning religious experience concerned power. Gunkel states simply, "For Paul the Spirit is a power," and if his teaching on the Spirit is to be understood, it must be in light of "his experience of the power and the depth of his spiritual inspiration."[58] Thus Bousset

---

54. R. Reitzenstein, *Hellenistic Mystery-Religions: Their Basic Ideas and Significance,* trans. J. E. Steely from 3rd (1926) German ed. (Pittsburgh: Pickwick Press, 1978) 113.

55. Reitzenstein, *Hellenistic Mystery-Religions,* 86–87; Wrede, *Paul,* 6–11.

56. Reitzenstein, *Hellenistic Mystery-Religions,* 426–500; Gunkel, *Influence of the Holy Spirit,* 77.

57. H. Gunkel, *Influence of the Holy Spirit,* 75; see also O. Pfleiderer, *Christian Origins,* trans. D. A. Huebsch (New York: B. W. Huebsch, 1906) 170–71.

58. Gunkel, *Influence of the Holy Spirit,* 92; see also Pfleiderer, *Christian Origins,* 178.

describes the Antiochene community at worship, "Over this whole swaying sea of inspiration reigns the Lord Jesus as the head of his community, with his power immediately present in breathtaking presence and certainty."[59] Thus also Gunkel can assert,

> An activity of the Spirit is not ascertained within the scheme of means and ends, but rather within the scheme of cause and effect. Belief in the Spirit is not for the purpose of grasping God's plan for the world, but for the purpose of explaining the presence of certain, above all inexplicable, phenomena by means of the transcendent.[60]

The history-of-religions school, furthermore, insisted that the religious phenomena of early Christianity must be understood within the context of the wider religious world of antiquity.[61] Otto Pfleiderer, in fact, raises the comparative method to the level of epistemological necessity: "It is a fact that only he really knows one religion who knows more than one religion. Not only does the study of comparative religions make us tolerant . . . but it also teaches us to understand our own religion better because of the clearer differentiation between the essential and the accidental, the perennial and the temporary."[62] Richard Reitzenstein, in particular, sought

59. Bousset, *Kyrios Christos,* 135.

60. Gunkel, *Influence of the Holy Spirit,* 32–33; note that in this statement, the "transcendent" has a functional rather than an essentialist denotation. For a similar emphasis on the experiential character of the Spirit, see H. Wheeler Robinson, *The Christian Experience of the Holy Spirit* (New York: Harper and Brothers, 1928) 1–45.

61. See O. Pfleiderer, *Das Urchristentum: Seine Schriften und Lehren in geschichtlichen Zusammenhang,* 2nd ed. (Berlin: Georg Reimer, 1902); English citations found in Kümmel, *The New Testament,* 207–10; also, Gunkel, *Influence of the Holy Spirit,* 3–5.

62. Pfleiderer, *Religion and Historical Faiths,* trans. D. A. Huebsch (London: T. Fisher Unwin, 1907) 65–66; still, we note the distinction between "essential"

specific connections between religious phenomena in disparate traditions in the hope of constructing out of separate fragmentary but parallel pieces some sense of a religious whole.[63]

The history-of-religions school also had deficiencies sufficiently severe to eclipse its genuine contributions and to enable the conclusion that the standard historical and theological approaches to the New Testament were necessary alternatives. The approach was overly dependent on philology and tended to draw large conclusions on the basis of small linguistic details.[64] It tended to place too much emphasis on Gnosticism and the Greco-Roman mysteries[65] and moved too easily from the detection of similarities to conclusions concerning identity and even dependence.[66] These

and "accidental," a theological interest found also in his *Urchristentum*, 1:vi–viii. This ultimate interest only in Christianity leads Boers to remark correctly that the movement might better be translated as "history of religion school" in the singular (Boers, "Die Religionsgeschichtliche Schule," 18).

63. Reitzenstein, *Hellenistic Mystery-Religions*, 113–14.

64. Reitzenstein's self-designation as "philologist" enabled him to adopt an angle on religion that was not privileged theologically and thus come to new insight (see ibid., 4 and 360); at the same time, there is no question that his fascination with linguistic parallels led him to precipitous conclusions (see ibid., 320–37 and 364–425. And Bousset's determination to locate the cult of the *kyrios* on gentile territory led him to suppress the counter-evidence offered by 1 Cor 16:22 (see *Kyrios Christos*, 129).

65. This is certainly more the case with Reitzenstein, *Hellenistic Mystery-Religions*, e.g., 148–49 (although see his disclaimer, p. 4) and Pfleiderer, *Religion and Historic Faiths*, 267–70, than it is with Gunkel, Bousset, and J. Weiss, each of whom also stressed the influence on early Christianity of some form of Judaism (see Kümmel, *The New Testament*, 226–80).

66. For the range of Reitzenstein's (often very subtle) observations on this point, see *Hellenistic Mystery-Religions*, 148–49, 184–85, 190–91, 258–59, 284; nowhere is he so crudely reductionistic as O. Pfleiderer, *Christian Origins*, who in a discussion of Antioch, says, "*Here* for the first time, it is likely that the belief in the resurrection of Christ was cast in its final mould as the Evangelical Easter Legend; particularly the dating of the resurrection 'on the third day' (or 'after three days') which Paul found there (1 Cor 15:4) and which he

tendencies culminated in the hypothesis of a pre-Christian redeemer myth,[67] a construct for which there was so little positive evidence and for which such sweeping causal claims were made,[68] that its dismantling led inevitably to the discrediting of the entire approach as well.[69]

The distinctive and noteworthy virtues of the history-of-religions approach — in particular its attention to religious experience and language — were ultimately vitiated by its captivity to the dominant paradigm within which it operated. Its religious focus, like that of the tradition shared by these scholars, was rather more on the individual than on the community.[70] It reduced religious responses to psychological conditions.[71] Finally, it was theologically embarrassed

could not have heard from the early Apostles, finds simplest explanation: the heathen-Christians of Antioch continued their popular celebration of the resurrection of Adonis ('the Master') as an old habit, but transferred the worship to the new Master, Christ" (p. 189).

67. See especially R. Reitzenstein, *Poimandres: Studien zur griechisch-aegyptischen und frühchristlichen Literatur* (Leipzig, 1904); *Das Iranische Erlösungsmysterium* (Bonn, 1921); "Iranischer Erlösungsglaube," *ZNW* 20 (1921) 1–23; W. Bousset, *Das Hauptprobleme der Gnosis* (FRLANT 10; Göttingen, 1907); R. Bultmann, "Die Bedeutung der neuerschlossenen mandäischen und manichäischen Quellen für das Verständis des Johannes-Evangeliums," *ZNW* 24 (1925) 100–147.

68. See, e.g., Bousset, *Kyrios Christos*, 245–81; R. Bultmann, "Der religionsgeschichtliche Hintergrund des Prologs zum Johannes-Evanglium," *Eucharistērion* (Gunkel Festschrift; FRLANT 36, Teil 2; Göttingen, 1923) 3–26; idem, *The Gospel of John: A Commentary*, trans. G. Beasley-Murray *et al.* of the 1966 ed. (Philadelphia: Westminster Press, 1971); W. Schmithals, *Gnosticism in Corinth*, trans. J. Steely (Nashville: Abingdon Press, 1971); idem, *Paul and the Gnostics*, trans. J. Steely (Nashville: Abingdon Press, 1972).

69. See C. Colpe, *Die religionsgeschichtliche Schule: Darstellung und Kritik ihres Bildes vom gnostischen Erlösermythus* (FRLANT 78; Göttingen: Vandenhoeck & Ruprecht, 1961); and E. M. Yamauchi, *Pre-Christian Gnosticism: A Survey of the Proposed Evidence*, 2nd ed. (Grand Rapids: Baker Book House, 1983).

70. See, e.g., Reitzenstein, *Hellenistic Mystery-Religions* 113–14; Pfleiderer, *Christian Origins*, 167.

71. See Bousset, *Kyrios Christos*, 285; Pfleiderer, *Christian Origins*, 167.

by the religious data it analyzed, as shown by the insistence that although Paul inherited such lively religious expressions, he purified them by giving them theological and ethical direction.[72] Finally, as the myth of the *Urmensch* illustrates, the movement was less concerned with religious phenomena themselves as with the desire to place them in some diachronic, developmental scheme. The ancient mysteries were of interest not for themselves or for how they illumined aspects of early Christian religious experience, but insofar as they could be positioned as a form of religion out of which Christianity developed[73] or a stage of development within the Christian movement itself.[74]

The discrediting of the history-of-religions school enabled the historical-critical approach to early Christianity to ignore its virtues — its attention to the language of religious experience — while perpetuating its vices. Walter Bauer's *Orthodoxy and Heresy in Early Christianity* reinvigorated investigation of early Christianity within a modified conflict model in which theology rather than religion was once more the focus of

---

72. See Pfleiderer, *Religion and Historic Faiths,* 267–69; and Bousset, *What Is Religion?* trans. F. B. Low (London: T. Fisher Unwin, 1907) 247–49; in these popular lectures, Bousset is unusually frank concerning his own theological convictions: Judaism represents captivity, Christianity freedom (p. 218); the personality of Jesus is the heart of Christianity (p. 235); Jesus' proclamation was about inwardness, and Paul delivered the good news from all traits of nationality (pp. 218–19); the simple gospel was overlaid with ritual and doctrine (pp. 231–32) and went into a decline that was reversed only by the Reformation (pp. 249–59), which was a "freeing of evangelical piety and morality from a mass of external observances which had accumulated in the course of history" (p. 261); among these apparently is belief in the divinity of Christ, which Bousset explicitly denies by appeal to the words of Jesus himself (pp. 279–82), and anything smacking of the miraculous: "We moderns can no longer hold fast to this belief in miracles. Here again it is not merely that it contradicts our whole mode of thought, but is in direct contradiction to our changed belief in God" (p. 285).

73. Reitzenstein, *Hellenistic Mystery-Religions,* 148–49.

74. Bousset, *Kyrios Christos,* 129–52; O. Pfleiderer, *Christian Origins,* 189.

attention.[75] The discovery of the Nag-Hammadi documents in 1947 helped to legitimate a renewed historical analysis of Christian origins. Now, however, the bounds of the canon are decisively dissolved and all Christian writings are placed into putative "trajectories" through time.[76]

Two highly questionable premises fuel this new form of history. The first is that literary compositions can confidently be divided and subdivided on the basis of stylistic or ideological seams. The second is that each dissected strand of literature adequately represents the ideology of a separate "community." The historical-critical method had from the first connected history to the dating of literature (since it lacked the external controls provided by a firm chronology and extensive outside evidence).[77] But now the history of nascent Christianity becomes simply the tracing of text-fragments through putative stages of redaction.[78] Since every textual tension is dissolved by dissection into separate strands representing separate theologies, it is no surprise that more and more varieties of Christianity are discovered.[79] The

75. W. Bauer, *Orthodoxy and Heresy in Earliest Christianity* (1934) 2nd ed. G. Strecker (1964); ed. and trans. R. A. Kraft and G. Krodel (Philadelphia: Fortress Pres, 1971).

76. Explicitly adopting Bauer's perspective, J. M. Robinson and H. Koester's *Trajectories through Early Christianity* (Philadelphia: Fortress Press, 1971) has set the agenda for a large portion of late-twentieth-century historical analysis of early Christianity.

77. Note the tribute paid by A. Jülicher to F. C. Baur, "He has taught us to regard the books of the New Testament from a truly historical point of view as the products of and the witnesses to the Christian Spirit of a definite age," and declares in response to Harnack's complaints against excessive "literary criticism" (=source criticism), "But is it possible to write history at all without including literary criticism?" *An Introduction to the New Testament,* trans. J. P. Ward (1st German edition, 1894; New York: Putnam, 1904) 21 and 27.

78. See, for example, R. E. Brown's attempt to trace the "history" of Johannine Christianity through a redactional analysis of the extant literature in *The Community of the Beloved Disciple* (New York: Paulist Press, 1979).

79. Or, more cynically, "invented," as in the so-called "Q Community"

premise "In the Beginning was Diversity" has been elevated into a dogma as absolute as any decreed by a pope.[80] Indeed, these tendencies have made it increasingly difficult to speak of "earliest Christianity" in any sense that meets general agreement. The study of Christian origins appears as the classification of a loose congeries of movements that inexplicably continue to operate in the name of Jesus after his death.[81]

The present situation with respect to the academic study of early Christianity, then, is decidedly odd. On one hand, over the past thirty years an army of researchers has expanded our knowledge of first-century Mediterranean culture and of the literature generated by the Christian movement. Research into Greco-Roman moral discourse has illuminated great patches of both epistolary and narrative literature, showing how Christians not only used the form and substance of Hellenistic moral teaching but were also engaged in the task of shaping communities of character.[82] Analysis of its social world has yielded insight not only into the ways

---

constructed by B. Mack in *The Lost Gospel: The Book of Q and Christian Origins* (San Francisco: Harper San Francisco, 1993).

80. As well stated by G. MacRae, "It is now as much a dogma of scholarship as its opposite used to be: orthodoxy is not the presupposition of the church but the result of a process of growth and development," in "Why the Church Rejected Gnosticism," *Jewish and Christian Self-Definition,* vol. 1: *The Shaping of Christianity in the Second and Third Centuries,* ed. E. P. Sanders (Philadelphia: Fortress Press, 1980) 127.

81. Precisely this fragmentation is made programmatic by B. Mack, *A Myth of Innocence: Mark and Christian Origins* (Philadelphia: Fortress Press, 1988), and expanded into a complete account of the formation of the New Testament in *Who Wrote the New Testament? The Making of the Christian Myth* (San Francisco: Harper San Francisco, 1995). For a solid if not sufficient effort to balance the picture, see A. Hultgren, *The Rise of Normative Christianity* (Minneapolis: Fortress Press, 1994).

82. On the first point, see the survey article by A. J. Malherbe, "Hellenistic Moralists and the New Testament," *ANRW* II.26.1 (1992) 278–93; on the second, see W. A. Meeks, *The Origins of Christian Morality* (New Haven: Yale University Press, 1993).

nascent Christianity intersected Mediterranean and imperial social structures and dynamics but also the ways in which the cultural valences attached to social systems both influenced and challenged this movement.[83] Attention to the literary character of the Christian writings has enabled analysis of the way they fit into ancient literary conventions and thereby function within their social world.[84] Finally, the rediscovery of the rhetorical character of New Testament compositions has led to a deeper understanding of the way the language of these writings functions as an instrument of persuasion.[85] Rhetorical criticism, in fact, brings all the research into the intertextual, moral, and social worlds of early Christianity to an exegetical point, demonstrating that the language of the New Testament can by no means be considered *simply* as expressive but must be taken seriously in its argumentative character and persuasive intent.[86]

83. With some overlap, such research has tended to fall into three categories: (a) description of the social world, as in G. Theissen, *The Social Setting of Pauline Christianity: Essays on Corinth,* trans. J. Schütz (Philadelphia: Fortress Press, 1982); and W. A. Meeks, *The First Urban Christians: The Social World of the Apostle Paul* (New Haven: Yale University Press, 1982); (b) anthropological analysis of culture, as in B. J. Malina, *The New Testament World: Insights from Cultural Anthropology* (Louisville: John Knox Press, 1981); and J. Neyrey, *Paul in Other Words: A Cultural Reading of His Letters* (Louisville: Westminster John Knox Press, 1990); (c) use of theoretical sociological perspectives, as in J. G. Gager, *Kingdom and Community: The Social World of Early Christianity* (Englewood Cliffs, N.J.: Prentice-Hall, 1975); and J. H. Elliott, *A Home for the Homeless: A Sociological Exegesis of 1 Peter* (Philadelphia: Fortress Press, 1981).

84. See, e.g., K. Berger, "Hellenistiche Gattungen im Neuen Testament," *ANRW* II.25.2 (1984) 1031–1432, and S. K. Stowers, "Social Typifications and the Classification of Ancient Letters," in *The Social World of Formative Christianity and Judaism,* ed. J. Neusner *et al.* (Minneapolis: Fortress Press, 1988) 78–89.

85. See, e.g., B. L. Mack, *Rhetoric and the New Testament* (GBS; Minneapolis: Fortress Press, 1990); G. A. Kennedy, *New Testament Interpretation through Rhetorical Criticism* (Chapel Hill: University of North Carolina Press, 1984); M. Warner, ed., *The Bible as Rhetoric: Studies in Biblical Persuasion and Credibility* (London: Routledge, 1990).

86. The most ambitious attempt to address these dimensions of the text

On the other hand, not only have these approaches failed to yield significant insight into the language of religious experience in early Christian writings, they seem to have moved even further away from such an appreciation.[87] For one thing, social-scientific approaches tend to privilege etic or outsider discourse rather than insider or emic discourse.[88] But something else is also at work. I have noted how much of the language of experience in the New Testament involves language about power as a positive reality. The development of what is sometimes called the "hermeneutics of suspicion" within scholarship and of "ideological criticism" as its methodological manifestation, however, leads to quite a different perception of power and language about power.[89] If

within a single comprehensive approach is represented by V. K. Robbins, *The Tapestry of Early Christian Discourse: Rhetoric, Society, and Ideology* (London: Routledge, 1996). While some of his specific observations may be disputed, he provides a useful mapping of the contemporary interpretive landscape; see also his "Social Scientific Criticism and Literary Studies: Prospects for Cooperation in Biblical Studies," in *Modelling Early Christianity: Social Scientific Studies of the New Testament in Its Context*, ed. Ph. Esler (London: Routledge, 1995) 274–89.

87. A noteworthy exception can be found in J. J. Pilch, "The Transfiguration of Jesus: An Experience of Alternate Reality," in *Modelling the New Testament*, 47–64.

88. See the introductory comments in *The Social World of Luke-Acts: Models for Interpretation*, ed. J. Neyrey (Peabody, Mass.: Hendrickson, 1991) ix–xviii, 3–23; as well as J. Neyrey, *Paul in Other Words*, 11–20.

89. See the extensive and subtle discussion in C. Bell, *Ritual Theory, Ritual Practice* (New York: Oxford University Press, 1992) 86–223. For a sense of how this applies to the reading of the New Testament, see, e.g., the first two chapters in E. Schüssler Fiorenza, *In Memory of Her: A Feminist Theological Reconstruction of Christian Origins* (New York: Crossroad, 1983) 3–67; and her "Feminist Theology as a Critical Theology of Liberation," in *Discipleship of Equals: A Critical Feminist Ekklesia-logy of Liberation* (New York: Crossroad, 1993) 53–79; see also the essays in *Feminist Perspectives on Biblical Scholarship*, ed. A. Y. Collins (SBL Biblical Scholarship in North America 10; Chico, Calif.: Scholars Press, 1985); N. K. Gottwald, *The Bible and Liberation: Political and Social Hermeneutics* (Maryknoll, N.Y.: Orbis Books, 1983); and *Stony the Road We Trod: African American Biblical Interpretation*, ed. C. H. Felder (Minneapolis: For-

religious symbols generally are taken to be epiphenomenal to human struggles for social and political position, then power, rather than a transcendental reality that is encountered as Other is invariably an instrument of control wielded in behalf of interested parties.[90] Claims to the experience of transcendent power should be demystified as camouflage for political position-taking within religious traditions.[91]

tress Press, 1991). The tendency to read Christian literature as fundamentally ideological in character and in function, however, is as old as the Tübingen School, as repristinated by W. Bauer's *Orthodoxy and Heresy* and given classic expression by B. Mack's, *Who Wrote the New Testament?* 225–73.

90. A fascinating example of how a theoretical interest can both enable and disable perception is found in W. Wink's trilogy on the *Powers.* He acknowledges at the beginning of his first volume that "the language of power pervades the whole New Testament," *Naming the Powers,* 2, but the only language about power he analyzes is that pertaining to the "powers and principalities," which he perceives as the symbol for social and political domination: "the powers are the inner aspect of material reality," 104. He further suggests in his second volume that "The recovery of these concepts and *a sense of the experiences that they named* can play a crucial role in eroding the soil from beneath the foundations of materialism" (*Unmasking the Powers,* 6, emphasis added). But he never says anything more about what "the experiences" might have been. Instead, he returns to the structural, social analysis: "Power must become incarnate, institutionalized or systemic in order to be effective. It has a dual aspect, possessing both an outer, visible form (constitutions, judges, police, leaders, office complexes) and an inner, invisible spirit that provides it legitimacy, compliance, credibility, and clout" (ibid., 4).

91. Elizabeth A. Castelli's *Imitating Paul: A Discourse of Power* (Louisville: Westminster/John Knox Press, 1991) is a particularly instructive example. Taking her cue from Michel Foucault, she reads Paul's call to imitation of himself in 1 Corinthians as a form of ideological domination through mimesis, which has as its corollary the rejection or suppression of difference. Her actual analysis of the text of 1 Corinthians is slight and does not take into account the register of language I have described here. But this is not surprising, given her assumption that language about power is inevitably language about politics: "It is precisely because of this marginal status that the discursive and ideological factors for constructing power relations became so important in the first centuries of Christian practice. *Other forms of power were inaccessible,* and ideological power became the *single possible mode* of articulating a powerful and compelling stance" (p. 52, emphasis added). But see also Bell's comments

The specific readings of the New Testament literature that have been generated by the hermeneutics of suspicion are less than satisfying. They are first of all anachronistic: it is one thing to manipulate authority within the framework of well-established structures; it is another to attempt to hold newly founded and fragile communities in existence. They are also simplistic: it is difficult to sustain the fantasy that all literary production is nothing else but ideological. Finally, they are in the most obvious sense reductionistic: by insisting that the language of religious experience has only a mystifying and not a mystical import, they fail to account for the specific shape and function of the symbols and thereby miss entirely the specifically religious dimension of early Christianity. We shall see that religious experience is inevitably connected to linguistic, social, and, yes, ideological constructs. But attention to those constructs should not amount to an implicit elimination of the experiential itself.

The Case of Jonathan Z. Smith

The present situation can perhaps best be illustrated by Jonathan Z. Smith of the University of Chicago, whose great learning in the religious traditions of antiquity is unquestionable and whose allegiance to the study of religion within the framework of the human sciences rather than within the framework of theology is explicit and emphatic. Smith's fortuitous location within a field called "History of Religions" also invites comparison between his approach and that of earlier scholars such as Bousset and Pfleiderer.[92]

on how ritual also *empowers* those who participate in it (*Ritual Theory, Ritual Practice*, 207–18).

92. Smith has been remarkably consistent in his self-understanding and approach. For characteristic early and later statements, see, e.g., "Coup d'Essai," *Criterion* 9 (1969) 19–20; " 'Religion' and 'Religious Studies': No Dif-

In an early essay, Smith expressed regret that the specific categories of the history of religions, such as those found in Mircea Eliade's *Patterns of Comparative Religion,* had been so little applied to ancient Judaism and Christianity, and suggested that the explanation for such neglect was an apologetic attitude among scholars in both traditions, who worried that a thoroughly comparative approach would prove reductionistic and miss (speaking tongue in cheek here) the "'something more' that makes our Western traditions unique and true."[93]

Over the years, however, Smith's statements about Eliade became less positive than his early praise of the one who had taught us "how and what to see; and, far more important, how to understand what we have learned to see."[94] He subjected Eliade's often careless reading of sources to scathing criticism.[95] And he became steadily more dismissive of the epistemological premises lodged in Eliade's phenomenological approach to religion. Eliade's merging of the language of Rudolf Otto and Emile Durkheim led, said Smith, to a view of the sacred, not as a construct of consciousness, but as a reality that "imposes itself on humans from without."[96]

Smith's own explicit espousal of a post-Kantian epistemology demanded his rejection of an understanding of the sacred as something "out there" rather than as a pattern of cognition.[97] It is striking that when Smith characterizes

---

ference at All," *Soundings* 71 (1988) 231–44; "Scriptures and Histories," *Method and Theory in the Study of Religion* 4 (1992) 97–105.

93. "Earth and Gods" (1960), in *Map Is Not Territory,* 107–8.

94. "Wobbling Pivot" (1972), in *Map Is Not Territory* 90.

95. See *To Take Place: Toward Theory in Ritual* (Chicago Studies in the History of Judaism; Chicago: University of Chicago Press, 1987) 1–13.

96. "The Wobbling Pivot" (1972), in *Map Is Not Territory,* 92.

97. Smith's rationalist stance is stated clearly in the "Discussion" devoted to his essay "The Domestication of Sacrifice" in *Violent Origins: Walter Burkert, René Girard and Jonathan Z. Smith on Ritual Killing and Cultural Formation,* ed. R. G. Hammerton-Kelly (Stanford, Calif.: Stanford University Press, 1987):

Eliade's understanding of the sacred, he uses the terms "real, being, power, creativity," but when he describes the profane, he contents himself with "unreal, 'absolute non-being,' and chaotic,"[98] leaving out the term *power*, which was for Eliade an essential component that enabled the sacred to organize human activity around itself.

Note the implication of Smith's departure from Eliadean presuppositions in his own later discussion of sacred space: "Ritual is not the expression of a response to 'the sacred'; rather, something or someone is made sacred by ritual."[99] Smith's refusal to entertain the possibility that humans actually may encounter something real and powerful that "imposes itself on them" is fundamental to his developed sense of what religion is and what the study of religion is about:

> What we study when we study religion is one mode of constructing worlds of meaning... religion is the quest, within the bounds of the human, historical condition, for the power to manipulate and negotiate one's "situation" so as to have "space" in which to meaningfully dwell. It is the power to relate one's domain to the plurality of environmental and social spheres in such a way as to guarantee the conviction that one's existence "matters."
> ... What we study when we study religion is the variety of attempts to map, construct and inhabit such positions of

"I stand squarely in the rationalist tradition. I have an uncompromising faith in reason and intellection. My intellectual ancestors are the Scottish Enlightenment figures. Not surprisingly, I accord religion no privilege" (p. 206); and later, "For me, things are surface: there simply is no depth; there simply is no original; and there is no concealment. It's all out there, it's plain, it's ordinary, it's largely uninteresting, and it's utterly — in fact overwhelmingly, that's the problem for a scholar — accessible" (p. 211).

98. "Wobbling Point" (1972), in *Map Is Not Territory*, 91.

99. *To Take Place*, 105.

power through the use of myths, rituals and experiences of transcendence.[100]

We see in this double definition that both religion and its study are purely human endeavors, that both are fundamentally cognitive in character, a question of "mapping" human existence. More pertinent to my present topic, we see that the term *power* here occurs entirely as something exerted by humans rather than something exerted on humans: it is their "power to manipulate and negotiate" situations for existential significance.

Whereas Eliade thought that analysis of religious experience could "open up the reality" that such experiences signified,[101] Smith progressively moves toward an explicit rejection of any such reality. In one of his earlier essays he was willing to grant a tension between "the subjects' sense of the unique and the methodological requirement of the analysis,"[102] but in "Good News Is No News," he places inverted commas around the term "experience" when speaking of Levi's encounter with Apollonius of Tyana.[103] To some extent, Smith's strictures can be seen as methodological fastidiousness. If the student of religion is essentially a historian, then there can be "no privilege to myth or other religious material. They must be understood primarily as texts in context…no privilege to the so-called exotic. For there is no primordium — it is all history. There is no 'other' — it is all what we see in Europe every day."[104] Adherence to a

---

100. *Map Is Not Territory*, 290–91. In this still-early statement, Smith uses the phrase, "experiences of transcendence," but does so in an instrumentalist way: with myths and rituals, such "experiences" are the means to inhabit positions of power.

101. "Wobbling Pivot" (1972), in *Map Is Not Territory*, 94.

102. "Adde Parvum Parvo" (1971), in *Map Is Not Territory*, 243.

103. "No News Is Good News" (1975), in *Map Is Not Territory*, 191.

104. Jonathan Z. Smith, *Imagining Religion: From Babylon to Jamestown*

consistent historical methodology thus eliminates revelation in any traditional sense of the term; all of history has been brought to the level of the observer.[105] If the study of religion is exclusively an academic enterprise, in fact, then statements as startling as this one appear logical:

> Religion is solely the creation of the scholar's study. It is created for the scholar's analytic purposes. Religion has no independent existence apart from the academy. For this reason, the student of religion must be relentlessly self-conscious. Indeed, this self-consciousness constitutes his primary expertise, *his foremost object of study.*[106]

The effect of this, of course, is to make academic discourse the actual subject of religious studies.[107]

Smith's concern that religious studies not become a covert form of theology (or *sapientia*) and insistence that it be located within the human sciences (as *scientia*) makes intelligible his privileging of the general over the particular, for it is not the "territory" but the "map" that is of interest:

(Chicago Studies in the History of Judaism; Chicago: University of Chicago Press, 1982) xiii; see also "Coup d'Essai," 19; *Violent Origins,* 195–96.

105. Although Smith's phrasings are always fresh and vivid, one sees in his statements the same historiographical principles enunciated by Ernst Troeltsch: criticism, analogy, and correlation; see E. Troeltsch, "Historical and Dogmatic Method in Theology" (1898), in *Religion in History,* trans. J. L. Adams and A. F. Bense (Minneapolis: Fortress Press, 1991) 11–32. For the pervasive influence of Troeltsch on contemporary discussions, see, e.g., V. A. Harvey, *The Historian and the Believer* (New York: Macmillan, 1966) 3–37; and J. Bowden, *Jesus: The Unanswered Questions* (Nashville: Abingdon Press, 1989) 148–64.

106. *Imagining Religion,* xi. Emphasis in original.

107. By no means is Smith unaware of this conclusion; indeed, he takes delight in emphasizing it: see " 'Religion' and 'Religious Studies'," 231–44.

For the self-conscious student of religion, no datum possesses intrinsic interest. It is of value only insofar as it
can serve as *exempli gratia* of some fundamental issue in
the interpretation of religion. The student of religion
must be able to articulate clearly why "this" rather than
"that" was chosen as an exemplum....This effort...is
all the more difficult, and hence all the more necessary, for the historian of religion who accepts neither
the boundaries of canon nor of community in consti-
tuting his intellectual domain, in providing his range of
examples.[108]

Given these perceptions and presuppositions, we can
better understand why Smith, whose training is in "the religions of the Mediterranean world during the Hellenistic
Period,"[109] apparently finds so little in Christianity to interest him. In the Hellenistic period, after all, what we mainly
have are discrete particulars and reports of experiences,
rather than well-defined patterns that might serve as *exempla* to illuminate major issues in religious studies. In "The
Temple and the Magician," first published in 1976, Smith brilliantly identified the ways in which reformation perceptions
had affected the study of "pagano-papism," and developed a
theoretical position to which he returned later concerning
"locative" traditions and "utopian" movements.[110] In "Good
News Is No News: Aretalogy and Gospel," published in 1975,
he used a comparative literary approach to relativize any
claim of Christian Gospels to uniqueness.[111] In "Adde Parvum
Parvo Magnus Acervus Erit," first published in 1971, Smith

---

108. *Imagining Religion*, xi.

109. "Coup d'Essai," 19

110. See *Map Is Not Territory*, 172–89; for the discussion of pagano-papism,
see p. 188.

111. See ibid., 190–205.

illumined the gray areas shared by ancient religion and magic.[112] Aside from some initial interest in the social description of early Christianity,[113] these essays are (so far as I have determined) the main pieces in Smith's prodigious scholarly output that deal with specifically Christian materials.[114] Earliest Christianity did not seem a good source for the *exempla* Smith finds pertinent to broad issues in the study of religion.

Against this backdrop, the appearance in 1990 of *Drudgery Divine,* which is subtitled *On the Comparison of Early Christianities and the Religions of Late Antiquity* was of obvious interest to scholars in the field of religious studies.[115] It appeared that Smith would finally direct his methodological precision and enormous learning to the clarification of the problem that most befuddled and finally betrayed the first history-of-religions school.

One of the most interesting things about Smith's book, however, is the way in which he does not meet this expectation, but does so with great brilliance. It is in the odd way his polymathic prowess turns ultimately into a kind of shrug that we find in this book perhaps the parable of contemporary study of early Christianity. The pattern shows itself first

112. Ibid., 240–64; see also idem, "Towards Interpreting Demonic Powers in Hellenistic and Roman Antiquity," *ANRW* II Principat 16.1 (1978) 425–39.

113. See Smith, "The Social Description of Early Christianity," *Religious Studies Review* 1 (1975) 19–25; and idem, "Too Much Kingdom, Too Little Community," *Zygon* 13 (1978) 123–30.

114. I may well have missed some of his essays, even important ones, but the ones I have listed here are those that have surfaced after a reasonable search.

115. The book began as the fourteenth Jordan Lectures in Comparative Religion, given at the School of Oriental and African Studies, University of London, in 1988, and was published in the Chicago Studies in the History of Judaism, edited by W. S. Green and C. Goldscheider (Chicago: University of Chicago Press, 1990).

in the way that Smith's unquestioned learning — his astonishing knowledge of the most obscure texts and his capacity to interrogate them in the minutest detail — seems finally not to go anywhere. Take for example his chapter, "On Comparing Words," which takes as its topic the occurrence of the term *mystērion*.

The essay ranges widely across secondary scholarship and primary sources, moves into technical subdiscussions of the most exquisite subtlety and out again to the most sweeping comprehension of the broad and complex Hellenistic world. In the process, Smith makes some individual points of great significance, among them that philology has been used as much for apologetic as for historical ends, that words taken out of context are insufficient and misleading, and that the use of *mystērion* by the Septuagint shows that the New Testament could have used such language quite comfortably. But in the end, his argument serves much more to indict Christian scholars of bad faith for the ways in which they have avoided the issue, than it does actually to clarify the issue of *mystērion* language in the New Testament.

The pattern is found also in his castigation of Protestant scholars for their rejection of "pagano-papism," which Smith correctly, I think, connects to the polemics of anti-Catholicism.[116] He sees clearly that for such scholars,

> Judaism has served a double (or, a duplicitous) function. On the one hand, it has provided apologetic scholars with an insulation for early Christianity, guarding it against "influence" from its environment. On the other hand, it has been presented by the very same scholars as an object to be transcended by early Christianity.[117]

116. *Drudgery Divine*, 1–35, 114–15.
117. Ibid., 83.

We might expect such a demystification to be turned to a positive argument that would say that, in fact, Christianity is deeply influenced by Judaism and just as deeply influenced by the mysteries. This would be the logical opposite of the apologetic protectionist stance. By showing how thoroughly the New Testament was immersed, like Judaism, in the language of the mysteries, Smith could rescue earliest Christianity from its Protestant protectors and restore it to its messy but Catholic birth.

Instead, however, Smith seems much more intent on denying that Christianity was an identifiable religious entity at all. At the end of the chapter, he quotes David Aune disapprovingly as representing both apologetic tendencies he has identified. Aune says, "The Christianity of the New Testament is a creative combination of Jewish and Hellenistic traditions transformed into a *tertium quid* (a 'Third Something'): that is, a reality related to two known things but transcending them both."[118] Why is Smith so disapproving? Aune seems only to be saying that Christianity was a new thing distinguishable from its environment. Two things must bother Smith. The first is Aune's use of the word *transcending,* which Smith hears as implying uniqueness or superiority rather than (as probably intended) simply difference. For Smith, transcendence suggests origination, a category he emphatically rejects.[119] Once one grants any substantial reality to

118. David Aune, *The New Testament in Its Literary Environment* (Philadelphia: Westminster Press, 1987) 12, cited in *Drudgery Divine,* 83 n. 43.

119. See, e.g., *Violent Origins,* 235: "Talk of privilege is about presuppositions that we hold because of who we are, presuppositions that we see as self-evident. I understand "roots and origins" to be that kind of presupposition. It's not just a linguistic notion. *It's the notion that religion was formed at some point in time, and that an understanding of that point in time is a privileged understanding.*" I have underscored the last sentence to show how Smith tends to identify two distinct things. To claim origins does not mean that origins defines essence (although he is right, scholars often have). And the (correct)

earliest Christianity, then one acknowledges the importance of "origins," and (for Smith) one is not far from another sort of "transcendence," namely, the claim to the revelation of an Other and therefore the claim to a unique religious validity.[120]

The worry that granting Christianity any distinctiveness must lead to a triumphalistic trumpeting of its superiority leads to Smith's effectively seeking to dissolve Christianity into its Greco-Roman and Jewish milieu. Notice that the subtitle of his book is *On the Comparison of Early Christianities!* It is perhaps in this light that we can understand Smith's slighting characterization of "the Christ event" as the purported start of the religion,[121] and his remarkable recommendation of Burton Mack's *The Myth of Innocence* as the "first study of 'Christian origins' which may be taken up, with profit, by the general student of *religion.*"[122] I call the recommendation remarkable because of the deeply flawed character of Mack's work.[123] One suspects that Smith's approbation has less to do with the adequacy of Mack's account than with Mack's sharing Smith's own presuppositions: history dissolves all claims to revelation and thereby deprives Christianity of any special claim to uniqueness. Indeed, rather than a coherent religious movement generated by a resurrection experience,

---

denial of the privileged *interpretive* stance of origins should not lead to the denial that specific religions do have origins — at the very least, that they emerge as distinguishable entities at some historical point! Smith's worry about the epistemological (and axiological) issue seems in the case of Christianity to lead him to a peculiar historical rigidity.

120. Note the strong rejection of the "experiential" because of its apparently inevitable connection to the concept of revelation, in *Divine Drudgery,* 54–55.

121. Ibid., 142–43.

122. Ibid., 110 n. 43.

123. See my brief discussion of Mack's work in *The Real Jesus,* 15, 50–54, 100–101, as well as in my review essay, "The Crisis in Biblical Scholarship," *Commonweal* 120/21 (1993) 18–21.

Christianity is dissolved into a loose arrangement of competing political and ideological claims within the Jewish version of Hellenistic culture.

By placing the seal of academic correctness on Mack's effort, Smith is once more consistent: no more than any religion can earliest Christianity be about a human experience of power that opens up a deeper reality inaccessible to history. It can only be about the manipulation of human power within the closed system of history, "what we see in Europe every day."

As we might expect, Smith's book shows no interest in the sort of religious experiences the Greco-Roman and Jewish mysteries might have involved for their participants or how these experiences might have thrown light on the experiences of those who were part of the earliest Christian movement. For Smith to acknowledge the validity of the concept of "Christian experience" would mean to acknowledge that there was an "origin" to this religion that was something more than the confluence of disparate strands. But to ignore the language of religious experience in early Christian writings is to neglect the specific historical character of this movement and thereby to make its historical continuation and success all the more difficult to understand.

The issue here is not, as Smith seems to think, that Christianity's distinctiveness is equivalent to a claim to its uniqueness and therefore its privileged character as revelation. The issue is whether, by ignoring the specific contours of a historical phenomenon and allowing them to be absorbed into a general theoretical framework, we can say we have done history at all. If Jonathan Z. Smith represents the best and most methodologically consistent work in religious studies, and if his work ends up ignoring the specific religious language of the New Testament, then it is appropriate to ask whether in this case also the historical paradigm has not, in its implicit — and sometimes explicit — claim to unique epistemological validity, simply led scholarship into a dead end. We need to ask whether another way of thinking about religion might help us deal with the language that the scholarship we have reviewed has so completely missed or misapprehended.

GETTING AT
CHRISTIAN EXPERIENCE

Despite its impressive erudition on so many points, scholarship on earliest Christianity has somehow managed to leave out of account the most interesting thing about the first Christians, namely, their claims to having specific religious experiences. I have suggested that the best effort to capture the significance of such claims was made by the history-of-religions school, but that recent scholarship has increasingly moved from a concern with religious experience toward an analysis of religion in terms of a manipulation and mapping of human ideological and political interests.

We learn thereby something about the sociology of knowledge, which is as applicable to the community of scholars as it is to any group they study.[1] There are fashions in scholarship that function as structures of plausibility and need to be recognized as such. What the scholarly guild recognizes as significant may not be what is actually most important. But what its methods or presuppositions do not allow to be seen, might as well not exist.[2] We also thereby, I hope, learn

---

1. See K. Mannheim, *Ideology and Utopia: An Introduction to the Sociology of Knowledge,* trans. L. Wirth and E. Shils (New York: Harcourt, Brace and Company, 1936) 264–311; P. L Berger and T. Luckmann, *The Social Construction of Reality: A Treatise in the Sociology of Knowledge* (New York: Doubleday, 1966); and P. Berger, *The Sacred Canopy: Elements of a Sociological Theory of Religion* (New York: Doubleday, 1967).

2. The point is given classic expression by Stanley Fish, *Is There a Text in*

something even more fundamental about epistemology: reality is richer and more complex than can be apprehended by any single mode of cognition, and an exclusive commitment to one mode of knowledge inevitably excludes as much as it includes.[3]

The writing of Jonathan Z. Smith illustrates both points. Smith has repeatedly and shrewdly demonstrated how certain "Protestant presuppositions" within scholarship have precluded a fair assessment of the religious character of early Christianity.[4] But his statements also reveal a set of presuppositions of his own that are at least as distorting of the data

This Class? The Authority of Interpretive Communities (Cambridge: Harvard University Press, 1982), esp. the chapter "What Makes Interpretation Acceptable?" 338–55.

3. It is certainly the case that every method of inquiry must be implicitly imperialistic and reductionistic. That is, it must seek to explain everything it can in terms of its perspective, and it cannot *apriori* leave aside anything as privileged and unavailable for analysis. The mathematician is required to reduce everything possible to numbers. The psychologist is also correct in seeking to explain every phenomenon in psychological terms; functioning *as* psychologist, her analysis of religion must "reduce" religion to psychology. To do otherwise would be to betray the method. The same consistency is required also of the sociologist and historian: the first must seek to explain everything possible from the standpoint of social structures and dynamics, the second from the perspective of human events in time and space. The difficulty arises when this implicit reduction becomes explicit and negates the legitimacy of other modes of knowing or other dimensions of being not accessible to the method in question. Thus method becomes madness when the historian seeks to limit reality to "the historical," just as it is when the psychologist refuses to acknowledge any reality other than "the psychic." There is a subtle but important difference between saying, "Within the frame of historical methodology this experience does not exist," and saying *simpliciter,* "this experience does not (or cannot) exist."

4. See Jonathan Z. Smith, "The Temple and the Magician" (1976), in *Map Is Not Territory: Studies in the History of Religions* (Studies in Judaism in Late Antiquity 23; Leiden: E. J. Brill, 1978) 188; and idem, *Drudgery Divine: On the Comparison of Early Christianities and the Religions of Late Antiquity* (Chicago Studies in the History of Judaism; Chicago: University of Chicago Press, 1990) 1–35.

as those to which he objects. His theoretical refusal to acknowledge any reality beyond that capable of being described
"historically" leads to a methodological flattening of the very
subject being studied.[5]

If one's theory demands that language of religious experience is either meaningless or manipulative, then the
distinctive Christian claims to experience must either be ignored or reduced to political position-taking. This must lead,
in turn, to the dissolution of earliest Christianity itself —
either into ideologically competing factions or, because there
can be no *novum* in history so construed,[6] into the Greco-
Roman and Jewish *Umwelt*. The reason is simple enough. It is
impossible to "map" a religious world before it is constructed.
In the period of Christian nascence — the time when the New
Testament was being composed — there is not yet any such
stability. The indications of world-construction are inchoate
and not entirely coherent. Given Smith's theoretical perspective, then, and its methodological corollaries, there really is
not much to see and little to say about the "Christian religion"
as found in the writings of the New Testament.

Any theoretical starting point that disables engagement
with the classic and formative literature of a world religion
in its own terms might well be regarded as deficient. But
Smith's theoretical commitment to "history" — at least in the
way he defines it — can also be recognized as itself thoroughly ideological. The reduction of religion to a cognitive
"mapping of reality," and the premise that ancient people's
religious language was not expressive of real experience, is a

5. See, e.g., *Violent Origins: Walter Burkert, René Girard and Jonathan Z.
Smith on Ritual Killing and Cultural Formation*, ed. R. G. Hammerton-Kelly
(Stanford, Calif.: Stanford University Press, 1987) 198; Smith, *Drudgery Divine*,
54–55.

6. See *Violent Origins*, 195–96, and J. Z. Smith, *Imagining Religion: From
Babylon to Jamestown* (Chicago Studies in the History of Judaism; Chicago:
University of Chicago Press, 1982) xiii.

position that is neither self-evident nor demanded by the literature under examination. It is, rather, the expression of a philosophical commitment that is at root profoundly ahistorical, since it anachronistically projects onto the entire world of antiquity the demystified consciousness peculiarly characteristic of a certain segment of the educated population of post-seventeenth-century European culture.[7]

Smith's insistence that the past must be just like "what we see in Europe every day" represents a rejection of the "other" on the historical plane cognate to the rejection of "the Other" that religious language itself insists on speaking of — a flattening of the world to the profane place of human cognitive control and human political manipulation. But this is no longer history. It is certainly not a neutral analysis. It resembles, rather, an alternative a-theology.[8]

For the study of earliest Christianity adequately to engage its religious language, then, it must not only abandon

7. In this respect, Smith interestingly exemplifies Eliade's portrayal of "the modern societies of the West"; see M. Eliade, *The Sacred and the Profane: The Nature of Religion,* trans. W. R. Trask (New York: Harcourt, Brace and World, 1959) 201–13; and idem, *Cosmos and History: The Myth of the Eternal Return,* trans. W. R. Trask (New York: Harper and Row, 1959) 147–59. Eliade, in fact, spoke of his conviction "that Western philosophy is dangerously close to 'provincializing' itself (if the expression is permitted): first by jealously isolating itself in its own tradition and ignoring, for example, the problems and solutions of Oriental thought; second by its obstinate refusal to recognize any 'situations' except those of the man of the historical civilizations, in defiance of the experience of 'primitive' man, man as a member of the traditional societies." *Cosmos and History,* xii.

8. In " 'Religion' and 'Religious Studies': No Difference at All," *Soundings* 71 (1988) 231–44, Smith dismisses not only any distinction between religion and the study of it, but also anything distinctive to religious studies itself, and finally any solid distinction between the humanities and social sciences. He considers any appeal to a "special subject" to be a disguised form of apologetics. For a review of the way in which Smith's intellectual influence has become a political issue in religious studies departments, see C. Allen, "Is Nothing Sacred? Casting the Gods from Religious Studies," *Linguafranca: The Review of Academic Life* 6/7 (1996) 30–40.

the apologetic tendencies that have denied or suppressed the presence and implications of such language. Equally important is that such study employ an epistemology appropriate to the subject. In this chapter I argue that historical analysis must be complemented (not replaced) by a phenomenological approach to earliest Christianity's religious language and behavior.

I use the expression "phenomenological approach" as lightly as possible. I want to exploit the fundamental advantages of the philosophical outlook and approach associated with Edmund Husserl,[9] without getting enmeshed in the endless technical disquisitions and disputations that every philosophy engenders.[10] For my purposes here, I understand "phenomenological" to be a critical inquiry into consciousness and its contents, taking with equal seriousness the *noesis* (or knowing subject) and the *noema* (or subject known) in all their delicate interplay, while bracketing (holding in

9. Part of the difficulty in pinning down phenomenology is that much of what it is about was present even before Husserl, and its manifestations after Husserl are both multiple and complex; see H. Spiegelberg, *The Phenomenological Movement: A Historical Introduction,* 2 vols. (Phaenomenologica 5; The Hague: Martinus Nijhoff, 1971). Husserl's writings are voluminous and mostly untranslated; in English, see *Ideas: General Introduction to Pure Phenomenology,* trans. W. R. B. Gibson (London: George Allen & Unwin, 1931); *Phenomenology and the Crisis of Philosophy,* trans. Q. Lauer (New York: Harper and Row, 1965); and *Husserl's Shorter Works,* ed. P. McCormick and F. A. Elliston (Notre Dame, Ind.: University of Notre Dame Press, 1981).

10. For a sense of internal conversations and of the variety of topics considered phenomenologically, see, among many others, *Descriptions,* ed. D. Ihde and H. J. Silverman (Selected Studies in Phenomenology and Existential Philosophy 11; Albany: State University of New York Press, 1985); *Life-World and Consciousness: Essays for Aron Gurwitsch,* ed. L. E. Embree (Northwestern University Studies in Phenomenology and Existential Philosophy; Evanston: Northwestern University Press, 1972); *Phenomenological Perspectives: Historical and Systematic Essays in Honor of Herbert Spiegelberg,* ed. P. J. Bossert (Phaenomenologica 62; The Hague: Martinus Nijhoff, 1975); A. Schutz, *On Phenomenology and Social Relations,* ed. H. R. Wagner (Heritage of Sociology; Chicago: University of Chicago Press, 1970).

suspension) judgments concerning the extramental existence or non-existence of such states of consciousness. I take it to be fundamentally a kind of contemplation of, and reflection on, that which appears before us, an attempt to "see" a *phenomenon* from as many perspectives as possible, as fully as possible, trying to tease out "what is this before us." It is a mode of analysis that by concentrating on a single subject in all its visible connections enables a distinctive and valuable sort of understanding.[11]

By advocating a phenomenological approach to the religious experiences of early Christians, however, I do not want to locate my investigation within that ambiguous body of literature which has been termed the "phenomenology of religion," even though some of my interests and sensibilities are similar.[12] Nor is my call for a phenomenological approach the construction of a new "method" that purports to yield predictable results. I am not so much recommending a toolkit that can do new things as I am appealing for a willingness to

---

11. For particularly vivid presentations of what is involved in the *epoché*, see R. M. Zaner, *The Way of Phenomenology: Criticism as a Philosophical Discipline* (New York: Pegasus, 1970) 41–78; and J. G. Hart, *The Person and the Common Life: Studies in a Husserlian Social Ethics* (Phaenomenologica 126; Dordrecht: Kluwer Academic Publishers, 1992) 5–10.

12. The designation is used by, or of, a variety of approaches to the study of religions; for a sense of this variety, see *Phenomenology of Religion: Eight Modern Descriptions of the Essence of Religion*, ed. J. D. Bettis (London: SCM Press, 1969), and esp. the full discussion of internal criticism and variation in *Experience of the Sacred: Readings in the Phenomenology of Religion*, ed. S. B. Twiss and W. H. Conser Jr. (Hanover, N.H.: Brown University Press, 1990) 1–74. A taste of the substantial and sustained criticism levelled at the approach, especially as exemplified by M. Eliade, can be found in H. Penner, "Is Phenomenology a Method for the Study of Religion?" *Bucknell Review* 18 (1970) 29–54; H. Penner and E. A. Yonan, "Is a Science of Religion Possible?" *Journal of Religion* 52 (1972) 107–33; R. A. Segal, "In Defense of Reductionism," *Journal of the American Academy of Religion* 51 (1983) 97–124; G. Dudley, *Religion on Trial: Mircea Eliade and His Critics* (Philadelphia: Temple University Press, 1977); and B. S. Rennie, *Reconstructing Eliade: Making Sense of Religion* (Albany: State University of New York Press, 1996) 119–212.

look at texts with a certain sensibility out of a conviction that such seeing is not without point.

A phenomenological approach has three virtues that recommend it, especially since they are virtues that the purely historical paradigm lacks. First, phenomenology is good at dealing with the particular as opposed to the general; its whole point is the accurate and if possible adequate perception of a specific phenomenon, demanding of its practitioner the patience to see something from every angle, staying with the particular until it reveals itself more fully, without precipitate categorization or reduction to some "general law or issue."[13] Second, phenomenology is comfortable with language that expresses experience, with the specifically emic dimension of human reality that the social sciences — and the history of religions shaped by a social-scientific attitude — find scientifically negligible.[14] Third, despite my uneasiness about some of its practices, the classic literature of the

13. In my own reading, this quality has been best exemplified by the remarkably rich and evocative reflections of Gabriel Marcel, e.g., *Homo Viator: Introduction to a Metaphysic of Hope*, trans. E. Craufurd (New York: Harper and Row, 1962); idem, *Creative Fidelity*, trans. R. Rosthal (New York: Farrar, Straus & Co., 1964). And this is one of the ways in which the "phenomenology of religion" as practiced by Gerardus Van der Leeuw, William B. Kristensen, Rudolf Otto, and Eliade, actually fails to employ phenomenological method: too frequently catalogues of "empirical" observations are adduced in service of some "essential" element of religion; the actual *description*, so critical to phenomenology properly executed, is missing.

14. See, e.g., P. Ricoeur's "Phenomenology of 'Confession'" in *The Symbolism of Evil*, trans. E. Buchanan (Boston: Beacon Press, 1967) 3–24; see also pp. 306–57. Although appearing in a remarkably confused argument, Eliade's observation on the value of the emic is worth noting: "Paul Radin felt he has the right to reject the conclusions reached by the missionary Gusinde in his researches because his inquiries were limited to one man. Such an attitude would be justified only if the object of the inquiry were a strictly sociological one: if it were the religious life of a Fuegian community at a given time; but when it is a question of discovering what capacity the Fuegians have of experiencing religion, then the position is quite different." *Patterns in Comparative Religion*, 6.

phenomenology of religion is specifically attentive to the element of *power* as a key element in religion, both as a component of experience, and as the organizing point for the social expressions of experience.[15] Since, as I have already indicated, the New Testament is literally filled with the language of power, it would seem logical to appropriate the diagnostic categories provided by this literature.

Assessing Experience

I appreciate why the very idea of experience is one that historians and social scientists alike would find so frustrating that they ignore or suppress it, for the category is, in all honesty, an extraordinarily difficult one with which to work, even if we modestly limit our investigation to "human experience."[16] Experience is, unlike events, connected to individuals as individuals. We can speak of historical or social events as encompassing crowds (as rock concerts do) or nations (as wars and battles do). And such events can, at least in rough and ready fashion, be defined. Spatial and temporal lines of enclosure can be drawn around them, so that analysts

15. This is above all the case with G. Van der Leeuw, who makes power the key diagnostic category in his *Religion in Essence and Manifestation: A Study in Phenomenology*, 2 vols., trans. J. E. Turner (1st German ed. 1933; New York: Harper and Row, 1963); see esp. 1:1–51, 101–58, 169–87. See also R. Otto, *The Idea of the Holy: An Inquiry into the Non-Rational Factor in the Idea of the Divine and Its Relation to the Rational*, trans. J. W. Harvey (1st German ed. 1917; London: Oxford University Press, 1923) 19–24; M. Eliade, *Patterns in Comparative Religion*, trans. R. Sheed (New York: World Publishing Co., 1963) 13–26; M. Eliade, *Myth and Reality*, trans. W. R. Trask (New York: Harper and Row, 1963) 19, 30, 34, 36–37, 51; W. B. Kristensen, *The Meaning of Religion: Lectures in the Phenomenology of Religion*, trans. J. B. Carman (The Hague: Martinus Nijhoff, 1960) 173–86, 285.

16. See the remarks of W. Proudfoot, *Religious Experience* (Berkeley: University of California Press, 1985) 155–89.

can work with an agreed upon "stop frame": we are talking here about the "Landing at Anzio" not the "Normandy Beachhead."

Yet reflection makes clear that the experience of any event is communal only by extension and abstraction. To speak of a "group experience," then, is to speak analogously. At a concert, each musician and each listener experiences the music differently, as they do also all the other sensory and psychic dimensions of the event. In war, battles are notoriously experienced differently by their individual participants: at Normandy some men were shot on beaches, others slept under hedgerows. And whereas an "event" can at least in principle and for the purpose of analysis be assigned a beginning and end, experience is not so easily demarcated into an "experience of X" as opposed to an "experience of Y"; the realm of experience is one of flow and flux more than that of discrete and isolated moments. The problem for the scientist in the individual character of experience is patent: the need endlessly to gather data is an obstacle to generalization.

The reason why human experience is irreducibly individual is that it is inexorably somatic. Two bodies can no more occupy the identical place or perceive from the same perspective than they can experience identically. But to say that experience involves bodies does not go far enough. Experience is not simply somatic, it is also psychosomatic. The experience of pain is not only the reflex of nerves to a stimulus, it is also the *consciousness* of the reflex. Hearing music is more than the simple stimulation of nerve endings in our ears by vibration; it involves as well the mental activity of somehow "following" and "connecting" sounds. The psychosomatic character of experience renders it both ineluctably individual and incredibly complex to analyze.[17]

17. See D. Leder, *The Absent Body* (Chicago: University of Chicago Press, 1990) esp. 1–99.

When we reflect on it, for example, we realize that human experience always involves (so to speak) both an inner and outer aspect. The body, indeed, is something of a bridge: across it moves the (outer) external encounter, the (inner) realm of psychic apprehension and the (outer) sphere of physical expression. Of course, such spatial language can be misleading, for there is surely an "inwardness" to the body as well, and experience can be generated by movements within as much as from encounters without. The phenomenology of body is itself made extraordinarily complex by the difficulty of discerning between the body as that which one is and the body as that which one has.[18]

Because of this inward dimension of human experience — even that involving the sheerest collision between bodies — analysis of experience necessarily depends on some sort of report from the one experiencing. For the scientist, such mediation presents still another nightmare; experience is inaccessible except through subjective consciousness and the communication of that consciousness. At a concert, for example, it is impossible to tell from bodily posture alone what an individual is experiencing. Closed eyes could signify ecstasy or boredom. Rhythmic movement could be in response to the music or to a psychic twitch. In battle, does a soldier's hand shake? It could be from fear or from cold or from excited anticipation. Does the soldier lie on the ground and moan? It could be shell-shock or exhaustion or dysentery. Body language gives us some clues, but they are not sufficient. Some outward expression by symbolic gesture or speech is necessary if we are to have closer access to another's experience than that made possible by the reading of tics and grimaces. Even then, as the sad story of human rela-

---

18. See G. Marcel, "Outlines of a Phenomenology of Having," in *Being and Having*, trans. A. and C. Black (London: Dacre, 1949; Collins Fontana Library, 1965) 168–89.

tions makes clear, much of what we experience is in any case strictly incommunicable. States of deep pleasure and great joy are notoriously incapable of being rendered by words, and no medium can adequately express pain, the uniquely subjective category for the presence or intensity of which we have no alternative but to rely on the other's testimony.[19]

For these same reasons, experience is also invariably an interpreted reality, that is, the experience itself is at least partially constituted by the interpretation of the experiencing subject. Interpretation does not follow only after the fact, as though to clothe a naked encounter but is itself an essential component of the experience. It follows that language (in the broadest sense of that term) plays a role not only in the communication of experience to others but also and above all in shaping the experience as it occurs. Language is therefore part of experience's embodiedness, for every individual subject's perception is particular and conditioned not only by the symbols available but also by that individual's apprehension of those symbols.[20]

It can even be said that certain linguistic/cultural symbols *enable* experiences that others do not. The claim that one has been touched by visitors from another place, or that one has ascended into heights above the earth, for example, has quite a different quality if the symbolism available for interpretation is that of science-fiction and space technology or the symbolism is that of the Bible. In one case, my "experience" of transport is one of a close encounter with

19. See F. J. J. Buytendijk, *Pain: Its Modes and Functions,* trans. E. O'Shiel (1943; Chicago: University of Chicago Press, 1961); see also the analogy between the analysis of religious experience and medical diagnosis in C. D. Batson and W. C. Ventis, *The Religious Experience: A Social-Psychological Perspective* (New York: Oxford University Press, 1982) 18–19.

20. This insight is fundamental to what is sometimes called the "existential-hermeneutical" phenomenology of religion; see Twiss and Conser, *Experience of the Sacred,* 54–70.

extraterrestrial aliens; in the other my flight is through the heaven with the angels surrounding the throne chariot.[21] The psychosomatic grounding of the respective *experiences* (whatever we may think of them) may be similar, but the meaning of the experience is dramatically divergent.

While giving full recognition to the way in which our shared symbols shape our experiences, however, it is also important that we not overstate the case, as though our symbolic worlds rigidly determined the shape of experience. The fact that symbols *change* in meaning, sometimes slowly, sometimes with amazing speed, is the surest indication that something more than human linguistic patterns are at work and that the term *experience* points to something real in the world that is not completely captured by our preset explanations and interpretations. The traffic, in short, moves both ways. Our language shapes our experience, but our experience also stretches, reshapes, and sometimes even shatters our language. Something happens to the phrase "Pearl River Swamp" once it is no longer a name on a map of Mississippi, but a miasmic morass in which I am lost. Likewise, the meaning of the word "terror" is altered when I have been suddenly and brutally attacked in the night. Some experiences can be contained within old symbols as variations on a theme, but some are so powerful that they give entirely new content to a symbol. Surely the word *holocaust* now has a specific weight of meaning that was available to no reader of the Bible before 1932.[22]

---

21. For the symbolism of Merkabah mysticism, see G. G. Scholem, *Major Trends in Jewish Mysticism* (New York: Schocken Books, 1961) 1–79; L. T. Johnson, "Gnosticism in the Rabbinic Tradition," *Resonance* 4 (1969) 5–17; and M. Himmelfarb, *Ascent to Heaven in Jewish and Christian Apocalypses* (New York: Oxford University Press, 1993).

22. For the reshaping of symbolic worlds in response to powerful experience, see L. T. Johnson, *The Writings of the New Testament: An Interpretation* (Philadelphia: Fortress Press, 1986) 11–18; for the impact of the Holocaust on the Jewish reading of the Bible, see, e.g., E. L. Fackenheim, *The Jewish Bible*

Given the individual, psychosomatic, interior, subjective, and interpretive character of experience, it is small wonder that scientists would rather not take it into account. Small wonder, when phenomenological studies themselves become so involved with separating out the observing subject from the experiencing subject that they sometimes appear as exercises in infinite regress,[23] seeming never to get anywhere definite. Although after going through them one seems somehow indefinably enriched, such studies however careful seem themselves never actually to get at the experience except as the penumbra of consciousness (that is, after all, only part of the experience). Small wonder that historians flee with gratitude to categories of perhaps coarser grain but of far greater visibility, like events!

Yet we must also recognize the loss involved in such flight. What, after all, is the meaning of any human event, if it is abstracted from all the personal experiences in which that event consists? What does it mean to speak of the Holocaust, for example, if the term is used only to demarcate the movement of physical and military and political bodies but takes no account of the testimony of individual, subjective, interpreted experience given by some of those particular bodies? Experience may be impossible for us adequately to analyze, but its reality and importance we must at all cost maintain. The denial or suppression of experience leads to what Giambattista Vico called the "conceit of scholars," that is, the arrogant

---

after the Holocaust: A ReReading (Bloomington, Ind.: Indiana University Press, 1990).

23. See, e.g., M. Merleau-Ponty, *The Primacy of Perception, and Other Essays on Phenomenological Psychology, the Philosophy of Art, History, and Politics,* ed. J. M. Edie (Northwestern University Studies in Phenomenology and Existential Philosophy; Evanston: Northwestern University Press, 1968); and idem, *The Visible and the Invisible: Followed by Working Notes,* ed. C. leFort, trans. A. Lingis (Northwestern University Studies in Phenomenology and Existential Philosophy; Evanston: Northwestern University Press, 1968).

assumption that the parts of reality that fit our cognitive grids equal all of reality.[24]

Nor should we ever agree that the patient unknotting of complex subjective testimony is somehow a form of self-indulgence by comparison with the serious business of statistical or social-scientific analysis. Each mode of knowing has its value, to be sure. But it is also surely the case that one could organize all the data concerning all the work and death camps run by the Nazis in World War II, including all logs and bills of lading and transport records and official communiques and records of fuel production and consumption, and never come to the meaning of the encounter with powerful evil we call the Holocaust that is given by the simple testimonies of experience given by Anne Frank or Elie Wiesel. And this is not because these narratives are more moving than the statistics; it is because without the individual human testimony by innocent people about their experience of gratuitous and systematic evil, the "event" of the Holocaust also is dissolved into the ordinary machinery of war, for that is all the truth that the statistics can ever yield.[25]

24. The expression occurs in G. Vico, *The New Science,* paragraphs 122–28; I came on it in J. S. Preus, *Explaining Religion: Criticism and Theory from Bodin to Freud* (New Haven: Yale University Press, 1987) 67–68. See also the comment by William James, "The first thing to bear in mind (especially if we ourselves belong to the clerico-academic-scientific type, the officially and conventionally 'correct' type, 'the deadly respectable' type, for which to ignore others is a besetting temptation) is that nothing can be more stupid than to bar out phenomena from our notice, merely because we are incapable of taking part in anything like them ourselves." *Varieties of Religious Experience* (New York: Longmans, Green and Company, 1902; Penguin American Library, 1982) 109.

25. It must also be admitted that the attempt to perceive experience phenomenologically involves its being "intuited" and "represented" in the perceiver's consciousness in a way that demands great empathy — knowing the other requires somehow identifying with the other without becoming the other; see, e.g., J. G. Hart, *The Person and the Common Life,* 178, 198–200.

Troubles with Religious Experience

Difficulties in analyzing any experience are multiplied in the case of religious experience.[26] There are also special problems with religious experience. One is that the purported cause of the experience is not visible or available for verification. The claim to experiencing pain gains greater plausibility for others when there is a visible trauma; millions of women can attest to the difficulty of convincing healers of "phantom pain" whose cause cannot be clinically determined. In the case of religious experience, the claim to visions or auditions or transformations are even harder to verify.

The second special difficulty derives from the first: for a variety of reasons, humans have found it profitable to fake religious experiences, not unlike the way some people fake the experience of pain for the sake of gain or attention. And when in principle such experiences lack the possibility of verification, the possibilities for widespread fraud and deception are obvious.

The third special problem is connected to the study of religious experience. Analysis of religious phenomena is never truly neutral; like the doctor whose willingness to recognize nonverifiable pain in a patient may have much to do with the physician's own theories about physiology, scholars' openness to religious experience is entangled in their theories about the way reality is structured.[27] Scholars have a stake in the construal of the evidence. Clear acknowledgment of these difficulties and their magnitude is necessary if the phenomenology of religious experience is to have any credibility.

---

26. The following analysis has taken into account the critical and chastening remarks in W. Proudfoot's *Religious Experience,* esp. 41–74 and 155–236; see also the useful discussion in Batson and Ventis, *The Religious Experience,* 25–170.

27. See Batson and Ventis, *The Religious Experience,* 14–15.

We are rightly wary, then, of efforts to isolate the "religious experience," as though it were totally separate from the continuum of other life experiences, recognizing in such efforts the attempt to transform experience into event, as well as an implied assertion concerning the uniqueness of religious as opposed to other experiences. We must acknowledge at once that whatever else we say about religious experiences, they are not utterly unique but can be located among other types of experiences more or less sharing their characteristics.[28]

In the same way, we should agree from the beginning that like all other experiences, religious experience also is irreducibly individual, distinctive for each subject involved, qualified by placement, perspective, capacity, and consciousness. Just as each participant in a concert experiences music diversely, so do participants in a charismatic prayer-meeting necessarily each have a distinct experience. It follows as well that like all other human experience, what we call religious experience is conditioned by historical, cultural, and linguistic particularity.[29] In short, before our conversation can go

---

28. It is difficult on this point to improve on William James: "These are each and all of them special cases of human experience of much wider scope. Religious melancholy, whatever peculiarities it may have *qua* religious, is at any rate melancholy. Religious happiness is happiness. Religious trance is trance. And the moment we renounce the absurd notion that a thing is exploded away as soon as it is classed with others, or its origin is shown; the moment we agree to stand by experimental results and inner quality, in judging of values — who does not see that we are likely to ascertain the distinctive significance of religious melancholy and happiness, or of religious trances, far better by comparing them as conscientiously as we can with other varieties of melancholy, happiness, and trance, than by refusing their place in any more general series, and treating them as if they were outside nature's order altogether?" *Varieties of Religious Experience,* 24. See also Eliade: "Obviously there are no *purely* religious phenomena; no phenomenon can be solely and exclusively religious." *Patterns in Comparative Religion,* xiii.

29. On this see, e.g., C. Geertz, *The Interpretation of Cultures* (New York: Basic Books, 1973); P. Ricoeur, *The Symbolism of Evil,* 306–61; C. B. Walker,

forward, we must agree on at least this: our subject matter is both elusive and disputable.

Such cautionary remarks are particularly appropriate because of the tendency in some phenomenology of religion to provide a universal definition of religious experience, or even "authentic religious experience," which then functions normatively.[30] Some sort of working definition is necessary if we want to move beyond the stage of simply cataloguing "the varieties of religious experience."[31] But if we lose sight of the fact that such working definitions are abstractions drawn from diverse examples, none of which fits the description exactly, or that they are of value as heuristic devices rather than as criteria for discernment of spirits, then we have shifted from phenomenology to a form of theology.

The danger in defining "authentic religious experience" is the implied claim that there is a universal essence to

---

ed., *Gender and Religion* (Boston: Beacon Press, 1986); H. Wheeler Robinson, *Christian Experience of the Holy Spirit* (New York: Harper and Brothers, 1928) 50.

30. Certainly, R. Otto's *Idea of the Holy* has had something of this effect; see the discussion of "Essential Phenomenology of Religion" by S. B. Twiss and W. H. Conser Jr. in *Experience of the Sacred*, 7–24, and the criticism of Otto in W. B. Kristensen, *The Meaning of Religion,* 16–18, 355–56; Kristensen thinks that the "essence" of religion is a philosophical question, whereas "Whoever seeks to know the essence of religion must possess a general picture of the different types of religious thinking and action, of ideas of deity and cultic acts; this is the material for his research. This is precisely what Phenomenology provides" (p. 9).

31. Even William James, whose interest was primarily in breadth of specific examples (p. 25), essayed a working definition of religion, "As I now ask you arbitrarily to take it, [religion] shall mean for us *the feelings, acts, and experiences of individual men in their solitude, so far as they apprehend themselves to stand in relation to whatever they may consider the divine." Varieties of Religious Experience,* 31 (emphasis in original). We can note that James's emphasis on experience correlates with his individualistic definition; contrast Durkheim's definition in *The Elementary Forms of the Religious Life,* trans. J. W. Swain (London: George Unwin, 1915; New York: Free Press, 1965) 62–63, which is entirely communal: "Religion should be an eminently collective thing."

religious experience and therefore, by implication, a certain essential reality to which such experiences respond. Eliade in particular slipped from the use of "sacred" as an adjective in functional contexts to the assertion of "the sacred" as a category of consciousness to the implication that the sacred is an extramental reality that forces itself on consciousness.[32] Such logical slippages may be understandable and may even be innocent. But they must be resisted, for the same reason that a clinician must maintain a necessary and delicate distinction between recognition that certain patterns of cell reproduction can legitimately be called cancerous, and the implication that there is something called cancer outside of and beyond such patterns.

Just as the definition of an "essential" religious experience can slide into an ontological affirmation of "the sacred," so can it also thereby suggest a universal sort of encounter with "the other" that transcends the specific clothing of cultural symbols and requires no interpretation. That is, if religious experience is designated as a unique sort of human event, a response to "something" that is always and everywhere essentially the same, then it can be regarded once more as a *brutum factum* independent of the subject's own perception and construal. We can observe this tendency in some of the phenomenology of religion's discourse on power. It is entirely appropriate to describe the way in which reli-

---

32. See, e.g., *Patterns in Comparative Religion*, 1, 9, 26, 30, and 460. For a detailed and balanced criticism of this aspect of Eliade's work, see A. B. da Silva, *The Phenomenology of Religion as a Philosophical Problem: An Analysis of the Theoretical Background of the Phenomenology of Religion, in General, and of M. Eliade's Phenomenological Approach, in Particular* (Studia philosophiae religionis 8; Lund: CWK Gleerup, 1982) esp. 227–31. J. Z. Smith criticizes the substantive use of "the Sacred," which he declares does not antedate Durkheim's *Elementary Forms;* see J. Z. Smith, *To Take Place: Toward Theory in Ritual* (Chicago Studies in the History of Judaism; Chicago: University of Chicago Press, 1987) 105–6; compare his specific criticism of Eliade on this point in "The Wobbling Pivot" (1972) in *Map Is Not Territory*, 91–94.

gious people themselves speak of their actions as a response to a power, and it is equally appropriate to observe and catalogue the ways in which their actions are organized around what they claim is the source of that power. But it is illegitimate to begin to refer to "power" as though it were an entity apart from such reports and such responses.[33]

The task of phenomenology, if the *epoché* is truly observed, is to observe and describe behavior and its discernible functions, rather than to draw ontological conclusions. When speaking casually, then, I may refer to "the organizing power of the Holy," but when speaking precisely, I need to indicate that what I mean is the way humans arrange themselves around what they perceive (or report as perceiving) a source of power that they regard as transcendent.

The term *transcendent* itself presents another sort of difficulty in talking about religious experience, especially for those scholars who are convinced that social-scientific categories provide the only appropriate approach to human behavior. They consider language about transcendence a surreptitious way of importing theology into religious studies, since the term suggests a "beyond" that is real although inaccessible to empirical verification. To speak of religious experience as a response to "transcendent power" appears to these critics as tantamount to an illegitimate normative judgment concerning the existence of a "power beyond" those modes of immanent power definable in mechanical, electronic, economic, political, or military terms. The suspicion is that transcendence suggests something absolute (and therefore divine) as opposed to relative (and therefore human).[34]

---

33. The hypostasizing of power is clearest in G. Van der Leeuw, as in this passage: "But even when Power is not expressly assigned a name the idea of Power often forms the basis of religion, as we shall be able to observe almost continually in the sequel." *Religion in Essence and Manifestation*, 1:27.

34. As in Eliade, *The Sacred and the Profane*, 116–19; see R. A. Segal, "In

I agree that language about transcendence can be used inappropriately and requires linguistic therapy. I take it as obvious that talking about "the Transcendent" is a form of reification, the mistaking of a noun for a reality, similar to the hypostatization involved in talking about "the Sacred." But I do not think that the cognates of "transcend" ought to be banished from religious discourse out of the fear of reification.

Transcendence can legitimately be used in a relative and functional sense. In the phenomenology of human experience, transcendence should be used with reference to the perception that something "goes beyond" the subject's available categories of comparison. The claim to encounter "transcendent power," in such usage, need not mean anything more than "a power beyond any I have encountered, understand, or can measure."[35]

Defense of Reductionism," *Journal of the American Academy of Religion* 51 (1983) 97–124; J. S. Preus, *Explaining Religion: Criticism and Theory from Bodin to Freud* (New Haven: Yale University Press, 1987) xviii.

35. Part of the difficulty for critics of the phenomenological approach to religion and religious experience is the way phenomenology asks for an empathetic relation to that which is known. If religious experience is the heart of religion, and to know "religious experience" one must "represent" that experience in one's own consciousness, the implication is that only the religious can "know" religion. Thus Kristensen: "In order to reach the right conclusions he must have a feeling for religion, an awareness of what religion attempts to formulate. Many historians are gravely lacking in this 'feeling.' " But then he adds, "But the reverse is just as true: the philosopher who wants to describe the essential element must work with historical data." *The Meaning of Religion,* 12. Precisely this dialectic seems to be missing from Otto's emphasis on re-experiencing the Holy: "It cannot be strictly defined. . . . he must be guided and led on . . . until he reach the point at which 'the numinous' in him perforce begins to stir, to start into life and into consciousness. . . . In other words our X cannot, strictly speaking, be taught, it can only be evoked, awakened in the mind; as everything that 'comes of the spirit' must be awakened." *The Idea of the Holy,* 7. Here we find precisely the ambiguity of which the critics complain: there is not only the "feeling with" the religious sensibility of others, but the "evoking of the spirit" within oneself: one can only know religious experience by having religious experience.

More important, certain situations require the usage, and without it our ability to speak about the richness of human experience would be weakened. To make this point, I remind you that transcendence connotes not only a "going beyond" but also a "going across." It suggests not only distance but also closeness. It is the term most appropriate, for example, to describe the experience of listening to the music of Mozart. What is meant by speaking of this experience as "transcendent" is not an essentialist claim that Mozart's music is "the greatest" or "the absolute."

Rather, it is simply the functional observation that the effect on listeners cannot be accounted for by the sum total of notes of paper, gestures in the air, the scraping of horsehair across wire strings, and the blowing of air in metal tubes. How scratches on a page from two hundred years ago can, through the crude alchemy of an orchestra's instruments, do what Mozart's music does to those who hear it, is not reducible to those disparate elements separately or even in combination. If we are unwilling to use the language of transcendence, then we must abandon all talk about mental and spiritual exchanges of any sort, and resign ourselves simply to the measurement of bodies in space. But then we are not religionists but physicists.

The difficulty of analyzing and speaking about religious experience must be taken seriously. But the category of religious experience, for all its elusiveness and ambiguity, remains necessary if we are not to deny or neglect certain important forms of human discourse and behavior. We need the category to account for people whose behavior, otherwise perfectly within the range of what we consider normal, appears in other respects to be organized around what they claim are convictions and experiences concerning powers that are neither reducible to immanent causes nor verifiable by neutral observation. Unless we are to follow the path of reduction that deems all such "binding" to unseen powers as a form of fraud, self-deception, or linguistic misdirection, then we must use some such category as religious experience. In this case we use language to identify what we assert to be real even if incapable of clear definition. By using such language, however, we do not assert that what people claim to have experienced is necessarily "real," or even that it is what they think it is. But we show ourselves willing to agree that their experience is real and that in their report of it they do not lie. By so doing we act like responsible clinicians whose definition of pain, despite being imprecise, enables a distinction between its presence and its pretense, and who are not bound, by their recognition of pain's presence, to agree with the patient concerning its aetiology.

A Working Definition of Religious Experience

Despite the dangers, therefore, some sort of working definition of religious experience is required, if only as a means of pointing to the sort of reality we mean and enabling us to distinguish it among its cognates. The benefit is heuristic and diagnostic.[36] In my study of religious phenomena, I use a modified version of the four-component description offered by Joachim Wach, the distinguished predecessor of Mircea Eliade at the University of Chicago: Religious experience is a response to that which is perceived as ultimate, involving the whole person, characterized by a peculiar intensity, and issuing in action.[37] I will comment on the separate components,

---

36. Note that this attempt to locate a certain kind of experience that can be called religious carries with it no implication that such experiences themselves define or are the essence of "religion." The matter is much more complex than that.

37. "The Nature of Religious Experience," in J. Wach, *The Comparative Study of Religions,* ed. J. M. Kitagawa (Lectures on the History of Religions, n.s. 4; New York: Columbia University Press, 1958) 27–58. I should add that my understanding of each of the terms in the definition is not necessarily that

each one of which is required, though not always in the same degree.[38]

First, religious experience is a response to what is perceived as ultimate. There are actually three separate elements contained in this careful formulation. Religious experience is a *response*. The experiencer does not consider himself or herself as the initiator of an encounter but as a responder. This dimension is sometimes thought to be too culturally conditioned, too closely tied to Western traditions of "encounter with God."[39] But if less dramatically expressed in other traditions, it is no less present in them.[40] Even when contact with the other is initiated through meditation or even more active forms of mediation, it is with the understanding that "the other" is there to be met and that even this active effort is a response to a antecedent reality.[41]

Religious experience, furthermore, is a response to the *ultimate*. It is at this point that the functional understanding of transcendence becomes useful or even necessary. The response is understood by the experiencer not as directed to any number of relative goods or powers or presences but to some good or power or presence that goes beyond such rivals in a fundamental way. This bring us to the last aspect of

---

of Wach, nor am I interested here in using the definition normatively, as he does, pp. 37–38; see Wach's essay, "Universals in Religion," in his *Types of Religious Experience, Christian and Non-Christian* (Chicago: University of Chicago Press, 1951) 30–47.

38. Wach, *Comparative Study of Religions*, 37.

39. For the phenomenology of religious orientations in which the character of "response" is more muted than in Otto and Eliade, see the excerpts by W. Earle, "Phenomenology of Mysticism," Katsuki Sekida, "Samadhi"; and C. P. Christ, "Nothingness, Awakening, Insight, New Naming," in Twiss and Conser, *Experience of the Sacred*, 98–111, 113–19, 121–28.

40. See the remarks in Wach, *The Comparative Study of Religions*, 49–50.

41. The term *antecedent reality* is more appropriate to those religious responses that are fundamentally mystical and unitive in character. By no means do I want the element of "response to the other" in this definition to be read exclusively in terms of classic Western theism.

this first part of Wach's formulation: the ultimate is *perceived* to be such by the experiencer. The qualification is critical, for it works to avoid the false projection and reification I discussed earlier: just because I perceive something as ultimate and transcendent does not mean that it is. Religious experience, like all experience, is perspectival. This or that object is ultimate with respect to this or that person. Recognition of the subjective and interpretive dimension enables us to speak about real religious experiences without entering into the endless and fruitless debate over the "authenticity" of such experiences based on whether the object to which a person responded was "really ultimate."[42]

Second, religious experience involves the whole person. Rudolph Otto insisted that religious experience is not to be reduced to a matter of the mind (a commitment to certain truths) or a matter of the will (a decision to act a certain way) or even a matter of a specific feeling (a sense of dependence).[43] Otto tried to get at the non-rational dimension of religious experience in terms of awe in the face of the *mysterium tremendum et fascinosum,* and he vividly evokes the psychosomatic dimensions of attraction and repulsion before the fearsomely "other" that give religious experience its distinctively "binding" quality: the participant can neither stay nor flee but is held in suspension between them.[44] Wach emphasizes the positive interaction of mind, will, and emotion,

---

42. "Every believer looks upon his own religion as a unique, autonomous and absolute reality. It is of absolute value and thus incomparable. This is true not only for the Christian, but just as surely for the adherent of a non-Christian religion." The statement occurs in a fine discussion of the dialectic between historical analysis (which always relativizes) and empathy (which enters into the experience) in Kristensen, *The Meaning of Religion,* 6–7. I have taken up this issue also in *Faith's Freedom: A Classic Spirituality for Contemporary Christians* (Minneapolis: Fortress Press, 1990) 31–59.

43. *The Idea of the Holy,* 8–11, 136.

44. Ibid., 12–40. James speaks of "polarizing and magnetizing us" in *Varieties of Religious Experience,* 57.

as well as the body.[45] It should be added that whereas religious experience can and does involve all dimensions of the human person, neither excluding any of these dimensions nor residing in any of them exclusively, no single experience necessarily involves all of them simultaneously and to the same degree.

Third, religious experience is characterized by a peculiar intensity. This term, I think, represents Wach's attempt to capture the element of experiential distinctiveness, similar to the common expression, peak experience. If such terms are understood only in terms of dramatic or loud or visible effects or psychosomatic pyrotechnics, then they are misleading, for the element of intensity can be as real in silent meditation. While this is the vaguest term in Wach's definition, it is not disposable. Intensity in this context is partly a matter of heightened awareness and partly a sense of contact with a heightened reality.[46]

Fourth, religious experience issues in action. Wach here provides the link between the psychological analysis of Otto and the social-organizational observations of Van der Leeuw and Eliade.[47] The point here is that the experience contains within itself an imperative, an ought: it is not a matter of just any action, therefore, but of one appropriate to the experience itself.[48] Religious experience organizes other aspects of life (often every aspect of life) around itself. I regard this as

45. *The Comparative Study of Religions*, 32–35.

46. *The Comparative Study of Religion*, 35–36. Compare James: "It is as if there were in the human consciousness a *sense of reality, a feeling of objective presence, a perception* of what we may call *'something there,'* more deep and more general than any of the special and particular 'senses' by which the current psychology supposes existent realities to be originally revealed." *Varieties of Religious Experience*, 58 (emphasis in original).

47. It is remarkable, in fact, how little these authors actually address the question of religious experience; see only G. Van der Leeuw, *Religion in Essence and Manifestation*, 2:459–62.

48. *The Comparative Study of Religions*, 36–37.

the critical element of the definition, enabling a distinction between religious and aesthetic experience that Otto did not manage.[49]

An experience of beauty, after all — as with our hypothetical concert — can possess the first three components of the definition: the music can be given a certain ultimacy and intensity and can certainly engage every aspect of the person. An aesthetic experience, however, is sufficient unto itself. The experience of beauty is enough. I leave the concert profoundly moved and perhaps even shaken, and I can't stop whistling *Eine kleine Nachtmusik,* but I return the next day to my ordinary life.

In contrast, the concert could be designated a religious experience for me if — given all the other elements of religious experience — I would then leave my job and take up the profession of a musician. Hearing a powerful sermon on Lazarus and Dives that I ponder and appreciate for its rhetorical elegance and for the way it moves me to tears is still only an aesthetic experience. If, after hearing the sermon, I divest myself of all my possessions and live among the homeless, then it can fairly be called a religious experience.[50]

Religious experience exercises power by organizing other activities around itself. In the most fundamental way, space and time are ordered around the when and where of what Eliade evocatively called the *kratophany* or appearance of power.[51] Specific religions are in reality ways of life organized

49. See *The Idea of the Holy,* 41–59, 65–71.

50. Notice that these two examples indicate the way in which religious experience is, for this analysis, contextual and functional. Hearing music that turns around a life must be considered *functionally* as religious as hearing a sermon that turns around a life. It should also be observed that such "religious experiences" are less easily identified with what is experienced in the pew every Sunday and more easily with what starts religions. Compare W. James, *Varieties of Religious Experience,* 30.

51. Eliade, *Patterns in Comparative Religion,* 14; see also E. Durkheim, *The Elementary Forms of the Religious Life,* 56: "Each homogeneous group of sacred

in such fashion as to mediate such power, through myth and ritual, doctrine and morality.[52] The somatic dimension of religious experience is particularly important here, for the way the body responds, not only in the moment but afterward in the restructuring of life, provides the clearest signal to the observer concerning the character of the experience itself. Because we cannot know until after the moment — sometimes not until long after the moment — whether and how life has been restructured around that moment, we cannot identify a religious experience while it is being experienced, but only after the fact, by examining its results, the degree to which an individual's or a community's life has or has not been changed.[53]

This is why the experience that turned Saul the persecutor into Paul the Apostle is one of the classic examples of religious experience in the full sense of the definition. It is well known that the accounts in Acts and in Paul's own letters do not entirely overlap,[54] and it is impossible to trace

---

things, or even each sacred thing of some importance, constitutes a centre of organization about which gravitate a group of beliefs and rites, or a particular cult."

52. Note how Wach, in *The Comparative Study of Religions,* develops his analysis of religious experience into "Expression of Religious Experience in Thought" (59–96), "Expression of Religious Experience in Action" (97–120), and "Expression of Religious Experience in Fellowship" (121–43). See also his *Sociology of Religion* (Chicago: University of Chicago Press, 1944) 17–53.

53. This final dimension of the definition also suggests how analysis of behavior patterns and analysis of discourse about experience can converge. If the etic analysis of the pattern of organization revealed by the behavior of an individual or group corresponds to what emic discourse claims is the power or presence experienced, greater weight must be given to such testimony, not necessarily with regard to the ontic reality of the claimed presence but with regard to the genuineness of the "experience of power" being reported. Even in such cases, of course, charlatanism is possible, as the ancient case of Alexander of Abunoteichos (see Lucian of Samosata, *Alexander the False Prophet*) and recent cases displayed regularly on television remind us. But counterfeit coinage thrives when genuine currency exists.

54. The Acts of the Apostles provides one narrative version (9:1-18) and

out completely the specific somatic,[55] psychic,[56] or symbolic dimensions[57] of what "seeing the Lord Jesus" months or years after Jesus' execution might have been. But what the accounts

two versions in Paul's defense speeches in 22:6-21 and 26:12-18. For the differences between them, see C. W. Hedrick, "Paul's Conversion/Call: A Comparative Analysis of the Three Reports in Acts," *Journal of Biblical Literature* 100 (1981) 415–32; D. M. Stanley, "Why Three Accounts?" *Catholic Biblical Quarterly* 15 (1953) 315–18). In Paul's letters, the main critical issue concerns which passages actually come from him (should Col 1:25, Eph 3:3, and 1 Tim 1:12-17 be included?) and which refer to his conversion/apostolic call: there is general agreement on 1 Cor 9:1; 15:8; Gal 1:12, 16, but less unanimity on 2 Cor 4:6; 12:1-5; Phil 3:6.

55. In Acts, Paul falls to the ground, hears a voice and answers it; he is blinded by the light until scales fall from his eyes and he can see again (9:4-8, 18; 22:11). The version in Acts 22:17-21 is distinctive for its report of a trance, in which Paul "saw" Jesus saying words and he himself responded. In Paul's own accounts, *vision* is present in 1 Cor 9:1 and 15:8, 2 Cor 4:6, and probably 1:16. In 2 Cor 12:1-5, Paul refers to "visions and revelations of the Lord" (12:1) that were either "in the body or out of the body, I do not know, God knows" (12:2,3), and to *hearing* "things that cannot be told, that man cannot utter" (12:4). Finally, there is the "thorn in the flesh" that was given so that he might not become too elated at "the abundance of revelations" (12:7): are we to understand this in physical terms and perhaps in connection with the *stigmata tou Iēsou* that Paul says he carried *en tō sōmati mou* (Gal 5:17)?

56. The phrase "in the body or out of the body I do not know, God knows" in 2 Cor 12:2, 3 can easily be read in terms of psychological dissociation or trance, just as the blindness reported in Acts 9:8-18 can be explicated in terms of a hysteric reaction. For interpretations of Paul's conversion/call in terms of the resolution of psychological dissonance, see, e.g., A. C. McGiffert, *The Apostolic Age,* rev. ed. (New York: Charles Scribner's Sons, 1906), and R. L. Rubenstein, *My Brother Paul* (New York: Harper and Row, 1972). The material for such analyses is primarily derived from Romans 7, although it is doubtful how much Paul's "speech in character" there reveals his own psychological state. See K. Stendahl, "The Apostle Paul and the Introspective Conscience of the West" (1963), in *Paul among Jews and Gentiles* (Philadelphia: Fortress Press, 1976) 78–96.

57. The references in Paul's letters, especially that in 2 Cor 12:1-5, are compatible with the prayer experiences associated with Merkabah mysticism. See, e.g., A. F. Segal, *Paul the Convert* (New Haven: Yale University Press, 1990) 34–71. The narrative in Acts 9:1-9 uses the literary conventions of Judaism associated with theophanies, the overcoming of oppressors, and conversion;

and all of Paul's activities do make clear is that whether sudden or slow, whether spectacular or subtle, this encounter completely restructured his life[58] and, for that matter, the life of much of the world.

Religious Experience in Early Christianity

In the next chapters, I will turn to aspects of religious experience in earliest Christianity as we find it in the pages of the New Testament. I will address in turn rituals of initiation, glossolalia, and meals. In each case, insights from the contemporary social-scientific study of religion, as well as information from religious parallels in antiquity, will be brought to bear; our data are so skimpy that we need all the perspectives we can get. But my analysis, despite employing the technique of comparison, will remain focused on the specific religious phenomena. I will seek to comprehend them as fully as possible in themselves rather than as examples for generalizations concerning religion or the history of religions in general.

My analysis of specific religious activities and experiences will employ both the definition I have just elaborated and the cautions I have acknowledged. I approach the analysis with assumptions that religious experiences in earliest Christianity existed in a continuum with other experiences in complex combinations; that different persons had such experiences within a variety of perspectives; that the experiences were contextualized by the cultural settings and symbolic worlds

see the discussion in L. T. Johnson, *The Acts of the Apostles* (Sacra Pagina 5; Collegeville, Minn.: Liturgical Press, 1992) 161–70.

58. The sense of the "imperative" in religious experience that dictates "appropriate action" is clear not only in the Acts accounts (9:6; 22:10, 18-21; 26:16-18), but also in Paul's own references to the *consequences* of his having "seen the Lord" (see 1 Cor 9:16-19; 15:10-11; 2 Cor 11:22-12:10; Gal 1:11-24; Phil 3:4-16; Col 1:24-29).

within which the first believers dwelt and which dwelt within them; that our engagement with such experiences can only be indirect, through the medium of discourse which is itself most often indirect and always linguistically conditioned; that because our only access to these experiences is through intentional literary compositions the specific rhetoric of such compositions must also be engaged if we hope to speak about the experiences.

I hope that the analyses will be received with the same spirit of experimentation in which they are undertaken. It remains to be seen whether so simple yet difficult a task can be accomplished, or whether the yield is worth the effort. But if scholarship cannot speak in an accurate and disciplined fashion about the experiential aspects of earliest Christianity, then it misses what is most interesting, and quite likely what is most distinctive, about this puzzling and paradoxical religious movement.

3

RITUAL IMPRINTING
AND THE POLITICS
OF PERFECTION

If religious experience issues in the organization of life around a perception of power,[1] first of all in the demarcation of sacred time and sacred space,[2] then the study of ritual provides an obvious point of access to the religious experience of the earliest Christians.[3] For ritual — broadly defined as repetitive communal patterns of behavior[4] — we need not

1. For the organization of life around the perception of power, see G. Van der Leeuw, *Religion in Essence and Manifestation,* trans. J. E. Turner (New York: Harper and Row, 1933) 1:27–28, 191–205; 2:339–42; J. Wach, *Sociology of Religion* (Chicago: University of Chicago Press, 1944) 17–34.

2. See E. Durkheim, *The Elementary Forms of the Religious Life,* trans. J. W. Swain (1915; New York: Free Press, 1965) 52–55; M. Eliade, *The Sacred and the Profane: The Nature of Religion,* trans. W. R. Trask (New York: Harcourt, Brace and World, 1957) 20–113.

3. For the connection between ritual and the demarcation of sacred time and space from very different perspectives, see M. Eliade, *Cosmos and History: The Myth of the Eternal Return,* trans. W. R. Trask (New York: Harper and Row, 1959) 3–92; J. Z. Smith, *To Take Place: Toward Theory in Ritual* (Chicago Studies in the History of Judaism; Chicago: University of Chicago Press, 1987) 102–8; C. Bell, *Ritual Theory, Ritual Practice* (New York: Oxford University Press, 1992) 124–30.

4. Compare Bell, *Ritual Theory, Ritual Practice,* 91–92. Note that my definition includes rituals that are not necessarily or specifically "religious," although — like some college sporting events — they may indeed *function* religiously. Compare the definition of ritual by E. M. Zuesse, as "conscious and

rely entirely on reports about personal experience, for ritual is embodied and visible, and often, though not always, public.[5] It therefore enables us to move from ritual gestures, with their symbolic valences, in two directions. We can move laterally to compare ritual patterns, and we can move inward — tentatively to be sure — from the public gesture to the personal experience.

In the case of nascent Christianity, the ritual of baptism offers the best possibility for such analysis. It is the most pervasively attested ritual activity in the New Testament. The evidence is insufficient to reconstruct completely either the ritual or its significance, but it is adequate to support some reasonable hypotheses. As a ritual of initiation into an intentional community, furthermore, baptism can be compared with similar ritual activities in religious communities contemporaneous with nascent Christianity. Finally, crosscultural anthropological studies of rituals of initiation provide us with a fuller sense of what the experiential and social dimensions of baptism might have been. In sum, baptism allows the sort of convergence of perceptions that enriches a phenomenological analysis.[6]

---

voluntary, repetitious and stylized symbolic bodily actions that are centered on cosmic structure and/or sacred presences." In "Ritual," *Encyclopedia of Religion,* ed. M. Eliade (New York: Macmillan, 1987) vol. 11/12: 405. J. Z. Smith offers a number of partial characterizations in *To Take Place:* "Ritual is, first and foremost, a mode of paying attention (p. 103) . . . is, above all, an assertion of difference (p. 109). . . . Ritual represents the creation of a controlled environment where the variables (the accidents) of ordinary life may be displaced precisely because they are felt to be so overwhelmingly present and powerful. Ritual is a means of performing the way things ought to be in conscious tension to the way things are (p. 109). . . . Ritual, concerned primarily with difference, is, necessarily, an affair of the relative" (p. 110).

5. See Bell, *Ritual Theory, Ritual Practice,* 94–117, on recent attention in scholarship to the "ritual body."

6. Compare W. Burkert's attempt at a "comparative phenomenology of Ancient Mysteries," in *Ancient Mystery Cults* (Cambridge: Harvard University Press, 1987) 4.

Reconstructing the Ritual

Although the author of Ephesians speaks of "one baptism" as an identifying mark of unity among believers,[7] we cannot assume that the ritual took the same form or had the same significance everywhere it was practiced.[8] Some things, however, can be stated with some degree of probability, especially if we suppose — as it seems we should — some degree of continuity between the baptism practiced by John and received by Jesus,[9] and that practiced by Christians in the name of Jesus.[10] Our reconstructive effort must take into account all the possible allusions to baptism in the epistolary literature,[11] as well as schematic descriptions in New Testament narratives.[12]

7. "There is one body and one spirit, just as you were called in the one hope that belongs to your call, one Lord, one faith, one baptism, one God and Father of us all, who is above all and through all and in all" (Eph 4-6). We will see the connection between "one baptism" and "one God" again later.

8. My language here is deliberately cautious, for there are even cases in which we cannot be sure baptism was practiced at all. See C. J. A. Hickling, "Baptism in the First-Century Churches: A Case for Caution," in *The Bible in Three Dimensions,* ed. D. J. A. Clines *et al.* (JSOTS 87; Sheffield: Sheffield Academic Press, 1990) 249–67.

9. See Matt 3:1-16; 11:11; 14:2; 16:14; 17:13; 21:25; Mark 1:4-9; 6:25; 8:28; 11:30; Luke 3:7-21; 7:19-20, 33; 9:19; 20:8; John 1:25-33; 3:22-26; 4:1-2; Acts 1:5, 22; 10:37; 13:24; 18:25; 19:34.

10. See Matt 28:19; Mark 16:16; Acts 2:38-41; 3:12-28; 9:18; 10:47-48; 11:16; 16:15, 33; 18:8; 19:3-5; 22:16; Rom 6:3; 1 Cor 1:13-17; 12:13; 15:29; Gal 3:27; Eph 4:5; Col 2:12; 1 Pet 3:21. For the premise of continuity, see G. W. H. Lampe, *The Seal of the Spirit: A Study in the Doctrine of Baptism and Confirmation in the New Testament and the Fathers,* 2nd ed. (London: SPCK, 1967) 19–20.

11. In addition to the passages involving *baptizein* and *baptisma* given above, this means considering as well the references to "bath" (*loutron*) in Eph 5:26 and Tit 3:5, and "bathing" (*louein/apolouein*) in 1 Cor 6:11 and (possibly) Rev 1:5, and "sprinkling" (*rantizein*) in Heb 10:22.

12. The fullest description is that of the baptism of Jesus by John (Mark 1:9-11; Matt 3:16-17; Luke 3:21-22; John 1:32-34). Given the connections that will be shown below, it is highly likely that the depiction of this event in the Gospels has been at least in some degree affected by community practice

As the word itself suggests and as the language associated with it supports, baptism is first of all a washing, probably through immersion, in water.[13] In contrast to most other ancient lustrations, baptism is an initiation into an intentional community,[14] a *rite de passage* that marks a transition from outsider to insider status.[15] The circumstances of the ritual are not altogether clear. It seems to have been performed in public rather than in private.[16] It was passive rather than active: one did not bathe oneself but was "baptized," apparently by one other person,[17] when possible in the presence of others.[18]

Concerning the specific actions involved in the ritual,

and conviction. Other brief narrative accounts are in Acts 8:26-40; 9:17-19; 10:44-48; 16:15, 33; 19:1-7. For an attempt to flesh out the ritual in Pauline communities, see esp. W. A. Meeks, *The First Urban Christians: The Social World of the Apostle Paul* (New Haven: Yale University Press, 1983) 150–57.

13. See A. Oepke, *"baptō, baptizō,"* TDNT 1:529–46.

14. The question of proselyte baptism in Judaism will be discussed below. For the variety of washings in ancient traditions, see Oepke, *"baptō,"* TDNT 1:530–35; J. Delorme, "The Practice of Baptism in Judaism at the Beginning of the Christian Era," in *Baptism in the New Testament: A Symposium,* trans. D. Askew (Baltimore: Helicon, 1964) 25–60; G. Wagner, *Pauline Baptism and the Pagan Mysteries: The Problem of the Pauline Doctrine of Baptism in Romans VI, 1-11, in the Light of Its Religio-Historical "Parallels,"* trans. J. P. Smith (Edinburgh: Oliver & Boyd, 1967) 127–35; W. Burkert, *Ancient Mysteries,* 101–2.

15. See A. Van Gennep, *The Rites of Passage,* trans. M. B. Vizedom and G. L. Caffee (1908; Chicago: University of Chicago Press, 1960) 1–13. See also M. Eliade: "The term initiation in the most general sense denotes a body of rites and oral teachings whose purpose is to produce a decisive alteration in the religious and social status of the person to be initiated," in *Rites and Symbols of Initiation: The Mysteries of Birth and Rebirth,* trans. W. R. Trask (New York: Harper and Row, 1958) x. For further bibliography, see B. G. Meyerhoff, L. A. Camino, and E. Turner, "Rites of Passage," in *The Encyclopedia of Religion,* 11–12: 380–87.

16. See Matt 3:1-17; Mark 1:5; Luke 3:7, 21; Acts 2:41; 8:12; 10:47-48; 16:15, 33.

17. See Matt 3:11; Mark 1:8-9; John 1:26, 33; Acts 16:33; 19:5; 1 Cor 1:12-17. That Thecla "gave herself the bath" is clearly regarded as exceptional (see *The Acts of Paul and Thecla* 34, 40).

18. See Acts 2:41; 10:47-48; 16:15, 33; 19:5; 1 Cor 1:15.

we can only make informed guesses based on the symbolism associated with baptism in the New Testament writings. We cannot assume that they were part of every, or even any, baptismal ritual. The metaphor of taking off and putting on qualities, for example, which is used in the context of baptism, can with some likelihood be connected to ritual divestment and reclothing before and after immersion.[19] Similarly, language about illumination and enlightenment might be connected to the ritual use of lights such as candles, perhaps in a night-time ceremony.[20] It is conceivable that some form of ecstatic utterance accompanied the baptized person's emergence from the water.[21] Finally, it is likely that the ritual initiation of baptism also involved a longer or shorter period of instruction, the imparting of a body of lore concerning the significance of the ritual itself and of the larger mystery of which it was a part,[22] and some sort of profession of faith.[23]

19. See Gal 3:27; Col 3:9-10; Eph 4:22. See Meeks, *First Urban Christians*, 151, 157; G. Wainwright, *Christian Initiation* (Ecumenical Studies in History 10; Richmond, Va.: John Knox Press, 1969) 14–15.

20. See Wainwright, *Christian Initiation*, 15. Hebrews speaks of "having been enlightened" (*phōtisthentes*), with clear reference to the readers' initiation (6:4; 10:32). The statement cited by Eph 5:14, "Awake, O Sleeper, and arise from the dead, and Christ shall give you light," is plausibly connected to a baptismal ritual, given that composition's extensive use of darkness/light symbolism (compare Eph 1:18; 3:9; 5:8-9, 13). For other light symbolism possibly connected to baptism, see Rom 13:12; 2 Cor 4:6; Col 1:12; 1 Pet 2:9.

21. Note the reports of ecstatic speech in Acts 2:1-4; 10:46-47; and 19:6. Meeks, *First Urban Christians*, 151–52, makes the very plausible suggestion that the bilingual cry of *abba* (Gal 4:6; see Rom 8:15-17) may well have been one form of such utterance.

22. The imparting of knowledge is such a standard feature of all initiations (see J. La Fontaine, *Initiation* [Middlesex: Penguin Books, 1985] 15; Eliade, *Rites and Symbols of Initiation,* 3) and of ancient initiations in particular (see W. Burkert, *Ancient Mystery Cults,* 69, 153 n. 14), that we should take seriously such oblique indications as Acts 18:26; Heb 6:2; Luke 1:4, the explicit allusions to shared traditions (see esp. Rom 6:1-11), and possible samples of such instruction (1 Pet 3:18—4:6).

23. Note in particular the statement of faith in Acts 8:37 (v.l.); 16:15, 31;

In a 1907 essay, Sigmund Freud perceptively noted the similarity between obsessive behavior and religious ritual.[24] Both involve the repetition of patterned actions. But whereas obsessive acts like hand-wringing are pathological because they inhabit only a private world of meaning, religious rituals take their significance from a larger and more public symbolic world.[25] To those who do not share it, this symbolic world may appear as no less strange than that of the obsessive-compulsive. For its adherents, however, ritual both mirrors and models fundamental truths about the world.[26] To get closer to the experiential dimension of early Christian baptism, therefore, we must move beyond physical actions to a consideration of the symbols attached to these actions.

The most obvious religious symbolism for a ritual of washing is purification.[27] Some New Testament passages speak of baptism as cleansing the initiate.[28] Ritual purifications frequently have the effect of providing access to the sacred.[29]

and the element of "calling on the name" in Acts 2:38; 4:12; 8:16; 9:14, 21; 10:43; 22:16; 1 Cor 1:2; 6:11; as well as such creedal statements as Rom 10:9. See Meeks, *The First Urban Christians*, 152; and J. Crehan, *Early Christian Baptism and the Creed: A Study in Ante-Nicene Theology* (The Bellarmine Series 13; London: Burns, Oates & Washbourne, 1950) 8–22.

24. S. Freud, "Obsessive Acts and Religious Practices," in *The Standard Edition of the Complete Psychological Works of Sigmund Freud*, ed. J. Strachey (London: Hogarth Press, 1953-1974) 9:117–27; cited in Smith, *To Take Place*, 110–11.

25. Freud, "Obsessive Acts," 118–19.

26. See C. Geertz, "Religion as a Cultural System," in *The Interpretation of Cultures* (New York: Basic Books, 1973) 88–125, esp. 113–18.

27. See, e.g., G. Wagner, *Pauline Baptism and the Pagan Mysteries*, 127–35; W. Burkert, *Ancient Mystery Cults*, 101–2.

28. Eph 5:26; Tit 2:14; Heb 10:22; for possible allusions, see Acts 15:9; Heb 1:3; 9:14; 1 John 1:7.

29. This is obviously the case in the initiatory washing at Eleusis; see K. Kerenyi, *Eleusis: Archetypal Image of Mother and Daughter* (Bollingen Series 45:4; Princeton: Princeton University Press, 1967) 45–61; A. D. Nock, "Hellenistic Mysteries and Christian Sacraments," in *Essays on Religion and the Ancient World*, ed. Z. Stewart, 2 vols. (Oxford: Clarendon Press, 1972) 2:792–93.

Thus in Judaism, the cleansing of physical objects either results from contact with what is holy or enables access to such contact.[30] In Hebrew prophetic literature, in turn, the language of ritual purification was given an ethical dimension, so that purification could signal a conversion from patterns of idolatry and sin.[31] The same moral connotation is given to baptism in the New Testament, by the frequent connection to forgiveness of sins and admission to a sanctified people.[32]

A second symbolic dimension of Christian baptism is new life. Such symbolism is common in rituals of initiation, for behaviorally the initiate enters a community with distinctive observances and new obligations.[33] Thus we are not surprised to find baptism called the "bath of regeneration" (Tit 3:5), for *palingenesia* is widely attested in ancient literature for a variety of rebirths and new beginnings, whether cosmological, ethical, or mystical.[34] The language of "birth" or "rebirth" is closely connected to that of regeneration.[35] The most distinctive Christian symbolism for baptism, however, is that of death and resurrection, most clearly attested in Paul's letters

---

30. See LXX Exod 19:10; Num 8:21; 19:12; 31:23; Lev 16:19-20, 30; *m. Yad* 1:1-4:8; Matt 15:2; Mark 7:2-5.

31. See LXX Ps 50:1-12; Isa 57:14; 66:17; Jer 40:8; Ezek 36:25; 37:23.

32. Matt 4:11; Mark 1:4; Luke 3:3; Acts 2:38; 3:19; 15:9; 22:16; 1 Cor 6:11; Eph 5:26-27; Tit 2:14; 1 Pet 3:21; Heb 10:22. See also A. Y. Collins, "The Origin of Christian Baptism," *Studia Liturgica* 19 (1989) 28–46, esp. 40.

33. See M. Eliade, *Rites and Symbols of Initiation,* xii–xv; La Fontaine, *Initiation,* 15.

34. For discussion and references to primary sources, see M. Dibelius and H. Conzelmann, *The Pastoral Epistles,* trans. P. Buttolph and A. Yarbro (Hermeneia; Philadelphia: Fortress Press, 1972) 148–50.

35. See John 1:13; 3:3-8; 1 John 3:9; 1 Peter 1:3, 23. Paul's speaking of "giving birth" to individuals (Phm 10) or communities (1 Cor 4:15; Gal 4:19) may well be connected to the practice of baptism. Notice also how the language of "those born of the flesh / into slavery" in Gal 4:23-29 has as its explicit contrary "those born of the gospel," but by implication also "those born of the Spirit / into freedom," as in baptism (Gal 3:27-4:7). See F. Buechsel, *"gennaō"* and *"ginomai"* in *TDNT* 1:665–75 and 1:681–89.

but found elsewhere as well.[36] This symbolism most obviously connects the Christian ritual to the foundational narrative of Jesus' passion, death, and resurrection.[37]

A final aspect of baptismal symbolism is particularly complex. It can perhaps best be characterized as relational. Baptism establishes a bond between the initiate and two spiritual powers, themselves in some fashion interconnected. First, baptism brings the initiate into connection with a power designated as Holy Spirit.[38] The degree to which this power is perceived as personal is not clear, especially since *to pneuma to hagion* is itself brought into close association with the person of Jesus.[39] In the accounts of Jesus' baptism, we see that the

36. Romans 6:1-11 is the most obvious Pauline example. On this, see R. C. Tannehill, *Dying and Rising with Christ: A Study in Pauline Theology* (Beiheft zur Zeitschrift für die neutestamentliche Wissenschaft und die Kunde der Älteren Kirche 32; Berlin: A. Töpelmann, 1967); and R. Schnackenberg, *Baptism in the Theology of St. Paul* (New York: Herder and Herder, 1964) 105–70. 1 Cor 15:29 must certainly also be placed within this understanding, as also Col 2:12-15; 2:20-3:7. See also 1 Peter 3:18 . . . 4:2, and the implication of "the baptism with which I am to be baptized" in Mark 10:38-40. For the whole theme, see O. Cullmann, *Baptism in the New Testament* (Studies in Biblical Theology 1; London: SCM Press, 1950) 9–22.

37. By "foundational," I mean that the basic story of Jesus' passion and death was formed very early — probably the first part of the Jesus tradition to reach narrative expression — before the time of Paul and widely disseminated in non-Pauline as well as Pauline churches; see the argument in L. T. Johnson, *The Real Jesus: The Misguided Quest for the Historical Jesus and the Truth of the Traditional Gospels* (San Francisco: Harper San Francisco, 1996) 141–68. I thereby assume a position directly contrary to that held by B. Mack, *A Myth of Innocence: Mark and Christian Origins* (Philadelphia: Fortress Press, 1988); and idem, *Who Wrote the New Testament?* (San Francisco: Harper San Francisco, 1995), for whom the passion narrative is a late narrative elaboration of the "Christ Myth."

38. Acts 1:3, 8; 2:1-4, 38; 8:16-17; 9:17-19; 10:45-48; 11:16; 19:5-6; Rom 5:5; 1 Cor 12:13; Gal 3:27-4:6; Eph 4:4-6; Tit 3:5-6; Heb 6:4.

39. John 14:25; 20:21-23; Acts 2:33; 4:30-31; 10:36-45; Rom 1:4; 8:2-4; 9-11; 1 Cor 6:11, 15-19; 12:3, 12-13; 15:45; 2 Cor 3:18; 13:14; Gal 5:5-6; Eph 1:13; 2:21-22; Phil 2:1-5; 2 Tim 1:13-14; 1 Pet 3:18-20; 1 John 4:13-14; 5:6-8; Jude 20-21; Rev 1:9-10; 19:10.

descent of the Holy Spirit and the declaration of his divine sonship go together.[40] Paul's allusion to the "spirit of adoption" received by the baptized certainly seems to support the conclusion that the Holy Spirit was regarded as the medium through which the unique relationship between Jesus and God was transferred to others, so that at baptism this same filial relationship was established, as expressed by the initiate's shouting out the Aramaic caritative designation for God, *Abba.*[41]

Such a mystical identification is clearly understood as a form of status enhancement. It also points to the conviction that the Jesus who was crucified was now more powerfully alive as "Lord" and capable of contacting humans across time and space, touching them with this life through the Spirit, so that they could live a "new life" and a "resurrection life" according to the pattern of his own.[42] In short, Christian baptism not only signalled passage from one population to another but generated a new form of identity.[43] No

40. Matt 3:16-17; Mark 1:9-11; Luke 3:21-22; John 1:32-34.

41. "In Christ Jesus, you are all sons of God, through faith. For as many of you were baptized into Christ have put on Christ . . . and if you are Christ's, then you are Abraham's offspring, heirs according to promise . . . and because you are sons, God has sent the Spirit of his Son into our hearts, crying, 'Abba! Father!' So through God you are no longer a slave but a son, and if a son then an heir" (Gal 3:25—4:7).

42. Rom 6:1-11; 8:2-11; 12:1-2; 15:1-7; 1 Cor 2:16; 11:1; Gal 5:25-6:2; Eph 4:20-24; Phil 2:1-11; Col 3:10-17; 2 Tim 2:1-13; 1 John 4:17-19; 1 Pet 2:21-25; 4:1-6; Heb 13:12-13.

43. What is shocking, of course, is that this man, whose *nous* they now have (1 Cor 2:16), was executed as a criminal under Roman authority. The resemblance between this conviction and necromancy is obvious. In necromancy it is thought that those who have died, especially those who have died violently or criminally, have spirits that can operate powerfully when controlled by the appropriate mechanisms. Usually the dead are summoned for purposes of divination, but "the calling up of the dead may occur for purposes other than information seeking" (E. Bourguignon, "Necromancy," *Encyclopedia of Religion*, 10:345). Such a belief seems to lie behind the response of Herod to the

wonder baptism is the ritual constantly mentioned and most frequently recalled in the New Testament writings, for in this ritual Christians were both empowered and imprinted[44] — or, to use the language soon to become technical — they were "sealed."[45]

How Many Initiations?

A description like the one I have attempted can leave the impression of a uniformity of practice, understanding, and experience, that may not have existed. Precisely the notion of "ritual imprinting," however, can lead us to a closer consideration of what the actual experience of baptism may have involved for some early Christians. Suppose it be granted that baptism imparts a certain kind of identity or "seal-

wonders worked by Jesus: was it possible that the beheaded John the Baptist was more powerfully at work in this man whom he had baptized? Grasping how small a distance separates the phenomena of necromancy and baptism can, once we overcome resistance to what appears an intolerable reduction, help us understand the more vividly the realism, indeed, the sheer physicalism of some of the New Testament's language: The Holy Spirit was poured out over them (Acts 2:33; Tit 3:6), it was poured into them (Rom 5:5), it was drunk by all of them (1 Cor 12:13), they were "filled with the Holy Spirit" (Acts 4:31), and could therefore speak "in" the spirit (1 Cor 14:2) and live "by" the Spirit (Gal 5:25); and all of this is pretty much equivalent to speaking and acting "in the name of Jesus" (1 Cor 5:4) and "in the Lord" (1 Cor 7:39).

44. My use of "imprinting" here is metaphorical, borrowing partly from the ancient imagery of the seal, which shows identity, and partly from the psychological theory that certain early life experiences have a particularly important role in determining other sorts of responses. See, e.g., E. H. Hesse, *Imprinting: Early Experience and the Developmental Psychobiology of Attachment* (Behavioral Science Series; New York: Van Nostrand Reinhold, 1973) 1–61; and W. Sluckin, *Imprinting and Early Learning* (Chicago: Aldane Publishing Co., 1965) 1–15, 116–26.

45. See esp. the use of *sphragizein* in 2 Cor 1:22; Eph 1:13, 4:30; Rev 7:3-8. For this aspect of baptism, see G. Wainwright, *Christian Initiation,* 14, and G. W. H. Lampe, *The Seal of the Spirit,* 3–18.

ing": what is the corollary? Does it necessarily follow that baptism is the single and final initiation to be undergone, for example, or is it possible that Christians are to move through a series of rituals leading them progressively toward full perfection or maturity? This question lies at the heart of two letters attributed to Paul addressed to Christians in the territory of ancient Phrygia, namely, Galatians[46] and Colossians.[47]

The differences between the letters are obvious. In Galatians, Paul appears as the founder of the churches to whom he writes,[48] and the linked issues of his own apostolic authority and the observance of Torah figure prominently in his argument.[49] His language in Galatians is defensive and

46. I am using the expression "Phrygia" loosely, since the precise boundaries of what Luke in Acts 16:6 calls "the Phrygian and Galatian region" did not seem terribly clear to him, or for that matter to Pliny (*Natural History* 5:95) or Strabo (*Geography* 12, 7, 1–5). For the problems of ethnic, geographical, and political designations, see F. F. Bruce, "Phrygia," *The Anchor Bible Dictionary*, ed. D. N. Freedman (New York: Doubleday, 1992) 5:365–68. The debate over a "North Galatia" or "South Galatia" destination for the letter has at least something to do with reconciling Paul's founding of these churches with the account in Acts; see, e.g., J. B. Lightfoot, *St. Paul's Epistle to the Galatians* (London: Macmillan, 1914) 1–35; and F. F. Bruce, "Galatians Problems 2: North or South Galatia?" *Bulletin of the John Rylands Library* 52 (1970) 243–66.

47. The main critical issue pertaining to Colossians is its authenticity, which is not of particular importance in the present discussion. For arguments against authenticity from the perspective of literary connections, see E. P. Sanders, "Literary Dependence in Colossians," *Journal of Biblical Literature* 85 (1966) 28–45; and from the perspective of theological consistency, see E. Lohse, "Pauline Theology in the Letter to the Colossians," *New Testament Studies* 15 (1969) 211–20. An extensive argument in favor of authenticity is mounted by G. E. Cannon, *The Use of Traditional Materials in Colossians* (Macon, Ga.: Mercer University Press, 1983). The case for Colossians' authenticity, and indeed for its having been written from Ephesus *before* 1 Corinthians, has recently been made by J. Murphy-O'Connor, *Paul: A Critical Life* (Oxford: Clarendon Press, 1996) 237–39.

48. Gal 1:11; 4:13-20.

49. His apostolic authority: Gal 1:12; 1:17-2:10; 4:12-20; 5:2-3, 10-11; 16:17; the observance of Torah: Gal 2:3, 14-19; 3:2, 10-22; 4:21—5:4; 5:11, 18; 6:12-13.

passionate,[50] even as his argument is rhetorically shaped[51] and midrashically sophisticated.[52]

In contrast, Paul writes to believers in the city of Colossae,[53] not as the founder of their community[54] but as the senior colleague of Epaphras, from whom they learned Christ[55] and who is at the time of writing Paul's fellow-prisoner.[56] As we might expect in such circumstances, neither the issue of Paul's apostolic authority[57] nor his particular investment in

50. See 1:1, 6, 8, 9; 3:1; 4:11; 5:7, 12; 6:17.

51. For the use of rhetoric in Galatians, see H. D. Betz, *Galatians* (Hermeneia; Philadelphia: Fortress Press, 1979); B. H. Brinsmead, *Galatians: Dialogical Response to Opponents* (SBLDS 65; Chico, Calif.: Scholars Press, 1982); R. Hall, "The Rhetorical Outline for Galatians: A Reconsideration," *Journal of Biblical Literature* 106 (1987) 277–87; J. Smit, "Galatians: A Deliberative Speech," *New Testament Studies* 35 (1989) 1–26.

52. See, e.g., N. A. Dahl, "Contradictions in Scripture," in *Studies in Paul* (Minneapolis: Augsburg Publishing House, 1977) 159–77; M. Wilcox, " 'Upon the Tree: Deut 21:22-23 in the New Testament," *Journal of Biblical Literature* 96 (1977) 85–99; T. Callan, "Pauline Midrash: The Exegetical Background of Gal 3:19b," *Journal of Biblical Literature* 99 (1980) 549–67.

53. On the little that is known about the Phrygian city in the Lycus valley that disappeared from history after a devastating earthquake in 60 or 64 C.E., see C. E. Arnold, "Colossae," *Anchor Bible Dictionary*, 1:1089–90.

54. Paul has only "heard of" their faith (Col 1:4, 9); they have not "seen his face" (2:1), and Tychichus will report to them on Paul's affairs (4:7-8). It is possible that Colossians is part of a three-letter packet carried by Tychichus as he accompanied the slave Onesimus back to his owner, Philemon (see Col 4:9): the note to Philemon is a letter of recommendation for Onesimus, Colossians is a cover letter to the local church (similar to the one for the Laodiceans [see Col 4:16]), and Ephesians is a circular letter to Paul's gentile congregations. See L. T. Johnson, *The Writings of the New Testament: An Interpretation* (Philadelphia: Fortress Press, 1986) 353–55.

55. Paul refers to Epaphras as "one of yourselves" (4:2), and makes clear that they learned the grace of God in truth from Epaphras (1:6-7).

56. Paul calls himself a prisoner (4:3). And although in Colossians he does not call Epaphras a "fellow-prisoner" as he does Aristarchus (4:10), it is a fair inference, given the fact that Epaphras is with Paul, sends greetings, but is not returning to the church with Tychichus. The reference to Epaphras in Phm 23 as "fellow prisoner" is decisive.

57. Paul's authority is not under threat but assumed (1:1, 23, 25; 2:5; 4:2-4, 8-9, 18).

Torah emerge with the same vividness.[58] Instead, using language far less dialectical than that in Galatians, Paul works out the implications of what he considers shared traditions and understandings,[59] particularly concerning baptism and the identity of Christ.[60]

Despite these differences, the situations addressed have some striking similarities.

1. The ethnic and cultural background is gentile rather than Jewish: believers have turned to Christ directly from paganism.[61]

2. Whether under the influence of outside proselytizers or inside agitators,[62] some members in each community are seeking a further initiation beyond baptism. In the case of Galatians, it is clear that some believers are having themselves circumcised.[63] In Colossae, there is also apparently the desire for circumcision,[64] as well as some additional visionary experience.[65]

58. Not only is Torah not cited in this letter, the diction employed in 2:11-15 and 2:22 is, apart from the term *peritomē*, extremely general: *cheirographon tois dogmasin* and *entalmata kai didaslalias tōn anthrōpōn*.

59. See 1:5-7; 2:6-7; the conditional constructions in 2:20 and 3:1 also assume shared knowledge.

60. The argument in Colossians proceeds by intertwining the two: Christ (1:15-20, 27-29; 2:2-3, 6, 9; 2:14—3:1; 4:2); baptism (1:12-13, 21-23; 2:11-15; 2:20-3:4; 3:9, 12).

61. For Galatians, see 2:8, 15-16; 3:2; 4:8-9, 21; 5:2, 4; 6:12-13; for Colossians, see 1:21, 27; 2:13; 3:11; 4:11.

62. In both letters, Paul is either uncertain of the identity or remarkably circumspect. For Galatians, see 1:7, 9; 3:1; 4:17; 5:7, 10, 12; 6:12-13; for Colossians, see 2:8, 16, 18.

63. There is a note of coercion sounded in 2:3 and 6:12, but more of a voluntary desire in 4:21 and 5:2-4. Note Paul's apparent necessity to deny that he himself is a preacher of circumcision, in 5:11.

64. See the need to designate baptism as a "circumcision made without hands" and the "circumcision of Christ" in 2:11; the regulations against handling, tasting, and touching in 2:22; and the denial of distinction between Jew and Gentile in 3:11.

65. The key phrase is 2:18, which the RSV renders, "insisting on self-abasement and the worship of angels, taking his stand on visions...." The

3. In each group, such ambitions are connected to a desire for "perfection" or "maturity."[66]

4. In each case, there is the suggestion that those having additional initiations are in a superior position to those who have received only baptism into Christ.[67]

The most pressing *religious* question is why some Phrygian Christians were seeking an additional initiation beyond baptism. The question gains even more point when we remember that circumcision is, after all, a mutilation of the body which, when carried out on an adult male — as it would be in such cases — is also extraordinarily painful.[68] What impulse drove

---

term *embateuein* has definite associations with ritual initiations; see S. Eitrem, *"embateuō," Studia Theologica* 2 (1949) 90–94; and F. O. Francis, "The Background of *Embateuein* (Col 2:18) in Legal Papyri and Oracle Inscriptions," in *Conflict at Colossae,* ed. F. O. Francis and W. A. Meeks (Sources for Biblical Study 4; Missoula, Mont.: Scholars Press, 1975) 197–207. M. Dibelius, "The Isis Initiation in Apuleius," argued that the visionary experience involved an initiation into an Isis-style mystery after baptism (see *Conflict at Colossae,* 61–121. F. O. Francis, "Humility and Angelic Worship in Col. 2:18," argues for a form of Merkabah mysticism (*Conflict at Colossae,* 163–95. L. Cerfaux, "L'influence des 'mystères' sur les épîtres de S. Paul aux Colossiens et aux Ephésiens," thinks that a form of syncretistic Jewish mystery like that expressed by Philo is involved (*Recueil Lucien Cerfaux: Etudes d'Exégèse et d'Histoire Religieuse* (BETL 71; Leuven: Leuven University Press, 1985) 279–85.

66. Of particular importance in Galatians is the use of *epitelein* in 3:3. The RSV translates, "Having begun in the Spirit are you now ending with the flesh?" But the term has definite connections with the "perfection" that comes from the completion of initiation rituals; see R. S. Ascough, "The Completion of a Religious Duty: The Background of 2 Cor 8:1-15," *New Testament Studies* 42 (1996) 584–99, esp. the inscriptional evidence collected in 590–94. See also *plērōma* in Gal 4:4, *plēroun* in 5:14, *telein* in 5:16, and *anaplēroun* in 6:2. In Colossians, see *teleios* in 1:28 and 4:12; *teleiotēs* in 3:14; *plēroun* in 1:9, 25; 2:10; 4:17; *plērōma* in 1:19; 2:9; *plērophoria* in 2:2; and *plērophorein* in 4:12.

67. See Gal 4:17; 5:5; 6:12-13; Col 2:8, 16, 18, 23.

68. The debilitating effects of the procedure are graphically depicted in the story of Dinah and Shechem, in Gen 34:25. For an instance when Gentiles were compelled to be circumcised "as a condition of life among them

such an ambition? The letters to the Galatians and Colossians have rarely been read together, and even less frequently, if ever, with this question in mind. The reason is that our question is less historical than it is religious: we are asking a phenomenological question of ancient texts in order to apprehend better the human experience of ritual.

Because Colossians is often relegated to the ranks of the pseudonymous Pauline letters, in fact, the two compositions are rarely even brought together as evidence for religious practice in a specific region of the Mediterranean world, although, even if not both from Paul, they address remarkably similar situations in communities in the same region and within a relatively short timespan.[69] The letters are ordinarily studied to yield information about "Pauline opponents"[70] and

[the Jews]," see Josephus, *Life* 113; or themselves sought the procedure, see Josephus, *Antiquities of the Jews* 13:258; LXX Esth 8:17.

69. On the "Phrygian/Galatian Region," see n. 43 above. Galatians could have been written any time "fourteen years later" than his conversion (see Gal 2:1; 2 Cor 12:2) during his active ministry, therefore between 49–57. If Colossians is authentic, as I think, then it would be written during an imprisonment, therefore possibly between 57 and 64. Remember the presumed impact of the earthquake of 60/64 (n. 50, above). The convolutions required by the premise of pseudonymity are illustrated by W. A. Meeks, *The First Urban Christians*. He notes that we are dependent for locating the destination of Philemon (a universally recognized authentic letter) on Colossians (a disputed letter) (p. 210 n. 219). He even holds open the possibility that the letter could have been authorized by Paul (see his signature, 4:18) and written by Timothy under Paul's authorization (p. 125). It is difficult to see how this does not constitute "Pauline authorship" in the broad sense of the term (see Johnson, *Writings of the New Testament*, 255–57).

70. For Galatians, see, e.g., W. Schmithals, *Paul and the Gnostics*, trans. J. Steely (Nashville: Abingdon Press, 1972) 13–64; J. Tyson, "Paul's Opponents in Galatia," *Novum Testamentum* 10 (1968) 241–54; R. Jewett, "The Agitators and the Galatian Community," *New Testament Studies* 17 (1970) 198–212; J. Munck, "The Judaizing Gentile Christians," in *Paul and the Salvation of Mankind*, trans. F. Clarke (Richmond: John Knox Press, 1959) 87–134; for Colossians, see G. Bornkamm, "The Heresy of Colossians," in *Conflict in Colossae*, 123–45; A. J. Bandstra, "Did the Colossian Errorists Need a Mediator?"

the theological response made by the author.[71] In the eyes of most observers, the important action is that taking place between Paul and his rivals for his churches' allegiance. Little effort is spent trying to figure out what Paul's readers were themselves experiencing and thinking, or what the religious logic of their position might be. But precisely that should be of most interest to the study of religion. So we pose the question: what was the character of the experience of baptism for these Phrygian Christians such that they would seek further ritual initiations?

The clue is to be found, I think, in the fact that, on the evidence of both letters, these Christians were converted Gentiles. In the context of their symbolic world, it was natural for them to regard their baptism into Christ as initiation into a mystery.[72] Their cultural expectation (or imprinting, if you

in *New Directions in New Testament Study*, ed. R. Longenecker and M. C. Tenney (Grand Rapids: Zondervan, 1974) 329–43; C. A. Evans, "The Colossian Mystics," *Biblica* 63 (1982) 188–205.

71. For Galatians, see, e.g., M. Barth, "The Kerygma of Galatians," *Interpretation* 21 (1967) 131–46; L. Cerfaux, "Christ Our Justice," in *Christ in the Theology of St. Paul* (New York: Herder and Herder, 1959) 205–29; R. B. Hays, *The Faith of Jesus* (SBLDS 56; Chico, Calif.: Scholars Press, 1983); for Colossians, see, e.g., N. Dahl, "Christ, Creation, and the Church," in *Jesus in the Memory of the Early Church* (Minneapolis: Augsburg Publishing House, 1976) 120–40; F. O. Francis, "The Christological Argument of Colossians," in *God's Christ and His People*, ed. W. A. Meeks and J. Jervell (Oslo: Universitetsverlaget, 1977) 192–208; A. T. Hanson, "The Conquest of the Powers," in *Studies in Paul's Technique and Theology* (Grand Rapids: Eerdmans, 1974) 1–12.

72. Although the term *mystērion* occurs in Colossians (1:26; 2:2; 4:3), my suggestion is not based on terminology alone; nor am I debating the origins of Christian baptism. For the fruitless debates on these points, see J. Z. Smith, *Drudgery Divine: On the Comparison of Early Christianities and the Religions of Late Antiquity* (Chicago Studies in the History of Judaism; Chicago: Chicago University Press, 1990); there is no need to rehearse all the literature that he dissects so skillfully. There appear to be four basic approaches to the study of earliest Christianity in the context of the mysteries. The first is to ignore them completely and pay attention only to Jewish antecedents (and Palestinian Jewish ones, at that); see, e.g., O. Cullmann, *Baptism in the*

allow) was that one initiation would lead to another. The reasons for seeking circumcision, in other words, may have had much less to do with theology than with the logic of ritual practice in antiquity and the tendency of religious people to seek perfection, that is, to finish the course on which they have set themselves.

This proposal is far from purely speculative. It can, in fact, be supported by the convergence of four separate lines of evidence: testimony concerning the mysteries in the Greco-Roman world, language of the mysteries employed within Judaism, cross-cultural study of rites of initiation, and finally early Jewish and Christian practice.

New Testament (Studies in Biblical Theology 1; London: SCM Press, 1950), e.g., p. 14 n. 2; G. R. Beasley-Murray, *Baptism in the New Testament* (London: Macmillan, 1962). The second is to recognize the pervasiveness of mystery practice and language, but refuse to grant it any influence for nascent Christianity, reserving that for later "Catholic" development; see, e.g., G. Wagner, *Pauline Baptism and the Pagan Mysteries,* 259–75; B. M. Metzger, "Considerations of Methodology in the Study of the Mystery Religions and Early Christianity," *Harvard Theological Review* 48 (1955) 1–20; A. D. Nock, "Hellenistic Mysteries and Christian Sacraments," in *Essays on Religion and the Ancient World,* ed. Z. Stewart, 2 vols. (Oxford: Clarendon Press, 1972) 2:791–820, esp. 809–10. The third is to subsume early Christianity into the mysteries more or less completely; see, e.g., R. Reitzenstein, *Hellenistic Mystery-Religions: Their Basic Ideas and Significance,* trans. J. Steely (Pittsburgh: Pickwick Press, 1978); A. Loisy, *Les Mystères Païens et le Mystère Chrétiens,* 2nd ed. (Paris: E. Nourry, 1930); S. Angus, *The Mystery Religions and Christianity: A Study in the Religious Background of Early Christianity* (London: John Murray, 1925). The fourth is to be fundamentally open to the ways in which the symbolic worlds of the mysteries and Christianity may have intersected, without demanding causal connections in the strict sense and respecting the distinctiveness of the diverse cults; see H. Rahner, "The Christian Mystery and the Pagan Mysteries," in *The Mysteries: Papers from the Eranos Yearbooks,* vol. 2, ed. J. Campbell (Bollingen Series 30; Princeton: Princeton University Press, 1955) 337–401; O. Casel, *The Mystery of Christian Worship* (Westminster, Md.: Newman Press, 1962); L. Cerfaux, "L'influence des 'mystères' sur les épîtres de S. Paul aux Colossiens et aux Ephésiens," *Recueil Lucien Cerfaux* 3:279–85. My argument makes clear that I find the fourth position most congenial and, in fact, demanded by the sort of phenomenological analysis I am attempting.

Initiation in the Mysteries

Information about the ancient mysteries is notoriously and understandably difficult to assess.[73] The *disciplinum arcanum* functioned with sufficient rigor to make even our most explicit witnesses to ritual practice within the mysteries models of indirection and circumspection.[74] What is abundantly clear, however, is that initiation into one mystery by no means excluded initiation into another.[75] In the polytheistic system that dominated ancient Mediterranean cultures, even the most ardent devotion to a specific god allowed recognition of the dignity and importance of the other gods. Someone who boasted of initiation into a multitude of mysteries was not revealing religious unreliability but the most profound and catholic piety.[76]

73. The literature on the mysteries is obviously enormous. In addition to the works cited in n. 69, see B. M. Metzger, "A Classified Bibliography of the Graeco-Roman Mystery Religions, 1924–1973, with a Supplement, 1974–1977," *ANRW* II.17.3 (1984) 1259–1379; L. J. Alderinck, "The Eleusinian Mysteries in Roman Imperial Times," *ANRW* II.18.2 (1989) 1457–98; and R. Beck, "Mithraism since Franz Cumont," *ANRW* II.17.4 (1984) 2002–15. For basic orientation, see W. Burkert, *Greek Religion*, trans. J. Raffan (Cambridge: Harvard University Press, 1985) 276–304; idem, *Ancient Mystery Cults;* and M. W. Meyer, ed., *The Ancient Mysteries: A Sourcebook* (San Francisco: Harper and Row, 1987).

74. See A. Motte, "Silence et Sécret dans les Mystères d'Eleusis," in *Les Rites d'Initiation: Actes du Colloque de Liège et de Louvain-la-Neuve, 1984*, ed. J. Ries (Louvain-la-Neuve: Centre d'Histoire des Religions, 1986) 317–34; Alderinck, "Eleusinian Mysteries," 1477; Burkert, *Ancient Mystery Cults*, 90.

75. See A. D. Nock, *Conversion: The Old and New in Religion from Alexander the Great to Augustine of Hippo* (Oxford: Clarendon Press, 1933) 107–21, 155; Angus, *Mystery Religions*, 187–204.

76. Apuleius of Madura boasts of having undergone multiple initiations into mysteries (see *Apology*, 55). Libanius reports of the Emperor Julian that he "consorted with *daimones* in countless rites (*teletai*)" (cited in Nock, *Conversion*, 115). The extreme case is presented in Theophrastus's "Portrait of the Superstitious Person," who goes to the priests of Orpheus monthly (cited in G. Luck, *Arcana Mundi: Magic and the Occult in the Greek and Roman Worlds* (Baltimore: Johns Hopkins University Press, 1985) 65–66.

More pertinent to our present discussion, the most ancient and pervasively influential Eleusinian mysteries had well-defined multiple initiations, beginning with a purificatory bath, and moving through the "lesser mysteries" and "greater mysteries."[77] A first initiation into the cult of a specific god or goddess, then, could ordinarily be regarded as preliminary to still further initiations.[78] Our clearest direct evidence for this comes from Apuleius's *Metamorphoses (Golden Ass),* deservedly esteemed not only as a picaresque novel[79] but also as an account of religious conversion and transformation.[80]

After his careless dabbling in magic potions had turned him into an ass and vengeful Fortune had led him through a series of progressively more alienating experiences, Lucius encounters the goddess Isis on the moonlit beach at Cenchrae.[81] Isis saves him by restoring him to his humanity,[82] and Lucius becomes a devotee of the goddess.[83] Apuleius's veiled description of Lucius's initiation into the cult of Isis is

77. Clement of Alexandria, *Stromateis* 5:71-72, speaks of three stages, but there were actually four stages in the complete Eleusinian initiation: the purification, initiation into the lesser mysteries (at Agrae), then initiation into the greater mysteries (at Eleusis), and a year later, the *epopteia,* also at Eleusis. See Nock, "Hellenistic Mysteries," 792–93; Wagner, *Pauline Baptism and the Pagan Mysteries,* 71–88; K. Kerenyi, *Eleusis,* 45–102; Alderinck, "Eleusinian Mysteries," 1478–82.

78. For the seven degrees of initiation in the Mithras cult, see F. Cumont, *The Mysteries of Mithra,* trans. T. J. McCormack (Chicago: Open Court Publishing, 1910) 152–58; R. Merkelbach, *Mithras* (Königstein: Verlag Anton Hain, 1984) 86–145; Burkert, *Ancient Mystery Cults,* 42, 98–99.

79. See C. B. Conte, *Latin Literature: A History,* trans. J. B. Solodow (Baltimore: Johns Hopkins University Press, 1994) 559–69; T. Haegg, *The Novel in Antiquity* (Berkeley: University of California Press, 1983) 166–90.

80. Nock calls Apuleius's account "the high-water mark of the piety which grew out of the Mystery religions." *Conversion,* 138.

81. *Metamorphoses* X, 38; for text, translation, and full commentary, see J. G. Griffiths, *The Isis-Book (Metamorphoses Book XI)* (Leiden: E. J. Brill, 1975).

82. *Metamorphoses* XI, 3–15.

83. *Metamorphoses* XI, 26.

one of our most important sources of knowledge of the mysteries.[84] We note that it involves a purificatory bath[85] and the putting on of new clothing.[86]

However dramatic and decisive, however, Lucius's initiation is by no means final. It is really only a first step. He discovers that a still more advanced form of initiation into the cult of Osiris, the consort of Isis, is desirable,[87] and after some delay and considerable expense he undergoes that second initiation.[88] Nor is this the end. Soon he is informed that still a third initiation is available. Lucius begins to have questions about the good faith of those who had initiated him in the first place, but he undergoes a third initiation,[89] with the same result as with the first two: his expense is well repaid by the even greater prosperity he enjoys as a lawyer, and he gains an exalted status as a member of the priesthood of the Osiris cult.[90] While Lucius was hesitating before his third initiation, wondering if something had gone wrong in the first two times, he is reassured by a prophecy, which tells him:

> There is no reason to be afraid of this long series of ritual, as if something had been omitted before. Rejoice and be happy instead, because the deities continually deem you worthy. Exalt, rather, in the fact that you will experience three times what is scarcely permitted to others even

84. "It is the only first-person account of a mystery experience that we have." Burkert, *Ancient Mystery Cults*, 97.

85. *Metamorphoses* XI, 23.

86. *Metamorphoses* XI, 24.

87. *Metamorphoses* XI, 27; for the entire myth, see Plutarch, *Isis and Osiris* (Mor. 351D–384C).

88. *Metamorphoses* XI, 29.

89. *Metamorphoses* XI, 29; Nock notes, "The second and third initiations have been regarded as invented by the Roman priesthood for their personal gain . . . but it is possible that these additional ceremonies were genuine and due to a tendency elsewhere observed to multiple rites." *Conversion*, 150.

90. *Metamorphoses* XI, 30.

once, and from that number you should rightly consider yourself forever blessed.[91]

From Apuleius's story, then, we learn that multiple initiations within the same cult were not only possible but were to be expected as a progressive movement toward perfection; that the passage from Isis to Osiris was not considered an apostasy but an enhancement; and that each stage of initiation led to greater knowledge, dignity, and status within the cult. Ritual imprinting was toward the politics of perfection.

Mysterious Initiation in Judaism

The question of how much the language and sensibility of the mysteries had entered into the Judaism of the Hellenistic period remains disputed. At one extreme is Erwin Goodenough who argued that Hellenistic Judaism was, in effect, a form of Mystery, and who interpreted a variety of archaeological data and literary texts in support of that strong position.[92] For Goodenough, the discovery of the synagogue at Dura-Europos with its murals depicting Moses in the garb of a mystagogue was the key to unlocking the specific religiosity of Hellenistic Judaism as found above all in the writings of Philo, who for Goodenough is not an idiosyncratic but a representative figure.[93] At the other extreme is Arthur Darby

91. *Metamorphoses* XI, 29.

92. E. Goodenough, *By Light, Light: The Mystic Gospel of Hellenistic Judaism* (New Haven: Yale University Press, 1935); idem, *An Introduction to Philo Judaeus,* 2nd ed. (New York: Barnes and Noble, 1963).

93. E. R. Goodenough, *Jewish Symbols in the Greco-Roman Period,* 13 vols. (New York: Pantheon Books, 1953-1968). Before Goodenough, L. Cerfaux argued for widespread influence of the mysteries on Alexandrian Judaism, focusing esp. on Pseudo-Orpheus: see "Influence des Mystères sur le Judaisme Alexandrin avant Philon," *Le Museon* 37 (1924) 29–88, reprinted in *Recueil*

Nock, who, while recognizing the validity of many of Goodenough's discrete observations, resists the transmutation of Judaism in the Diaspora into a single coherent religious system fundamentally different than that of a halachically based Palestinian Judaism.[94]

What neither position can deny is the pervasive use by Philo of language that takes its origin in the mysteries yet is employed with direct reference to the practice and self-understanding of Judaism.[95] There is no question here of syncretism in the crude sense. As a passionate defender of Judaism, Philo engages in the same sort of rejection of the pagan mysteries that we find in *The Wisdom of Solomon*.[96] He speaks of "the lore of occult rites and mysteries and all such imposture and buffoonery," scorns their "mummeries"

Lucien Cerfaux, 1:65–112; for a full examination of the pertinent non-Philonic texts, see C. R. Holladay, *Fragments from Hellenistic Jewish Authors*, 4 vols. (SBL Texts and Translations; Chico, Calif. and Atlanta: Scholars Press, 1983-1996), esp. vol. 2: *Poets* (1989), vol. 3: *Aristobulus* (1995), and vol. 4: *Orphica* (1996). Certainly the vision of the heavenly man in *Joseph and Aseneth* 14–17 shares the same sensibility.

94. See in particular Nock's three reviews of Goodenough's *Jewish Symbols*, under the title "Religious Symbols and Symbolism I, II, and III," first published in *Gnomon* 27 (1955) 558–72; *Gnomon* 29 (1957) 524–33; and *Gnomon* 32 (1960) 728–36, now collected in *Essays on Religion and the Ancient World*, 2:877–94, 895–907, 908–19. In his "Hellenistic Mysteries and Christian Sacraments," Nock insists that Philo's language is no more than a "philosophic metaphor" and that his interests are the same as those of Palestinian Judaism (*Essays*, 802). A critical yet appreciative review of Goodenough's contribution is found in M. Smith, "Goodenough's *Jewish Symbols* in Retrospect," *Journal of Biblical Literature* 86 (1967) 53–68.

95. Nock grants, "Undeniably, Philo used Mystery terms for hidden theological truths," in "Religious Symbols II" (*Essays*, 899). Nock's reference to this usage as a "philosophical metaphor" (*Essays*, 802), derives from the fact that Plato had already employed the Eleusinian "lesser and greater mysteries" language with respect to spiritual transformation through knowledge (see *Symposium* 209E; *Phaedrus* 250B–C; Burkert, *Ancient Mystery Cults*, 91–93).

96. *Wisdom* 14:22-31; for Philo's rejection of an accommodation that would mean abandonment of ancestral customs, see *Migration of Abraham* 89–92; *Against Flaccus* 50.

and "mystic fables," and declares, "Let none, therefore, of the followers and disciples of Moses either confer or receive initiation to such rites."[97] In another place he associates the mysteries, especially that of Demeter, with exhibitions of licentiousness and effeminacy.[98]

What we find in Philo, then, is not a mingling of Judaism and the mysteries, but rather a conceptualization of Judaism as Mystery. Philo's loyalty to the literal prescriptions of the law, including the obligation of circumcision, cannot be doubted.[99] But he regards such observance, based on a literal reading of the text of scripture, as only the first stage of initiation. More is required if "perfection" is to be reached, namely, an initiation into a manner of reading that is allegorical and a transformation of the self that is spiritual in nature. It is the cultivation and perfection of the human soul through contemplation of the divine realities that is the real goal of scripture.

Philo employs the symbolism of the mysteries at three levels. First, he contrasts the stage of perfection available to the patriarchs to the higher level of knowledge and transformation available to Moses, who entered into the presence of God. The movement from the stories of Genesis (which provide protreptic in the virtues) to the revelation of the Law by Moses is the movement from the lesser to the greater mysteries. The moral virtues demonstrated by those *nomoi empsychoi* are available to all humans, but the divine secrets of the Law are available only by revelation. In this understanding, Moses is a mystagogue. Second, Moses is also the one who initiates into the higher, allegorical reading of the Law, so that the reader understands God's concern not to be simply with the cleansing of utensils and the separation of foods but always with the purification of

---

97. *Special Laws* 1:319.
98. *Special Laws* 3:37–42.
99. See *Migration of Abraham* 118.

the human mind and the separation of the spirit from earthly entanglements. Third, by displaying these two levels and by portraying them in terms of a mystery cult into which one can enter progressively through successive initiations, Philo has constructed himself also as hierophant, drawing his reader into deeper levels of knowledge and perfection.

If we scan Philo's language of perfection (*teleiosis*), we find that it focuses on the human soul (*psychē*) or mind (*nous*),[100] which, schooled in the virtues exemplified by the patriarchs[101] and guided by God,[102] reaches its perfection in divine knowledge[103] acquired by the vision of God.[104] His language concerning the mysteries, in turn, coincides exactly with that concerning perfection. The mind that still knows sensibly has not yet attained "the highest mysteries,"[105] and it is the mind that is the "initiate of the divine mysteries"[106] received by God's revelation.[107] The mind is purified by such initiation into the "great mysteries."[108] It can soar aloft and be initiated into the "mysteries of the Lord."[109] Those who have such knowledge deserve to be called "initiates."[110] The movement from sensible knowledge and the practice of the virtues to this higher apprehension of God is characterized as initiation respectively into the "lesser mysteries" and "greater mysteries."[111]

---

100. *On Husbandry* 133, 146, 165; *Migration of Abraham* 73; *On the Cherubim* 69.

101. *On Abraham* 26; *On Husbandry* 157; *On the Giants* 26.

102. *On Change of Names* 23–24.

103. *Sacrifices of Abel and Cain* 7.

104. *Rewards and Punishments* 36; *Who Is the Heir?* 121; *On Drunkenness* 82; *On Change of Names* 12; *Posterity and Exile of Cain* 132.

105. *On Abraham* 122.

106. *On Rewards and Punishments* 121.

107. *On the Cherubim* 42.

108. *Allegorical Interpretation* 3:100.

109. *Allegorical Interpretation* 3:71.

110. *On the Cherubim* 48; *Flight and Finding* 85.

111. *Sacrifices of Abel and Cain* 62.

For Philo, it is Moses who has uniquely entered into God's presence,[112] the "darkness of God" where he learned the "essence of unseen things,"[113] the "patterns and originals of the things of the senses."[114] It is Moses' mind that has been initiated into God's mystery.[115] Moses is therefore the one who can lead others into this greater mystery.[116] He is, indeed, a hierophant and teacher of the divine rites.[117] Moses is such through the oracles of the Law, which themselves bear clues, when properly detected, of how they are to be read at a deeper than literal level.[118] Even the Septuagint is to be received as the oracles of a mystery.[119] Logically, then, those who hear the oracles of the Law and learn to read them allegorically are themselves "initiated into the mysteries of the sanctified life."[120]

My point in this exposition is to demonstrate that in at least one writer roughly contemporaneous with Paul, Judaism was not only consistently portrayed in terms of a mystery, but one with multiple initiations. Philo states clearly, furthermore, that "initiation into the lesser mysteries must precede initiation into the greater,"[121] with Moses being the hierophant of the higher rites. The pertinence of this sequence to our present discussion should be obvious, especially in the case of Galatians, where an initial purificatory baptism into the messiah is considered as prelude to a higher "perfection" accomplished by initiation into Moses. Note how Paul

---

112. *On the Giants* 53–54; *Sacrifices of Abel and Cain* 53–54.

113. *Life of Moses* 1:158.

114. *On the Creation* 71.

115. *Allegorical Interpretation* 3:101–3.

116. *On the Virtues* 178.

117. *Posterity and Exile of Cain* 173; *On the Giants* 54.

118. *On Dreams* 1:164.

119. *Life of Moses* 2:40.

120. *Contemplative Life* 25, 28; see *On Abraham* 122; *Unchangeableness of God* 61.

121. *On Moses* 1:62; see *Sacrifices of Abel and Cain* 61–62.

addresses those seeking circumcision: "Tell me, you who *want to be* under the law, do you not hear the law?" (Gal 4:21). Philo intimates in one passage, in fact, that even more initiations might be possible: "I myself was initiated under Moses the God beloved into the greater mysteries, yet when I saw the prophet Jeremiah and knew him to be not only himself enlightened but a Hierophant of the holy secrets, I was not slow to become his disciple."[122]

Ritual Initiation and Status Elevation

A third line of evidence is provided by cross-cultural anthropological studies of ritual.[123] Analysis of initiation rituals from a variety of cultures indicates that the multiple initiations found among the ancient Greco-Roman mysteries are by no means exceptional.[124] The Hopi, for example, have a two-stage initiation, with the second occurring some years after the first.[125] The Navaho practice a four-stage initiation.[126] The Gisu and Samburu also practice multiple initiations.[127] Initiations into secret societies, which are almost always hierarchical, especially involve a series of initiations.[128] La Fontaine analyzes the intricate stages of initiation into the

---

122. *On the Cherubim* 49.

123. Richard Ascough's application of ritual theory to the ritual of baptism in the *Didache* ("An Analysis of the Baptismal Ritual of the *Didache*," *Studia Liturgica* 24 [1994] 201–13) reveals the tripartite movement described by Van Gennep and Turner but no evidence for a stage of liminality (see below).

124. See J. La Fontaine, *Initiation*, 145, 152–53.

125. Ibid., 90.

126. See A. Van Gennep, *The Rites of Passage*, trans., M. B. Vizedom and G. L. Caffee (Chicago: University of Chicago Press, 1960) 79.

127. La Fontaine, *Initiation*, 145.

128. Ibid., 39; see also V. Turner, *The Ritual Process: Structure and Anti-Structure* (The Henry Lewis Morgan Lectures; Ithaca, N.Y.: Cornell University Press, 1969) 190–94.

Chinese Triad societies[129] and refers to as many as ninety-nine levels of membership in the Poro associations of West Africa, each with its own initiation;[130] Van Gennep mentions the seven grades of initiation found among the Arioi in Tahiti and other parts of Polynesia, as well as the eighteen degrees of initiation into the Melanesian *suge*.[131] Such initiations involve an increase in both knowledge and power by the initiates,[132] especially in what Turner calls "rituals of status elevation."[133] Indeed, rituals of initiation consistently invest initiates with greater status within a specified group. In La Fontaine's precise formulation, "Maturity is a social status."[134]

Other anthropological aspects of initiation that might shed light on the present discussion are the frequent use of oaths and professions in such rituals,[135] the widespread symbolism of death and rebirth in connection with initiation,[136] the way that circumcision — especially in some African tribes — functions as an ordeal whose successful endurance proves maturity,[137] and the manner in which the suffering of an ordeal at initiation involves a pattern of submission to the authority of the initiator.[138] But of the greatest pertinence is Victor Turner's analysis of the dialectic of structure and structurelessness in the ritual process.

Turner used his fieldwork among the Ndembu of northwestern Zambia in Central Africa as a means of providing

129. La Fontaine, *Initiation*, 42–48.

130. Ibid., 94.

131. Van Gennep, *The Rites of Passage*, 84.

132. La Fontaine, *Initiation*, 15–17.

133. Turner, *The Ritual Process*, 167.

134. La Fontaine, *Initiation*, 104; see also M. Milner Jr., "Status and Sacredness: Worship and Salvation as Forms of Status Transformation," *Journal for the Scientific Study of Religion* 33 (1994) 99–109.

135. La Fontaine, *Initiation*, 15.

136. Ibid., 15, 102; see Eliade, *Rites and Symbols of Initiation*, 73–76, 89–93.

137. La Fontaine, *Initiation*, 112–14, 146–47.

138. Ibid., 147–85.

greater nuance to Van Gennep's classic analysis of *rites de passage*.[139] Van Gennep's work was a classic for two reasons. First, across a bewildering variety of specific ritual forms he was able to detect a basic pattern: in rituals negotiating a passage from one condition to another, he consistently saw the moment of separation, the moment of liminality, and the moment of reintegration.[140] Second, he saw that such rituals involved a social construction: puberty rituals, for example, did not mark a biological event but created a social event; what they effected was a transition from one social status to another.[141]

Turner gave his attention above all to the middle stage of liminality. Two of his observations are of special interest. The first is that the condition of liminality, experienced after the preliminary rites of separation and before the rites of reintegration, involves what Turner calls *communitas*,[142] namely, a sense of structureless cohesion and harmony that is frequently expressed by an absolute egalitarianism: "the passage from lower to higher status is through a limbo of statuslessness."[143] The second is that the condition of liminality is normally a temporary and preparatory condition. It prepares the way for the reintegration of the initiate at a higher status in society: "There is a dialectic here, for the immediacy of the *communitas* gives way to the mediacy of structure."[144]

Particularly those going through rituals of status eleva-

139. Turner, *The Ritual Process*, 4; see also V. Turner, *Process, Performance, and Pilgrimage: A Study in Comparative Symbology* (Ranchi Anthropology Series 1; New Delhi, Concept Publishing Company, 1979) 15–16.

140. Van Gennep, *The Rites of Passage*, 7–25.

141. Ibid., 65–70.

142. Turner, *The Ritual Process*, 102–28; idem, *Process, Performance, and Pilgrimage*, 40–44.

143. Turner, *The Ritual Process*, 97; idem, *Process, Performance, and Pilgrimage*, 98–101.

144. Turner, *The Ritual Process*, 129; idem, *Process, Performance, and Pilgrimage*, 44–45.

tion expect to pass through a stage of status reduction before reaching that higher state, "Such liminality may also, when it appears in *rites de passage,* humble the neophyte precisely because he is to be structurally exalted at the end of the rites." [145] If we were to apply Turner's analysis to the situation in Paul's Phrygian churches, we would say that those who had undergone an initial ritual of separation (such as baptism) could well agree with Paul that they were thereby "neither male nor female, neither Jew nor Greek, neither slave nor free" (Gal 3:28). But they would also have a great deal of anthropological evidence on their side if they were to add, " 'For the time being,' that is, until we are initiated into the higher status of initiation into Moses offered through the ordeal of circumcision."

Jewish and Christian Practice

Finally, we can consider the evidence concerning the multiple relations of baptism to other initiations within Judaism and nascent Christianity itself. Most obvious is the practice of proselyte baptism for Gentiles converting to Judaism. Our knowledge of the ritual is inadequate, but it seems to have been considered a preliminary initiation, to be followed later by circumcision. [146] The pertinence of this precedent to gentile converts to the messiah in Galatia should be obvious. There is also the baptism of John, which was extended to

145. Turner, *The Ritual Process,* 201.
146. The basic texts are *b.Yeb* 46a; *Pes* 8,8; 91b-2; Epictetus, *Discourses* II, 9, 9–21; *Sibylline Oracles* 4:62–78; Josephus, *Antiquities of the Jews* 20:38–48. For discussions, see G. R. Beasley-Murrray, *Baptism in the New Testament,* 18–31; J. Crehan, *Early Christian Baptism and the Creed,* 24; G. W. H. Lampe, *The Seal of the Spirit,* 24; O. Cullmann, *Baptism in the New Testament,* 9; J. Delorme, "The Practice of Baptism in Judaism at the Beginning of the Christian Era," in *Baptism in the New Testament: A Symposium,* trans. D. Askew (Baltimore: Helicon, 1964) 25–60.

Jews who had already been circumcised, including Jesus.[147] John's gospel provides slight evidence for a baptizing ministry of Jesus concurrent with that of John (John 3:22; 4:2). Thus we would have at least the theoretical possibility that a single individual could undergo, in sequence, Jewish proselyte baptism, circumcision, the baptism of John, and the baptism of Jesus.

The Acts of the Apostles shows those who heed Peter's proclamation at Pentecost being baptized "in the name of Jesus" (Acts 2:38). This group could well have included some who had also been baptized by John (see Acts 1:21-22). After his encounter with the risen Lord, Paul, a circumcised Jew, receives the Holy Spirit (9:17) and is then baptized (9:18). Finally, we see Paul baptizing "in the name of Jesus" those disciples who had been baptized by John (Acts 19:1-5), and then placing hands on them so that they received the Holy Spirit (19:6).[148] In light of these combinations, we should not wonder overmuch at a reference to "instruction about ablutions (=baptisms)" in the plural, as part of the "elementary doctrine of Christ" (Heb 6:1-2), nor should we be too much surprised if new gentile converts in Phrygia, recently baptized into Jesus, should think that perhaps still more initiations were in store for them.

By means of these separate lines of evidence, I have tried to move from the clues in the text of Galatians and Colossians to some sense of the *kind* of "religious experience" baptism was for them. Since in this case we have no direct emic evidence, we are obliged to move from the external pattern of

---

147. See Josephus, *Antiquities* 18.5.2; Matt 3:1-17; Mark 1:1-33; Luke 3:2-19; John 1:31-34; 3:22-24; 4:1-2; Acts 1:5; 18:25; 19:3-4; for discussion, see G. R. Beasley-Murray, *Baptism in the New Testament*, 31–44.

148. On the fruitless effort to derive some theological consistency on the question of the Holy Spirit in Luke's narrative by asking other than narrative questions, see W. H. Shepherd Jr., *The Narrative Function of the Holy Spirit as a Character in Luke-Acts* (SBLDS 147; Atlanta: Scholars Press, 1994) 11–26.

behavior toward some sense of the meaning of the ritual as suggested by ancient texts and modern studies. Yet the yield is not insignificant. We have put ourselves in the position of understanding why these Phrygian Christians would have wanted to receive circumcision and undergo additional initiations beyond baptism; the reason is simply that such was the symbolic imprinting of initiation, certainly in their world, and in most other worlds we have been able to survey as well. To be initiated once was to be separated from "the world" and enter the community of the "sanctified." It meant dwelling in a state of liminal *communitas*, where social differentiations between gender, race, and status were dissolved. But this was only to be a temporary and preliminary state of affairs. If one was to "mature" or "grow perfect" in this religion, then surely other initiations would follow, and with them, greater status. At the very least, we can appreciate that this desire was far from perverse, and was, in fact, the natural impulse of human religiosity within the symbolic world of the ancient mysteries.

The Character of Paul's Response

Paul's response to his churches becomes more intelligible when placed in this context. In Galatians 3:3, Paul's rhetorical question should be given its full ritual connotation. Rather than the RSV's neutral, "Having begun in the Spirit are you now ending in the flesh," we should read something like, "Having begun in the Spirit are you being perfected (*epiteleisthe*) now in the flesh?"[149] Paul perceives the logic of their endeavor.

Likewise, Paul's strange question in 4:8-9 becomes a little clearer: "Formerly, when you did not know God, you were in

---

149. See R. S. Ascough, "The Completion of a Religious Duty: The Background of 2 Cor 8.1-15," *New Testament Studies* 42 (1996) 584–99.

bondage to beings that by nature are no gods; but now that you have come to know God, or rather to be known by God, how can you turn back again to the weak and beggarly elemental spirits whose slaves you want to be once more?" Quite apart from the difficulty of identifying the "elemental spirits,"[150] how could Paul equate a desire for circumcision and the observance of Torah with a return to idolatry? The implied equation makes more sense against the backdrop I have sketched. To treat initiation into Christ as preliminary to initiation into Moses, is for Paul to deny the ultimacy of Christ and, finally, the oneness of God (see 3:30). It is to continue to act within the framework of polytheism, where initiation into a second deity in no way suggests rejection of the first. Paul's (to us) outrageous identification of Torah with idolatry makes sense if he is in fact opposing the logic of ritual imprinting in the mysteries.[151]

Above all, we can better understand why Paul hinges his entire argument on the reality of the gift of the Spirit the Galatians received when they accepted the proclamation of the crucified Messiah (3:2) and had "put on Christ" by baptism (3:27).[152] That Paul can appeal to their experience suggests that he knew they had indeed had the "working of powerful things among them." But he needs to convince them that this gift of the Spirit is indeed the fulfillment of God's promise (3:14), bringing them into full maturity before the one God: "Because you are sons, God has sent the Spirit

150. For the literature on *stoicheia tou kosmou* in Gal 4:3 and 8, see H. D. Betz, *Galatians* (Hermeneia; Philadelphia: Fortress Press, 1979) 204–5.

151. It may also be possible that Paul's polemical statement, "they desire to have you circumcised that they may glory in your flesh" (6:13) also fits within this framework, for success in recruiting devotees to higher stages of initiation also has implications for the authority of the mystagogue.

152. For the importance of the *experience* of the Holy Spirit in Paul's argument, see D. J. Lull, *The Spirit in Galatia: Paul's Interpretation of PNEUMA as Divine Power* (SBLDS 49; Chico, Calif.: Scholars Press, 1980) 53–152.

of his Son into our hearts, crying, 'Abba! Father!' So through God you are no longer a slave but a son and if a son then an heir" (4:6-7).

Paul therefore sets up a fundamental opposition between initiation in the Spirit and initiation "in the flesh" (that is, circumcision). So the desire to be circumcised cannot be something more added on by way of perfection, but a fundamental betrayal of the first gift. "If you receive circumcision, Christ will be of no advantage to you. . . . You are severed from Christ" (5:2-4). He extends the opposition also to the moral sphere. Paul declares, "If we live by the Spirit, let us also walk by the Spirit" (5:25), which means living according to the principles of *communitas* established by the gift of the Spirit: egalitarianism, mutual upbuilding, the positive "fruits of the Spirit" (5:22). In a word, Paul advocates living in what Turner would call a state of permanent liminality. For Paul, the desire to be initiated "in the flesh" is itself an expression of a "fleshly morality," which he spells out in terms of attitudes of rivalry, envy, self-seeking (5:19-21). In short, Paul argues for the sufficiency of baptism as a ritual of initiation because through it Christians enter into full inheritance of God's promise (Gal 3:27-4:7).

In Colossians, Paul's argument is based even more emphatically on the adequacy of the experience of God in Christ through baptism. Those seeking to disqualify others (2:18) or judge others (2:16) on the basis of circumcision (2:11) and ascetical regulations (2:21) and mystical initiation (2:18) are both deceiving and self-deceived. They are like people who chase after shadows but do not see the solid body that casts the shadow. Festivals and new moons and sabbaths are "only a shadow of what is to come; but the body is Christ's" (2:17). Their practices only puff them up (2:18) with the appearance of religious rigor (2:23) but do not really transform the person spiritually (2:23). Indeed the very fact that the promotion of further initiations leads to rivalry and judgment demonstrates that "they are of no value in checking the indulgence of the flesh" (2:23). Paul seeks to remind his readers that the power at work in Christ is the very power of God: "in him all the fullness of God was pleased to dwell" (1:19). Therefore, by their initiation into Christ through baptism (1:21; 2:11-12), they have entered into "the inheritance of the saints in light," for God has "qualified them" (1:12).

Once more, then, Paul exhorts his readers to follow through the ritual imprinting of baptism into the death and resurrection of Jesus. They are to live in a community where there is no "Greek and Jew, circumcised and uncircumcised, barbarian, Scythian, slave, free man, but Christ is all and in all" (3:11). They are to "put on" the qualities of meekness and compassion and harmony that reflect the state of *communitas.* The letter is filled with the language of mystery and maturity (see 1:6; 3:28; 4:12). But for Paul, the *mystērion* is above all the way in which God has reached out to the Gentiles through Christ, "in whom are hid all the treasures of wisdom and knowledge" (2:3). And perfection (see 1:28; 3:14; 4:12) consists above all in a deeper knowledge of this gift that has been given (1:6-7, 9-10; 2:2), a knowledge spelled out in a consistent manner of life that enacts the ritual imprinting of death and resurrection (1:10; 3:1-17).

Religion Trumps Theology

Paul's arguments are powerful, even compelling. And they tell us a great deal about *his* understanding of the experience of baptism.[153] But Paul's theological rhetoric had an uphill fight against the deep impulses of religious imprinting. We have no idea how successful he was in his ancient Phrygian

---

153. Note, however, that his arguments also depend on his readers' agreement that they had, in fact, experienced powerful things through baptism and the reception of the Holy Spirit.

battles.[154] We do know that he secured for baptism its unique status as a ritual of initiation for Christians and established the *nomos tou christou* (or law of the Christ), the pattern of the dying and rising Christ, as the ritual imprinting through which Christians would grow in perfection. But it is equally clear that the religious impulses of the Phrygian Christians were not confined to them. After not too many years, Christians everywhere followed the sacrament of baptism with the second initiation rite of Confirmation, and for those more dedicated still, a third initiation into the priesthood.[155] As with Apuleius in the cult of Isis, so with Augustine in the cult of the Christ. In this particular game, religion trumps theology.

154. We may wonder, however, what his Galatian and Colossian readers might have thought, had they heard him assure his Corinthian congregations that "We do speak a wisdom among the perfect (*teleiois*), but not a wisdom of this age nor of the rulers of this age who are being destroyed. But we speak a wisdom of God that has been revealed in a *mystērion*" (1 Cor 2:6-7).

155. Concerning confirmation, Gregory Dix notes that it performed the same function of excluding the less-than-fully-initiated from sacred meals in Christianity as circumcision did in Judaism: by the time of Hippolytus, "The old jewish [sic] rules against table-fellowship 'with men uncircumcised' have been transferred by the church to any form of table-fellowship 'with men unconfirmed.'" *The Shape of the Liturgy* (1945; New York: Seabury Press, 1982) 83

4

GLOSSOLALIA AND THE EMBARRASSMENTS OF EXPERIENCE

Even at Pentecost, speaking in tongues divided the crowd.[1] Since then, glossolalia has been singled out as either the supreme criterion for the direct action of the Holy Spirit in Christian lives[2] or the supreme example of how enthusiasm is a bad thing for Christian piety.[3] Opinions vary concerning

1. Even those positively impressed "were astonished and confused, asking each other what this meant" (Acts 2:12). The negative reaction resembles that repeated through the ages: "But others mockingly declared that they were filled with new wine" (Acts 2:13). For translation and discussion, see L. T. Johnson, *The Acts of the Apostles* (Sacra Pagina 5; Collegeville, Minn.: Liturgical Press, 1992) 41–47.

2. For examples, see F. D. Bruner, *A Theology of the Holy Spirit: The Pentecost Experience and the New Testament Witness* (Grand Rapids: Eerdmans, 1970) 19–149; E. J. Lawless, *Handmaidens of the Lord: Pentecostal Women Preachers and Traditional Religion* (Philadelphia: University of Pennsylvania Press, 1988) esp. 7, 23, 59–65, 99–101; Y. A. Obaje, *The Miracle of Speaking in Tongues: Which Side Are You?* (Nigeria: Abedayo Calvary Printers, 1987) 26–37; C. Garrett, *Spirit Possession and Popular Religion from the Camisards to the Shakers* (Baltimore: Johns Hopkins University Press, 1987).

3. In his classic study, R. A. Knox shows how glossolalia figures in some but not all manifestations of that religious impulse he calls *Enthusiasm: A Chapter in the History of Religion* (New York: Oxford University Press, 1950) 360–66, 380, 549–59, 564. Despite his basically positive appreciation, M. T. Kelsey, *Speaking with Tongues: An Experiment in Spiritual Experience* (London: Epworth Press, 1964), begins by noting the way tongues create controversy in churches (5–8).

the authenticity of tongues as a religious experience or as the expression of religious experience.[4] But no one denies that for some Christians it is the experience most highly prized, the palpable sign that their life has been taken over by the power of God.[5] What is more, such Christians claim that this experience is precisely the same as that reported in the New Testament of the first believers.[6] If present-day Christians have exactly the same experience of God, it is patent that their Christianity above all must be regarded as authentically continuous with that of earliest Christianity.[7] The present-day prevalence of this practice and the claims that continue to be made for it make the study of glossolalia of particular pertinence for any examination of religious experience in earliest Christianity.[8]

4. See M. Heyd, *"Be Sober and Reasonable": The Critique of Enthusiasm in the Seventeenth and Early Eighteenth Centuries* (Brill's Studies in Intellectual History 63; Leiden: E. J. Brill, 1995) 31–38, 51–64, 80–98, 239, for the way in which glossolalia was reduced either to a medical cause (*melancholia*) or the influence of demons. The general idea can be gained from the title of the work by M. Casaubon, *A Treatise Concerning Enthusiasme as It is an Effect of Nature: but is Mistaken by Many for Either Divine Inspiration or Diabolicall Possession,* 2nd ed. (London: Roger Daniel, 1656); similarly, J. Foster, *Natural History of Enthusiasm* 7th ed. (London: Holdsworth and Ball, 1834).

5. See M. T. Kelsey, *Speaking with Tongues,* 17, 78; E. G. Hinson, "The Significance of Glossolalia in the History of Christianity," in *Speaking in Tongues: Let's Talk about It,* ed. W. E. Mills (Waco: Word Publishing Co., 1973) 61–80; R. Laurentin, *Catholic Pentecostalism* (New York: Doubleday, 1977); L. N. Jones, "The Black Pentecostals," in *The Charismatic Movement,* ed. M. P. Hamilton (Grand Rapids: Eerdmans, 1975) 145–58.

6. See on this point W. G. MacDonald, "The Place of Glossolalia in Neo-Pentecostalism," in *Speaking in Tongues,* 81–93.

7. See C. G. Williams, *Tongues of the Spirit: A Study of Pentecostal Glossolalia and Related Phenomena* (Cardiff: University of Wales Press, 1981) 73.

8. The literature on glossolalia grew enormously under the impetus of the "charismatic movement" or "pentecostal movement" within both Protestantism and Catholicism in the 1960s and 1970s. For a helpful collection of articles, see W. E. Mills, ed., *Speaking in Tongues: A Guide to Research in*

The Nature of the Phenomenon

Determining the character of glossolalia is not easy.[9] The New Testament evidence is sparse and inconsistent.[10] In Acts, tongues are treated as real languages — Galileans speak "other tongues" (Acts 2:6-8) — and as a form of prophecy (Acts 2:16-18). In contrast, Paul emphasizes the unintelligibility of tongues (1 Cor 14:6-11) and explicitly contrasts this activity with that of prophecy (1 Cor 14:3-5).

The conflicts in our sources raise a number of questions. Should we assume that tongues takes a single consistent form? Then we might want to value one source more than another. Paul's report, for example, might be taken as that of a firsthand observer — indeed participant (see 1 Cor 14:18) — and therefore as more reliable. Acts correspondingly might be viewed as a narrative interpretation that camouflages the "real" phenomenon. Or should we begin with the assumption that even in the New Testament period glossolalia took several forms?[11] Then Paul and Acts might witness to a diversity of practice as well as of interpretation.

Another decision has to do with what evidence counts

Glossolalia (Grand Rapids: Eerdmans, 1986), esp. his full bibliography on pp. 493–528.

9. The term *glossolalia* derives from *glōssais lalein* (to speak in tongues) (see 1 Cor 14:6). The Greek word *glōssa*, which otherwise in the New Testament refers to the physical tongue (Luke 16:24), ordinary speech (1 John 3:18), or human language (Rev 5:9), is used in some passages for ecstatic utterance associated with possession by the Holy Spirit (see Mark 16:17; Acts 2:3, 4, 11; 10:46; 19:6; 1 Cor 12-14). See J. Behm, *"glōssa," TDNT* 1:719–27; R. A. Harrisville, "Speaking in Tongues: A Lexicographical Study," *Catholic Biblical Quarterly* 38 (1976) 35–48.

10. For surveys of the pertinent texts, see F. W. Beare, "Speaking with Tongues: A Critical Survey of the New Testament Evidence," *Journal of Biblical Literature* 83 (1964) 229–46; and W. G. MacDonald, "Glossolalia in the New Testament," *Bulletin of the Evangelical Theological Society* 7 (1964) 59–68.

11. See, e.g., D. Brown, "The Acts of the Apostle, Chapter 2: The Day of Pentecost," *Expositor* 1 (1875) 392–408.

in determining the nature of glossolalia in earliest Christianity. What weight should be assigned to similar phenomena in early Hebrew prophecy or Hellenistic mantic prophecy? Or how seriously should the experiences of contemporary glossolalists be taken, together with the claim that their experience represents the same "gift of the Holy Spirit" as that mentioned by Paul (1 Cor 12:10)?[12] Can the extensive studies of contemporary practice carried out by linguists, ethnographers, and psychologists, validly be employed to explicate the New Testament phenomenon?

Unfortunately, research into contemporary glossolalia is divided on such critical issues as whether tongues is a uniform or pluriform phenomenon,[13] whether it is invariably accompanied by or even to be identified with states of psychological dissociation,[14] and whether such parallel speech patterns as

12. Note J. M. Ford's dismissal of the hypothesis that tongues is ecstatic utterance: "It must be noted that no one who has ever heard the exquisitely beautiful choral singing in tongues at a quiet prayer meeting could ever declare this to be 'bedlam,' " and later, "All these articles appear to speak from the standpoint of persons who have no empirical experience of the phenomenon which they wish to evaluate." "Towards a Theology of Speaking in Tongues," *Theological Studies* 32 (1971) 3–29, reprinted in Mills, *Speaking in Tongues,* 268 and 270. Likewise M. T. Kelsey, *Speaking with Tongues,* 144, dismisses the work of a scholar on the grounds of unfamiliarity with the contemporary phenomenon. It is fascinating that some of the same writers who insist that tongues is absolutely unique to Christianity in antiquity and cannot be compared with Greco-Roman phenomena (e.g., Kelsey, ibid., 141), also assume that the contemporary phenomenon can, without more ado, be taken as equivalent to that addressed by Paul.

13. See W. J. Samarin, *Tongues of Men and Angels: The Religious Language of Pentecostalism* (New York: Macmillan, 1972) 129–49.

14. F. Goodman, *Speaking in Tongues: A Cross-Cultural Study of Glossolalia* (Chicago: University of Chicago Press, 1972) 124; Kelsey, *Speaking with Tongues,* 142; H. N. Maloney and A. A. Lovekin, *Glossolalia: Behavioral Science Perspectives on Speaking in Tongues* (New York: Oxford University Press, 1985) 112. Maloney and Lovekin provide a valuable survey and include a rich bibliography (pp. 263–79); see also J. P. Kildahl, "Psychological Observations," in *The Charismatic Movement,* ed. M. P. Harrington (Grand Rapids: Eerdmans,

those found in shamanism can be considered glossolalic.[15] Concerning antiquity, debate continues on the ecstatic character of the Hebrew prophets and the manifestations of mantic prophecy.[16]

Given this range of uncertainty, any definition of glossolalia in the New Testament must remain tentative, avoiding such easy characterizations as that expressed by the *Interpreter's Dictionary of the Bible* a generation ago, "The psychological aspects are patent."[17] Patience and discipline are particularly required in a phenomenological analysis of tongues. Neither a reductionistic assumption that tongues is attributable to charlatanism or self-delusion, nor an apologetic assumption that tongues is a direct result of divine inspiration, helps us understand the experience of glossolalia. Like any religious activity, glossolalia can be either sincere or phoney (or a complex mixture of both). Like other religious experiences, it can involve human and transcendental causes simultaneously.[18]

Scholars have generally worked with the hypothesis that glossolalia is a single phenomenon, and they have offered two standard definitions.[19] The first has it that tongues is the

1975) 124–42; and V. H. Hine, "Pentecostal Glossolalia: Toward a Functional Interpretation," *Journal for the Scientific Study of Religion* 8 (1965) 161–64.

15. See M. Eliade, *Le Chamanisme et les Techniques archaïques de l'Ecstase* (Paris: Payot, 1951) 98–102; L. Carlyle May, "A Survey of Glossolalia and Related Phenomena in Non-Christian Religions," *American Anthropologist* 58 (75–96) 1956.

16. C. G. Williams, "Ecstaticism in Hebrew Prophecy and Christian Glossolalia," *Science Religieuses* 3 (1974) 328–38; D. Aune, *Prophecy in Early Christianity and the Ancient Mediterranean World* (Grand Rapids: Eerdmans, 1983) 36–48; J. T. Bunn, "Glossolalia in Historical Perspective," in Mills, *Speaking in Tongues,* 36–47.

17. E. Andrews, "The Gift of Tongues," *Interpreters Dictionary of the Bible* (Nashville: Abingdon Press, 1962) 672.

18. See Maloney and Lovekin, *Glossolalia,* 249–51.

19. A third, rather odd, hypothesis, is that tongues are, literally, a heavenly language. The basis of this position, which is folkloric rather than scientific, is

divinely inspired ability to speak actual but untaught human languages, a skill technically known as *xenoglossia*.[20] In this understanding, the report in Acts 2:4-11 is determinative. The disciples receiving the Holy Spirit speak "other languages" that are understood by pilgrims from the Diaspora who also happen to speak those languages. Appeal is also made to Mark 16:17, which refers to "new tongues" (or "languages") as a sign that will accompany disciples. Some aspects of Paul's discussion in 1 Cor 14 are also isolated to support this hypothesis, for example, his comparison of tongues to known human languages of the earth (1 Cor 14:10-11).[21] Most of all, Paul lists with "tongues" another spiritual gift called "interpretation of tongues" (*hermeneia glōssōn,* 1 Cor 12:10). In light of 1 Cor 14:13, and especially 14:27-28, such interpretation is taken to mean "translating from a real but unknown language into another real but known language."[22] Modern glossalalists

---

Paul's phrase, "If I speak with the tongues of angels," in 1 Cor 13:1, his references to revealing mysteries (14:2) and speaking with God (14:28), as well as his cryptic allusion in 2 Cor 12:4 to heavenly visions that he is incapable of expressing in human speech. Paul's characterization has something in common with the ecstatic speech in the *Testament of Job* 48:1-50:3. The obvious problem with the hypothesis is that it is unhelpful for determining the linguistic or psychological dimensions of speech as it was practiced by early Christians. For a discussion of the texts, see S. D. Currie, "Speaking in Tongues: Early Evidence outside the New Testament Bearing on *Glōssais Lalein,*" *Interpretation* 19 (1965) 274–94.

20. May, "A Survey of Glossolalia and Related Phenomena," 63–68; See the reports given by I. Stevenson, *Xenoglossy: A Review and Report of a Case* (Charlottesville: University Press of Virginia, 1974); and idem, *Unlearned Language: New Studies in Xenoglossy* (Charlottesville: University Press of Virginia, 1984).

21. See T. W. Harpur, "The Gift of Tongues and Interpretation," *Canadian Journal of Theology* 12 (1966) 164–71; R. H. Gundry, "'Ecstatic Utterance'(NEB)," *Journal of Theological Studies* n.s. 17 (1966) 306. This is the position advocated as well by J. M. Ford, "Toward a Theology of 'Speaking in Tongues,'" *Theological Studies* 32 (1971) 3–29; and C. Forbes, "Early Christian Inspired Speech and Hellenistic Popular Religion," *Novum Testamentum* 28 (1986) 257–70.

22. J. G. Davies, "Pentecost and Glossolalia," *Journal of Theological Studies* n.s. 3 (1952) 231.

chime in with the evidence that their ecstatic speech is in fact a language unknown to them. A substantial oral tradition has it that such languages are spontaneously recognized by visitors from foreign climes who recognize in these utterances languages they themselves speak.[23]

The weight of textual evidence, however, does not support this understanding of tongues as real human languages. The Pentecost story does emphasize the intelligibility of the tongues spoken, but a careful reading indicates that the miracles occurred in the *hearing* rather than in the *mode of speaking*. The bystanders do not ask, "How can they all be speaking our native languages?" but rather, "Since all who are speaking are Galileans, how is it that *we hear them* in our own native languages?" (Acts 2:8).[24] The other references to tongues in Acts stress their source rather than their intelligibility. The isolation of Pentecost in this respect suggests that the element of communication was emphasized by Luke to suit his narrative purposes at that point in his story.[25]

The mention of "new tongues" in Mark 16:17 is too obscure to provide help in defining the nature of the phenomenon. The "longer ending of Mark" in which it occurs is certainly a later addition to the Gospel and indebted to other traditions, such as those found in Acts and Paul.[26] At best, the

23. W. J. Samarin, "The Linguisticality of Glossolalia," *Hartford Quarterly* 8 (1968) 55–57. For examples of such reports, see J. L. Sherrill, *They Speak with Other Tongues* (New York: McGraw-Hill, 1964) 98–107; and Kelsey, *Speaking with Tongues,* 160–63.

24. For the contrary view, see R. O. P. Taylor, "The Tongues at Pentecost," *Expository Times* 40 (1928-29), 300–303, and A. Beel, "Donum Linguarum juxta Act. Apost. ii.1–13," *Collationes Brugenses* 35 (1935) 417–20. But the divided response of the crowd is decisive: not all there heard in the same manner; some concluded from the apparently incoherent character of their raving that the speakers were in fact drunk (2:13). Peter's "interpretation," furthermore, was not of their discourse but of their ecstatic condition; see Johnson, *Acts of the Apostles,* 53–54.

25. See Johnson, *Acts of the Apostles,* 45–47.

26. The manuscript support for "new" (*kainais*) in the phrase "they will

phrase provides another witness to the practice of tongues among early Christians. As for Paul, he could hardly emphasize more strongly that, in his view — and he *was* a speaker in tongues himself (14:18) — glossolalia is an intrinsically noncommunicative form of utterance (1 Cor 13:1; 14:2, 4, 7-9, 16-17, 23). What, then, does he mean by "interpretation of tongues?" A study of the verb *diermeneuein* by Paul's Jewish contemporaries Josephus and Philo suggests that it often means simply "to put into words," or "bring to articulate expression."[27] When Paul tells the tongue-speaker to pray that he or she might "interpret," therefore (1 Cor 14:13), he does not mean "provide a translation," but "change to a mode of speech intelligible to the assembly."

The purported evidence offered by contemporary glossolalists that their utterance is real language, finally, is spurious. Careful linguistic study has demonstrated that glossolalia is not a "real but unknown language" but rather a "language-like patterning" of sound.[28] Observation of the "interpretation of tongues" in actual pentecostal practice, furthermore, shows that it is not the translation of a language, which would require some coincidence of sound-segment, but a separate utterance altogether, often lengthier by far than the glossolalic segment.[29] The stereotypical character of the reports of real languages being heard by native speakers, and the im-

---

speak with [new] tongues" (*lalēsousin kainais glōssais*) in Mark 16:17, furthermore, is even weaker than for the passage as a whole. For a discussion of the longer endings of Mark and variants, see B. M. Metzger, *A Textual Commentary on the Greek New Testament* (London: United Bible Societies, 1975) 122–28.

27. See A. C. Thiselton, "The 'Interpretation' of Tongues: A New Suggestion in the Light of Greek Usage in Philo and Josephus," *Journal of Theological Studies* n.s. 30 (1979) 15–36.

28. Samarin, *Tongues of Men and Angels*, 74–128; Maloney and Lovekin, *Glossolalia*, 38; Kildahl, "Psychological Observations," 362.

29. See the example that is provided by Maloney and Lovekin, *Glossolalia*, 32.

possibility of verifying such reports, suggests that they are essentially folkloric and legitimizing in character.[30]

The second major hypothesis concerning tongues is that it is not a real language but an ecstatic utterance which takes the form of an ordered babbling.[31] Paul clearly regards tongues as unintelligible, contrasting speech that is "in the Spirit" (*en tǭ pneumati*) but does not use the mind (*nous*), with speech that does use the mind and therefore builds up the community (1 Cor 14:14-15, 19). Because glossolalia is private and noncommunicative, God may be praised by it and the person praying may be edified, but neither the mind nor the community gain any benefit from the performance (1 Cor 14:2-3, 14, 17, 28).

This definition of glossolalia also better corresponds with most of ancient and contemporary parallel phenomena. In at least the older forms of Israelite prophecy, there is evidence of inspiration by God's Spirit, trancelike states with the physical indications of dissociation and the uttering of inarticulate cries (see, e.g., 1 Sam 10:5-13; 19:18-24). Whether classical Hebrew prophecy was also accompanied by ecstatic states remains a matter of debate.[32] An important parallel to early Christian glossolalia is the Hellenistic religious phenomenon known as mantic prophecy. In contrast to nonecstatic, "technical" prophecy, such as discerning the auspices or practicing divination,[33] such prophecy involved so complete a possession (*enthysiasmos*) by the divine spirit (*pneuma*) that the mind of the prophet (*mantis*) was inoperative and the

30. See D. Christie-Murray, *Voice from the Gods: Speaking with Tongues* (London: R. K. Paul, 1978) 248–52; Stevenson, *Xenoglossy,* 1–14; May, "A Survey of Glossolalia and Related Phenomena," 68–75.

31. See, e.g., C. G. Williams, "Glossolalia in the New Testament," in *Tongues of the Spirit,* 25–45.

32. See R. R. Wilson, *Prophecy and Society in Ancient Israel* (Philadelphia: Fortress Press, 1980) 21–35.

33. See Cicero, *De Divinatione* 18, 34.

oracles were literally spoken by the god.[34] The prophetic oracles delivered at Delphi played a key role through much of the religious and political life of ancient Greece.[35] Our evidence suggests that such oracles were linguistically intelligible, if obscure in meaning. Even so, they often required "interpretation" by qualified cultic personnel who were called "prophets" (*prophētai*).[36]

Such prophecy was highly esteemed, even by the philosophically sophisticated, as a sign of direct divine involvement with humans.[37] It is not certain, however, how inevitable was

34. For an orientation, see E. R. Dodds, *The Greeks and the Irrational* (Berkeley: University of California Press, 1966) 64–101. The classic monograph is E. Fascher, *PROPHĒTĒS: Eine sprach- und religionsgeschichtliche Untersuchung* (Geissen: Alfred Töpelmann, 1927); citations to comparative material can be found also in H. Kramer, *"prophētēs," TDNT* 6:784–96; H. Bacht, "Wahres und Falsches Prophetentum," *Biblica* 32 (1951) 237–62.

35. For a sense of the cultural importance of Delphi, see Herodotus, *Persian Wars* 1:51; 1:61; 1:67; 5:42-43; 5:62-63; 5:91; 6:52; 6:57; 6:66; 6:76; 6:86; 7:220; 7:239; 8:114; 8:141; Thucydides, *Peloponnesian War* 2,7,55; 3,11,92; 4,13,118; 5,15,17.

36. See Plato, *Timaeus* 72B; Herodotus, *Persian Wars* 8:135. The picture of ancient prophecy is made even more complex by the traditions concerning the Sibyls, who produced their prophecies in *mania* but did so in clear (and written) prose; see H. A. Parke, *Sibyls and Sibylline Prophecy in Classical Antiquity,* ed. B. C. McGing (London: Routledge, 1988).

37. See Plato, *Ion* 534A–D; *Phaedrus* 244A; *Timaeus* 71E–72B; Plutarch, *The E at Delphi* 387B, 391E; *Obsolescence of Oracles* 432A–D; *Oracles at Delphi* 399A, 397C. Once more, Philo's language and perceptions concerning prophecy are those of the Greek world: the divine *pneuma* "seizes" humans (*Questions on Genesis* 4:196), "falls on" them (*Life of Moses* 2:291), "possesses" them (*Life of Moses* 1:175), and "fills" their mind (*Questions on Genesis* 4:140). He consistently speaks of the *pneuma* replacing the human mind in prophecy (see *Special Laws* 4:49; *Who Is the Heir?* 264–65; *Questions on Genesis* 3:9; *Life of Moses* 2:188–92). This is how God "speaks through" the prophets (*Special Laws* 1:65). See M. J. Weaver, *Pneuma in Philo of Alexandria* (Ph.D. dissertation, Notre Dame University, 1973) 115–41; note in particular the comparison Weaver draws between this language and that used of the Pythian Oracle (131–34).

the state of trance or ecstasy (*furor, mania*) in such prophecy, although it is frequently mentioned.[38] Still less certain is the presence of glossolalic utterance.[39] Some references are made to the occurrence of strange sounds and garbled or foreign words,[40] but these tend to be associated with wandering prophets — especially the priests of the goddess Cybele — and soothsayers,[41] or with those attacked as charlatans,[42] than with the oracles of the fixed prophetic shrines like Delphi or Dodonna. That Paul himself considered tongues as equivalent — at least in manifestation — to such mantic prophecy seems certain from his word choice in 1 Cor 14:23, when he suggests that "ignorant and unbelieving" people (that is outsiders) who came across a whole congregation speaking in tongues would conclude, "you are raving" (*hoti mainesthe*), which, in context, should be understood as "you are prophesying in the way all cults do, in a frenzy."[43]

The understanding of glossolalia as a structured babbling, furthermore, corresponds with the best evidence provided by the linguistic analysis of modern tongue-speaking,[44] although the degree of ecstasy involved in the contemporary phenomenon is a matter of debate. Problems of definition are here obvious. Some observers virtually define glossolalia in terms

38. See, e.g., Plutarch, *On the Obsolescence of Oracles* 417C; Cicero, *De Divinatione* 32,70; Virgil, *Aeneas* VI, 42ff.

39. See Aune, *Prophecy in Early Christianity,* 30–35.

40. See Herodotus, *Persian Wars* 8.135; Plutarch, *On the Obsolescence of Oracles* 412A.

41. See Apuleius, *Metamorphoses* 8.27; Dio Chrysostom, *Oration* 10:23–24.

42. See Lucian, *Alexander the False Prophet* 13, 22, 27–28, 49, 51, 53.

43. Compare Homer, *Iliad* 6.131; Euripides, *Bacchae* 299; Pausanias, *Description of Greece* 2.7.5; Herodotus, *Persian War* 4.79; Plato, *Phaedrus* 244C. Paul's usage here must be taken, together with his emphasis that tongues does not use the *nous,* as decisive in pointing the phenomenon of glossolalia toward the manifestations of Greco-Roman prophecy. See E. Fascher, *PROPHĒTĒS,* 168: "Wenn Paulus I Kor 14:23 *mainesthe* von den Glossolalen gebraucht, dann heisst es 'rasen oder in Verzuchung reden.'"

44. Samarin, "The Linguisticality of Tongues," 55–73.

of psychological dissociation, considering it to be the oral expression of a trance state.[45] Others point out that the *initial* experience of tongues is often accompanied by dissociation but that subsequent performances frequently lack any signs of an altered consciousness.[46]

First-person accounts of the experience of glossolalia emphasize, especially with regard to the first occurrence, positive feelings of release, freedom, and joy.[47] Although some modern glossolalia occurs in private,[48] it is ordinarily a public and cultic activity. It is connected above all with the experience of conversion, being "born again" or "baptized in the Holy Spirit" (in explicit continuity with Acts 10:46 and 19:6), and to the practice of prayer (as in 1 Cor 14:2, 28).[49] The understanding of tongues as a form of prophecy (as in Acts 2:4-11) is rarer, as is the actual practice of "the interpretation of tongues."[50]

In summary, the convergence of evidence suggests that glossolalia is a verbal expression of a powerful emotional state. It is not a real language but a kind of structured or ordered babbling. Especially in its first manifestation, it is experienced by the speaker as a positive empowerment by a spiritual force, an empowerment that provides a sense of liberation and joy. For the individual, glossolalia can be characterized as the linguistic symbol of spiritual release; for a community, the manifestation of tongues is the linguistic

45. Goodman, *Speaking in Tongues,* 58–86.

46. Samarin, *Tongues of Men and Angels,* 26–34; Kelsey, *Speaking with Tongues,* 142.

47. Goodman, *Speaking in Tongues,* 24–57; Kildahl, "Psychological Observations," 359, 364; Kelsey, *Speaking with Tongues,* 221; Maloney and Lovekin, *Glossolalia,* 185.

48. See R. A. Hutch, "The Personal Ritual of Glossolalia," *Journal for the Scientific Study of Religion* 19 (1980) 255–66.

49. See Maloney and Lovekin, *Glossolalia,* 126–46.

50. See, however, May, "A Survey of Glossolalia and Related Phenomena," 68–70; Maloney and Lovekin, *Glossolalia,* 23–26.

expression of a powerful spiritual presence. It is human utterance whose entire significance lies in its directly expressing a certain kind of religious experience.

The Pervasiveness of the Phenomenon

It is impossible to determine how widespread glossolalia was in earliest Christianity. The evidence supports only that tongues were spoken by Paul and some members of the Corinthian congregation in the mid-fifties of the first century[51] and was thought by Luke to have been a feature of some early conversion experiences.[52]

Although Paul lists "tongues" and the "interpretation of tongues" among the spiritual gifts (*charismata*) in 1 Cor 12:10, it is noteworthy that neither appears in the two other Pauline lists of spiritual gifts (Rom 12:3-8; Eph 4:11). He makes no mention of the experience of tongues in connection with his

51. Clement makes no reference to the phenomenon when writing to them some forty years later.

52. Other evidence sometimes adduced in favor of larger claims is difficult to assess. Apart from the problematic longer ending of Mark (16:17), the Gospel tradition has nothing about glossolalia. Indeed, Jesus' condemnation of the "babbling" of Gentiles in prayer (Matt 6:7) could well have been taken by Christians as an implied criticism of glossolalia. Among passages that *could* be used with reference to glossolalia but need not be are Paul's mention of "spiritual hymns" by which Christians could praise God "in their hearts" (Col 3:16; Eph 4:19), his command to the Thessalonians not to "quench the Spirit" (1 Thess 4:19), and his claim that the Holy Spirit helps Christians when they do not know how to pray "with unutterable groanings (*stenagmois alalētois*)" (Rom 8:26). Still more difficult to assess are the traces of early Christian bilingualism. Certainly "amen" as a response to prayer could scarcely be thought of as an ecstatic utterance (see 1 Cor 14:16). But what about the Aramaic cry *maranatha* uttered in worship (1 Cor 16:22), and the Aramaic diminutive *abba*, the proclamation of which is directly connected by Paul to the experience of the Holy Spirit (Gal 4:6; see Rom 8:15)? Both words are wonderful candidates for the sort of "ordered babbling" that makes up glossolalia. Unfortunately, we have no way of positively linking these expressions to the practice of tongues.

own call (Gal 1:15-17) nor in connection with the conversion of others. The case of Gal 3:1-5 is particularly striking because of Paul's emphasis there on the work of the Spirit and its "powerful deeds." Indeed, we shall see that Paul is deeply ambivalent in his attitude toward tongues. But, for that matter, not even Luke connects tongues to Paul's conversion experience (Acts 9:3-8). Nor is tongues linked to the laying on of hands, except in Acts 19:6. Finally, there is no hint of the practice of glossolalia in any other Christian writing before the middle of the second century.

Even for the earliest period of the Christian movement, therefore, glossolalia appears as at best a sporadic and ambiguous phenomenon. Two inferences about that first period are therefore emphatically *not* supported by the evidence: that tongues was a normal and expected accompaniment of the Holy Spirit (and therefore, by implication, a necessary indicator of the authentic presence of the Spirit); and, that tongues demonstrates how the first Christians lived in a charismatic fog of trance or dissociation.

Evaluations of Glossolalia by New Testament Writers

The discussion of glossolalia is further complicated by the disparate evaluations of the phenomenon in the two New Testament sources that report it. Luke gives a completely positive valuation to glossolalia. As the tongues of fire at Pentecost are the *visual* sign of the Spirit's presence, which transforms followers into ministers of the word (see Luke 1:4), so the speaking in tongues is the *auditory* sign. It is the Holy Spirit who "gives them utterance" (Acts 2:4). In the Pentecost account, the first experience of tongues is an expression of praise: the disciples tell "of the great things of God" (2:11).

Peter's speech following this event provides Luke's own interpretation, not of the tongues, but of the experience of ecstatic utterance itself. He begins by citing Joel 3:1-5 (Septuagint), indicating thereby that this gift of the Spirit is in fulfillment of prophecy. Luke's emendations to the Joel citation, furthermore, have the effect of making this outpouring of the Spirit an eschatological event ("in the last days"), signalled by the spirit of prophecy (see 2:17-18), and by the "signs and wonders" worked by God (2:19).[53] These touches serve to make Pentecost a programmatic statement for the rest of Acts, in which the apostles are depicted as the prophetic successors to Jesus, filled with the same Holy Spirit he was and working as he did signs and wonders among the people.[54] By making the diverse tongues intelligible to Jewish pilgrims from all over the Diaspora, furthermore, Luke indicates that the prophetic Spirit is the fulfillment of the promises to Abraham, extended first to Abraham's descendents and only then to the nations of the earth (2:38-39).[55]

Glossolalia functions as a sign of the Spirit in the two other Acts passages, where it also marks a new stage in the mission. When the Spirit falls on the household of the gentile Cornelius, the Jewish Christians present at the scene can hear the tongues and conclude that the Gentiles had received the same Holy Spirit that they had at Pentecost (10:45). Likewise, when Paul lays hands on the former followers of John the Baptist in Ephesus and they begin "to speak in tongues and prophesy" (19:6), it shows that people of Asia have also received the Holy Spirit and that this baptism in Jesus is greater than that of John's (19:2-3; see Luke 3:16; Acts 1:5;

53. Johnson, *Acts of the Apostles,* 48–55.

54. For the notion of "programmatic prophecy" as a literary technique in Luke-Acts, see L. T. Johnson, *Luke* (Sacra Pagina 3; Collegeville, Minn.: Liturgical Press, 1991) 16; and for the depiction of the apostles as prophets in succession to Moses and Jesus, see ibid., 17–20.

55. Johnson, *Acts of the Apostles,* 47.

11:16). In short, Acts treats glossolalia as a nonambiguous symbol of the Spirit's presence and a sign of the mission's success.[56]

In contrast, Paul's attitude toward glossolalia is more complex and ambivalent, at least in part because of the problems he thinks it is causing in the Corinthian community.[57] The elitist tendencies in that assembly led some of them to regard all spiritual powers (*ta pneumatika*, 12:1) as a means of self-aggrandizement.[58] Just as some of them used "liberty" and "knowledge" in ways careless of community edification (8:1-2; 10:23), so the spectacular gift of tongues seems to have been claimed by some as a superior "sign of the Spirit." Indeed, some may well have been claiming that only tongues truly cer-

56. While rejecting the historicity of the Cornelius episode in Acts 10:44-48, P. F. Esler argues that, together with the evidence in 1 Cor 12-14, it provides genuine historical evidence that speaking in tongues among Gentiles functioned as a sign for their admission into the church; see his "Glossolalia and the Admission of Gentiles into the Early Christian Community," in *The First Christians in Their Social Worlds: Social Scientific Approaches to New Testament Interpretation* (London: Routledge, 1994) 37–51.

57. For discussions of Paul's treatment of glossolalia and prophecy in 1 Cor 12-14, see L. T. Johnson, "Norms for True and False Prophecy in First Corinthians 12-14," *American Benedictine Review* 22 (1971) 29–45; T. Callan, "Prophecy and Ecstasy in Greco-Roman Religion and in 1 Corinthians," *Novum Testamentum* 27 (1985) 125–40; A. R. Hunt, *The Inspired Body: Paul, the Corinthians, and Divine Inspiration* (Macon, Ga.: Mercer University Press, 1996) 18–30; T. W. Gillespie, *The First Theologians: A Study in Early Christian Prophecy* (Grand Rapids: Eerdmans, 1994) 97–164; F. D. Bruner, *A Theology of the Holy Spirit*, 283–319; W. A. Grudem, *The Gift of Prophecy in 1 Corinthians* (Washington, D.C.: University Press of America, 1982).

58. D. B. Martin, "Tongues of Angels and Other Status Indicators," *Journal of the American Academy of Religion* 59 (1991) 547–89; and idem, *The Corinthian Body* (New Haven: Yale University Press, 1995) 87–103, is certainly on target concerning the ways in which the Corinthians themselves were using tongues, although the evidence he adduces for ecstatic speech as a broad cultural status enhancer, while provocative, is not probative. J. Neyrey reads both 11:2-16 and 14:1-34 in light of Mary Douglas's analysis of societal freedom and control, in his *Paul in Other Words* (Louisville: Westminster/John Knox Press, 1990) 128–35; he also touches briefly on the question of honor/shame on pp. 67–68.

tifies a spiritual person: "tongues is a sign for believers" (see 1 Cor 14:22).[59]

Paul acknowledged from the start of this letter that his readers had been "enriched with all speech and knowledge" (1:5). But when he takes up the issue of tongues explicitly in 1 Cor 12-14, it is to relativize the claims being made for it. He begins by reminding them that there is a difference between *ta pneumatika*, which can refer to any sort of "spiritual phenomenon," and *ta charismata*, the term Paul uses for the gifts given by the Holy Spirit (see 1:7; 12:4, 9, 28, 30, 31).[60] He does not deny the reality of *ta pneumatika* but stresses their ambiguity. When they were still pagans, such impulses led them away into idolatry (12:1-2).[61] Ecstasy is not self-validating but must be tested by its results. Thus the gift of the Holy Spirit leads to the confession, "Jesus is Lord" (12:3),[62] and every *charism* given by that Spirit must be shaped according

59. J. C. Hurd, *The Origin of First Corinthians* (London: SPCK, 1965) suggests that the Corinthian letter to Paul (see 1 Cor 7:1) contained this line of questioning, "Concerning spiritual gifts: how is it possible to test for the Spirit? How can we (or anyone else) distinguish between spiritual men? When you were with us and spoke with tongues you gave us no instructions on this point" (p. 195), but recognizes that behind the question lay the vested interests of the glossolalists (p. 192). See also B. C. Johanson, "Tongues: A Sign for Believers?" *New Testament Studies* 25 (1979) 186–90.

60. E. Käsemann notes that it is with his choice of terms that Paul begins his theological critique; see "Ministry and Community in the New Testament," in *Essays on New Testament Themes* (London: SCM Press, 1964) 66.

61. The text is very difficult, but its basic sense is clear enough: "Il est fort naturel que l'Apôtre rappelle ici les phénomènes extatiques d'un passe païen; c'est pour rappeler aux Corinthiens qu'ils sont pas en soi une manifestation du Saint-Esprit" ("It is entirely natural that the apostle here recalls the ecstatic phenomena of a pagan past; it is to recall to the Corinthians that they are not in themselves a manifestation of the Holy Spirit"). J. Hering, *La premiere Epître de St. Paul aux Corinthiens* (Neuchatel: Delachaux et Niestle, 1959) 108. See also K. Maly, "I Kor 12:1-3: Eine Regel zur Unterscheidung der Geister?" *Biblische Zeitschrift* 10 (1966) 82–95, esp. 86.

62. On the issue of the opposing formula, "cursed be Jesus," see N. Brox, *"ANATHĒMA IĒSOUS,"* *Biblische Zeitschrift* 12 (1968) 103–11; B. Pearson, "Did

to the "mind of Christ" (2:16), that is, in service to the up-building of the messianic community (1 Cor 8:12; 10:31-33).[63] Each part of the messianic body should work for the common good rather than for the benefit of individual members (12:7).[64] Although Paul acknowledges "tongues" and "the interpretation of tongues" as gifts of the Holy Spirit, therefore, he already relativizes their importance by placing them last, after the "foundational" gifts that build up community identity (12:8-10), and by emphasizing that private experience is secondary to the good of the whole body (12:12-31).

In chapter 13, Paul continues to diminish the importance of tongues — as indeed of all the gifts of speech — by asserting *agapē* as the most fundamental expression of God's Holy Spirit (compare Rom 5:5). *Agapē* is defined in terms of service to the other in preference to personal gain. Using himself as an example, Paul declares that "the tongues of humans and of angels" are meaningless without *agapē* (13:1).[65] Tongues is a gift that will pass away (13:8), and Paul clearly intimates that it is among the "childish" things that must be put aside if real maturity is to be reached (13:11).[66]

When he turns to the discussion of the "higher gifts"

the Gnostics Curse Jesus?" *Journal of Biblical Literature* 86 (1967) 301–5; Maly, "I Kor 12:1-3," 93–95.

63. Hunt, *The Inspired Body*, 125–27; Gillespie, *The First Theologians*, 142–55.

64. For Paul's appropriation of a common rhetorical *topos*, see M. M. Mitchell, *Paul and the Rhetoric of Reconciliation: An Exegetical Investigation of the Language and Composition of 1 Corinthians* (Louisville: Westminster/John Knox Press, 1991) 157–64; Martin, *The Corinthian Body*, 92–96.

65. That chap. 13 functions rhetorically as an *exemplum* in the same fashion as chap. 9 is shown decisively by C. R. Holladay, "1 Corinthians 13: Paul as Apostolic Paradigm," in *Greeks, Romans and Christians: Essays in Honor of Abraham J. Malherbe*, ed. D. L. Balch *et al.* (Minneapolis: Fortress Press, 1990) 80–98.

66. It is difficult to imagine that Paul did not intend to connect the rebuke to the Corinthians' "childishness" in 3:1-3, this declaration that "when I became a man, I put away childish things" (13:11), and his command with reference to tongues in 14:20: "Brethren, do not be children in your thinking;

that the community should pursue (12:31), Paul makes glossolalia the foil for prophecy, which he considers superior in every respect (14:5). Prophecy uses the mind, whereas ecstatic babbling does not (14:14-15). It builds up the identity of the community, whereas tongues improves only the speaker (14:3-4). It is intelligible, whereas tongues are not (14:6-10). Glossolalia also escapes the discernment of the entire community, which Paul considers essential for the healthy expression of the spiritual gifts. He regards glossolalia as an optional form of prayer, but one which can be abandoned with no great loss. He speaks in tongues himself but would gladly give them up for the sake of building up the community (14:18-19). He can leave the impulses of the prophets to the prophets themselves since they are under rational control (14:31-32), but he must impose rules for glossolalia: tongues are restricted to their function of private prayer (14:13-16). The only time they can be spoken in public is when they can be followed by "interpretation" (14:27-28).[67]

Paul's evaluation of glossolalia is best summarized by 14:20-25. He reverses the glossolalists' claim by suggesting that tongues are far from an unambiguous sign of belief: they can mean anything, can come from anywhere.[68] If the assembly has glossolalia as its dominant mode of speech, outsiders can legitimately conclude that this assembly is simply a cult like every other one (14:23).[69] Only if prophecy is active can they be brought to recognize that God is at work in this

be babes in evil, but in thinking be mature." See also Hunt, *The Inspired Body*, 102–5, 129–32.

67. See W. Richardson, "Liturgical Order and Glossolalia in 1 Cor 14.26c-33a," *New Testament Studies* 32 (1986) 144–53; E. Schweizer, "The Service of Worship: An Exposition of 1 Cor 14," *Interpretation* 13 (1959) 405.

68. See B. C. Johanson, "Tongues: A Sign for Unbelievers?" *New Testament Studies* 25 (1979) 186–90; P. Roberts, "A Sign: Christian or Pagan?" *Expository Times* 90 (1978-79) 199–203.

69. "Paul has the unbeliever mistake the Christian prayer meeting as just one more enthusiastic Hellenistic cult. The scandal here, in the strict sense,

community (14:25). To make tongues more than an interesting variety of private prayer is to think like a child and not like an adult (14:20; compare 13:11).

The Ambiguous Character of Glossolalia

Paul's delicately nuanced treatment of glossolalia suggests that it was, at least in his eyes, a deeply ambiguous phenomenon. To elicit dimensions of this religious experience that lie just below the surface of the text, some controlled use of the imagination is required.

There is every reason to suppose that for the Corinthians who spoke in tongues, the gift was unequivocally positive. Such ecstatic babbling must have seemed to them — as it does to us — all the more dramatic a "religious experience" because of its exotic character. Here is not a concept about God or the will to please God. It is instead a somatic invasion by God's own power, lifting not only their feelings to states of joy and liberation but even their tongues to lalic freedom. For the speakers themselves, the gift (see 12:10, 28) must have indeed have seemed a pure expression of *ta pneumatika* (12:1; 14:1), in which one "drank the Spirit" (12:13) and was activated and directed by the Spirit (12:11). Since it was the Holy Spirit itself that activated their speech (12:6, 11), furthermore, it must have appeared to them that the overwhelming of their *nous* was all the more impressive a sign of God's immediate presence, literally inside them and speaking through them! In their speech, God spoke as through angels, God clashed the cymbals, God made music on the harp, God blew the trumpet (13:1; 14:7-8). What could be a more unmistakable sign of God's empowering

---

is that the distinctive word of the Gospel is not heard." Johnson, "Norms for True and False Prophecy," 41.

and transformative presence than to have their speech directed, not by their own puny minds, but by the direct breath of God![70] For that matter, how could the truth of the resurrection — that Jesus is Lord — be more emphatically expressed than by them speaking ecstatically "in the spirit" (see 12:3)?

For those seeing and hearing the tongue-speakers, the phenomenon was undoubtedly impressive as well. Surely in such Spirit-driven speech could be found the "powerful deeds" energized by the Spirit as a sign of faith (Gal 3:1-5), the palpable demonstration that the kingdom of God does not consist in speech but in power (1 Cor 4:20). For the observers as much as for the speakers themselves, the phenomenon of glossolalia among those gathered in the name of Jesus must have served as proof that he was alive and powerfully present among them (see Matt 18:20). Especially if tongues was regarded (as it was by Luke and by the wider gentile world) as a form of prophecy, then glossolalia served as well to demonstrate that the age of prophecy had now been reborn in this messianic sect of Judaism. As a result, this sect had a legitimate if not compelling claim to be considered as the authentic people of God, the rightful heir of the biblical tradition. In short, by enlivening their hearts and by liberating their tongues, this gift of the Holy Spirit made clear to all that prophecy was alive and that Jesus was alive as well.

If Paul was a glossolalist as he claimed to be (14:18), then his appreciation for this gift must have been real. Indeed, he does call it a *charisma* of the Holy Spirit (12:10, 30), and he does "thank God" that he can speak in tongues more than any them (14:18). But his appreciation, as we have seen, is

---

70. Compare H. Gunkel, *The Influence of the Holy Spirit: The Popular View of the Apostolic Age and the Teaching of the Apostle Paul*, trans. R. A. Harrisville and P. A. Quanbeck (1888; ET, Philadelphia: Fortress Press, 1979) 77–86.

muted by equally real apprehensions. What sort of concerns led him to emphasize what he considered prophecy, namely, rational discourse, in preference to glossolalia?

Two of Paul's concerns are explicit. The first is his worry that the form of glossolalia might be mistaken for the mantic prophecy prevalent in Greco-Roman culture. His caution in 1 Cor 12:1 that *ta pneumatika* drew them away to idolatry when they were pagans, and his conclusion in 14:23 that outsiders would assume that an assembly of glossalalists "are raving as mantic prophets rave" both point in this direction. In a sense, Paul wants to protect the "one Spirit" here just as he did the "one baptism" in Galatia, as a means of affirming the "one God."[71] His concern here is a variation of the command in 1 John 4:1 to "test the spirits to see if they are from God."

Paul's second manifest concern is the way in which tongue-speaking can lead to disorder in the assembly. He suggests that an ecstatic cannot exercise self-control in the way that the "spirits of prophets are subject to prophets" (14:32). Out of the conviction that God is a God of peace and not of confusion, therefore (14:32), Paul himself sets limits on glossolalia. At most, two or three should speak in tongues; but if there is no one to "interpret," a glossolalist should "keep silence in church and speak to himself and to God" (14:28). Paul's stringency here stands in contrast to his leniency with prophets: "You can all prophesy one by one so that all may learn and be encouraged" (14:31).

Thus far the surface of the text and the surface reasons for limiting glossolalia's expression. But are there unexpressed issues as well? It may be that glossolalia was not only messy but also a challenge to established, and especially male, authority. We can take our first clue from social-scientific work on contemporary glossolalia. More

---

71. See my discussion in chap. 3.

recent psychological studies reject the older view that glossolalia is intrinsically connected to psychopathology.[72] On the other hand, glossolalia appears to be mimetic behavior; that is, new speakers in tongues follow the patterns of sounds uttered by the lead glossolalist.[73] Not surprisingly, extroversion, the ability to be hypnotized, and a willingness to submit to authority, are positively correlated with the experience.[74] For the most part, while the experience of tongues has an integrating effect on the individual, it also fosters among those who practice glossolalia a sense of elitism that proves disruptive in communities.[75] These findings throw possible light on the divided allegiances in the Corinthian community (1 Cor 1:10-12). Certainly Cephas was a glossolalist by reputation (Acts 2:4-11) and Paul by self-acknowledgment (1 Cor 14:18). It is certainly conceivable that the party spirit of those who cried out, "I am for Paul" or "I am for Cephas" (1 Cor 1:12) could be correlated with the sociopsychological tendencies of submission to authority

72. J. T. Richardson, "Psychological Interpretations of Glossolalia: A Reexamination of Research," *Journal for the Scientific Study of Religion* 12 (1973) 199–207; Maloney and Lovekin, *Glossolalia*, 93; J. R. Coulson and R. W. Johnson, "Glossolalia and Internal-External Locus of Control," *Journal of Psychology and Theology* 5 (1977) 312–17; see also the survey of studies in C. G. Williams, *Tongues of the Spirit*, 125–91.

73. For tongues as learned behavior, see Kildahl, "Psychological Observations," 355; M. K. Mayers, "The Behavior of Tongues," in Mills, *Speaking in Tongues*, 112–27.

74. J. P. Kildahl, *The Psychology of Speaking in Tongues* (New York, 1972) 50–53; Kildahl, "Psychological Observations," 353, 365; Maloney and Lovekin, *Glossolalia*, 77; H. E. Gonsalvez, *The Theology and Psychology of Glossolalia* (Ph.D. dissertation, Northwestern University, 1978) 107; Kelsey, *Speaking with Tongues*, 220.

75. Kildahl, *Psychology of Speaking in Tongues*, 66–75; Kildahl, "Psychological Observations," 365–66; despite his overall positive evaluation of tongues, M. T. Kelsey emphasizes their tendency to breed arrogance and elitism in the individual, and consequently divisiveness within groups (*Speaking with Tongues*, 223, 231).

figures, elitism, and divisiveness attributed to contemporary glossolalists.[76]

Such speculation is given some support by I. M. Lewis's classic study of spirit possession and shamanism.[77] Lewis makes no mention of glossolalia. But he does demonstrate how, in cultures that have a generalized belief in transcendental spiritual powers, claims to the possession of such powers have specific sociological implications. In particular, spirit possession serves to empower groups otherwise marginal within a society. "In its primary social function, peripheral possession thus emerges as an oblique aggressive strategy."[78] The claim to spirit possession does not rupture relationships but helps vent frustrations among those who do not enjoy overt power within the group.[79] Such claims would understandably have more appeal among the lesser orders,[80] enabling them functionally to destabilize a given authority structure[81] while also grasping a share of power by providing what is, in such contexts, an obvious status enhancement.[82]

Lewis's analysis is most pertinent, and provocative, for our present topic, however, because of the role that spirit-possession plays in gender battles. Lewis shows how certain ritualized forms of sickness, which are interpreted by males as a form of demonic possession, are evaluated quite differently by the women involved: "What men consider demoniacal sickness, women convert into a clandestine ecstasy."[83] Specifically with regard to women's possession cults, Lewis notes that they

76. Esler suggests that the Corinthians may well have imitated Paul's glossolalic practice; see "Glossolalia and the Admission of Gentiles," 48.

77. I. M. Lewis, *Ecstatic Religion* (Baltimore: Penguin Books, 1971).

78. Ibid., 32.

79. Ibid., 121.

80. Ibid., 101, 104–6, 110.

81. "Enthusiasm thrives on instability," ibid., 175.

82. Ibid., 109–10.

83. Ibid., 30; see also 77.

are "thinly disguised protest movements directed against the dominant sex."[84]

If Lewis's analysis has any pertinence to ancient glosso-lalia as an expression of spirit-possession, then we are led to still another aspect of Paul's treatment of tongues, namely, his general difficulties with the speech of *women* in the Co-rinthian church. We note that the discussion of glossolalia is framed at either side by Paul's efforts to control women's speech in the assembly. In 11:3-16, the topic is the veiling of women who "pray or prophesy";[85] in 14:33b-36, Paul is-sues a blanket directive for women to "keep silent in the assembly."[86] The apparent contradiction in the two passages is notorious and has led to various resolutions.[87] In the first instance, some sort of ecstatic speech is clearly at issue, for "prayer and prophecy" are included among the *charis-mata.*[88] The second case appears to involve teaching, for

---

84. Ibid., 31.

85. For a analysis of the passage as a whole in the light of recent literature, see M. C. Black, "1 Cor 11:2-16: A Re-Investigation," in *Essays on Women in Earliest Christianity,* 2 vols., ed. C. D. Osburn (Joplin, Mo.: College Press, 1995) 1:191–218.

86. The critical issues attaching to this passage are discussed, with recent literature, by C. D. Osburn, "The Interpretation of 1 Cor 14:34-35," in *Essays on Women in Earliest Christianity* 1:219–42.

87. Including considering one or both passages interpolations: For 11:2-16, see W. Walke Jr., "1 Cor 11:2-16 and Paul's Views Regarding Women, *Journal of Biblical Literature* 94 (1975) 94–10; L. Cope, "1 Cor 11:2-16: One Step Further," *Journal of Biblical Literature* 97 (1978) 435–36; J. Murphy-O'Connor, "The Non-Pauline Character of 1 Corinthians 11:2-16?" *Journal of Biblical Literature* 95 (1976) 615–21. For 4:33b-36, see J. Murphy-O'Connor, "Interpolations in 1 Corinthians," *Catholic Biblical Quarterly* 48 (1986) 90–92; H. Conzelmann, *A Commentary on First Corinthians,* trans. J. W. Leitch (Her-meneia; Philadelphia: Fortress Press, 1975) 246; G. Fee, *The First Epistle to the Corinthians* (Grand Rapids: Eerdmans, 1987) 699–702.

88. In the present passage, we have "every man praying or prophesying" (*proseuchomenos ē propheteuōn,* 11:4), to which corresponds "every woman who prays or prophesies," 11:5, and "it is fitting that every woman be covered while praying," in 11:13. In 1 Cor 14, we find prayer in 14:13, 14, and 15,

Paul instructs the women to learn from their husbands at home rather than speak in the assembly.[89] Nevertheless, both instances involve women's speech.

We observe furthermore that in both discussions Paul appeals to the custom of the other churches concerning the roles of women.[90] More strikingly still, in both places, Paul invokes the concept of shame (*aischros*).[91] Finally, we note the element of specifically sexual embarrassment that appears to be connected with the uncovering of women's heads, in Paul's appeal to what "nature (*physis*) itself teaches us" (1 Cor 11:14) or what is "proper" (*prepei*) in women's public behavior (1 Cor 11:13). Even if his alternatives of wearing short hair or having the head shaved (1 Cor 11:5-7) do not necessarily refer, as sometimes thought, to prostitution,[92] the probable

and prophesying in 14:1, 3, 4, 5, 24, 31, 39. We cannot be certain that Paul uses the terms with absolute consistency, but if chap. 11 is to be fitted to the distinctions Paul draws in chap. 14, then the "praying" may be discourse in tongues (and therefore ecstatic), and "prophesying" rational discourse (using the *nous*).

89. The passage obviously resembles 1 Tim 2:11-15, which is one reason some want to find it an interpolation (see R. Scroggs, "Paul and the Eschatological Woman," *Journal of the American Academy of Religion* 40 (1972) 283–303; for a discussion of similarities, see L. T. Johnson, *Letters to Paul's Delegates: 1 Timothy, 2 Timothy, Titus* (New Testament in Context; Valley Forge: Trinity Press International, 1996) 132–41.

90. In 11:2, "I commend you because you remember me in everything and maintain the traditions even as I have delivered them to you," and in 11:16, "If any one is disposed to be contentious, we recognize no other practice, nor do the churches of God." In 14:33c, "As in all the churches of the saints, women should keep silent," and in 14:36, "What! Did the word of God originate with you, or are you the only ones it reached?"

91. He declares that it is shameful — *aischron estin* — for a woman to pray with unveiled head or to speak in public (11:6, 14:35). The expression is all the more stunning for occurring only here in all of Paul's letters (see only Eph 5:12 and Tit 1:11) and only in these closely connected passages. Note also in 11:14 the contrast between "dishonor" (*atimia*) and "honor" (*doxa*).

92. Black cites a text from Dio Chrysostom to the effect that a woman caught in adultery should have her head shaved and be a harlot, but also

allusion to the lust of the angels (1 Cor 11:10)[93] sexualizes women's unveiled ecstatic speech.

Elisabeth Schüssler Fiorenza and Antoinette Clark Wire have placed Paul's delimitation of women's speech in the context of the activity of "women prophets" in the Corinthian community.[94] Paul's concern with veiling can thus be connected to the practices of ecstatic speech among women prophets in shrines such as that of Apollo at Delphi: the tossing of the unveiled and unbound hair by the enthused maiden was a notable feature of such prophecy.[95] Just as Paul was concerned that ecstasy could "lead them off to

gives evidence that a shaven head can be associated with mourning, in "1 Cor 11:2-16: A Re-Investigation," 206.

93. Gen 6:1-4. See the argument in Martin, *The Corinthian Body*, 242–46, and G. Patterson Corrington, "The 'Headless Woman': Paul and the Language of the Body in 1 Cor 11:2-16," *Perspectives in Religious Studies* 18 (1991) 223–31. The passage in *Joseph in Aseneth* 15:2 is also pertinent: in the presence of the "man from heaven," Aseneth is told to remove her veil, so that her head is "like that of a young man."

94. See A. C. Wire, *The Corinthian Women Prophets: A Reconstruction through Paul's Rhetoric* (Minneapolis: Fortress Press, 1990) 116–58; E. Schüssler Fiorenza, *In Memory of Her: A Feminist Theological Reconstruction of Christian Origins* (New York: Crossroad, 1983) 226–36. Schüssler Fiorenza in particular argues that the inconsistency in Paul's argument and the cultural probabilities suggest that the issue is not one of veiling but rather of wearing the hair loose or bound. While I agree with Martin, *The Corinthian Body*, 233, that veiling is at the heart of the passage, I think it a false dilemma: not wearing a veil when prophesying in a *furor* would in all likelihood lead to its loosening and thus to the sexual and cultic associations suggested by both Schüssler Fiorenza and Martin.

95. In his account of the restrictions placed on the cult of Dionysius in Rome (ca. 186 B.C.E.), Livy lists among the troubling aspects of the cult that it involved sexual misbehavior, men prophesying with contorted bodies, and women with dishevelled hair (*Annals of Rome* 39:13). He adds that in the Roman decree concerning the matter, it was noted that "a great part of them are women, and they are the source of this mischief" (*Annals* 39:15). See the references in Schüssler Fiorenza, *In Memory of Her*, 227; and R. and K. Kroeger, "An Inquiry into Evidence of Maenadism in the Corinthian Congregation," *Society of Biblical Literature Seminar Papers* 14 (1978) 2:331–46.

dumb idols" (12:2) and that an assembly of glossalalists could be mistaken for a seance of mantic prophets (14:23), so he feared that women speaking ecstatically with unveiled or loose hair could be regarded as a manifestation of the Pythian spirit. And if Lewis is correct, Paul might also, at some level, have intuited that such speech among women might prove threatening to the orderly patriarchal world constructed by "the law" (1 Cor 14:34).

We can, however, go one step further. Why does Paul's discussion sexualize such ecstatic speech and speak of it in terms of shame? Here the recent research by Dale Martin and Mary Foskett concerning the ways in which the body was construed in Greco-Roman medical and moral discourse offers significant insight.[96] If serious medical opinion considered male sperm as bearing the *pneuma* of life into a woman's womb;[97] if some ancient physiology pictured the woman's body as a receptive vessel, open both at the mouth and vagina;[98] if the ravings of the Delphic Oracle sitting over the smoking tripod came from her being suffused from below by the *pneuma* of Apollo, so that the god spoke out above through her mouth;[99] and if these ravings could be heard, by clients as

96. Martin's discussion of this passage is provocatively and appropriately entitled, "Prophylactic Veils," in *The Corinthian Body*, 229–49, and he adduces convincing evidence from the medical literature. One is only surprised that he, unlike Schüssler Fiorenza, does not explicitly connect this discussion to the one on glossolalia. M. F. Foskett advances this research by connecting it explicitly to the cultural construction of virginity in the Greco-Roman world and the frequent link between virginity and prophecy; see *A Virgin Conceived: Virginity as a Character-Indicator in Luke-Acts and the Protevangelium of James* (Ph.D. dissertation, Emory University, 1997).

97. See Aristotle, *Generation of Animals* 1:20; the entire discussion of *sperma* is in 1:17–21.

98. Aristotle, *History of Animals*, 10:5; Hippocratic Aphorisms, V.51; see Martin, *The Corinthian Body*, 237–39.

99. See the vivid story of Apollo closing the throat of the Oracle in prophecy in Lucan, *Pharsalia*, V.160–97; Plutarch, *The Obsolescence of Oracles* (*Mor* 432 D–E; 404E; 405C); Martin, *The Corinthian Body*, 239–40.

well as by critics, as a sort of orgasmic frenzy,[100] then the sexual connotations of female prophecy in this culture are obvious. If any of these associations were in Paul's mind (and the allusions to sex and shame are his, after all), it is small wonder that he was worried not only about the disorder that glossolalia could create but also about the deep confusion over the sort of *pneuma* by which Christians were being possessed. In this light, his restrictions are less surprising than his willingness to credit this ecstatic gift and give it some degree of expression. He does conclude, after all, "do not forbid speaking in tongues, but let all things be done decently and in order" (1 Cor 14:39-40).

Glossolalia and Deviance

In the second and third centuries, glossolalia appears only infrequently. The most noteworthy outburst is associated with the figure of Montanus (ca. 160) and the two women prophets who accompanied him.[101] Montanus apparently regarded himself as a passive instrument of the Holy Spirit, "like a lyre struck with a plecton."[102] He understood his "strange speech" (*xenophonein*) as a form of prophecy, and his speech was accompanied by the frenzy associated with mantic prophecy.[103] Even in Montanism, however, such inspired utterance did not seem long to survive the founders,[104] although the Montanist Tertullian does evoke the presence of

---

100. Virgil, *Aeneas* VI, 77–101; Martin, *The Corinthian Body,* 240–42.

101. See Eusebius, *Ecclesiastical History* V, 15–18; Hippolytus, *Refutation of All Heresies* 8,12.

102. Epiphanius, *Panarion* 48, 4, 1.

103. Eusebius, *Ecclesiastical History* V, 16, 7–10.

104. Ibid., V, 17, 4; but see Epiphanius, *Panarion,* 49, 1–3.

ecstatic speech in his community as a proof against Marcion of its authenticity.[105]

Irenaeus of Lyons (ca 200) also claims acquaintance with tongues, although his report is succinct and influenced by Pauline language: "We have heard many brethren in the church having prophetic gifts and speaking through the spirit in all tongues and bringing to light men's secrets for the common good and explaining the mysteries of God. Such persons the Apostle calls spiritual."[106] Irenaeus apparently understands tongues to mean "other languages." But he also reports on the activities of a Valentinian gnostic called Marcus, whom Irenaeus regards as a charlatan and magician, but whose repertoire includes prophecy. According to Irenaeus, Marcus seduces women and coaxes them to prophecy, and the manner of their speech once more suggests glossolalia or mantic prophecy.[107] It is worth noting that in the case of Montanism and Gnosticism, glossolalia is associated with women.

Apart from these notices, there are only the occasional patches in gnostic compositions of strung-together syllables that resemble transcribed glossolalia,[108] and the numerous concatenations of sounds in the magical papyri that are used in spells. Phenomenologically it is difficult to distinguish these from "praying in tongues."[109] In such cases, however, it is impossible to determine what sort of oral activity generated or was generated by the literary text. Some preachers

---

105. Tertullian, *Against Marcion,* 5, 8.

106. Irenaeus, *Against Heresies* 5, 6, 1; see also Eusebius, *Ecclesiastical History,* V, 7, 6.

107. Irenaeus, *Against Heresies,* 1, 14–16.

108. See *Pistis Sophia* 4, 142; *Gospel of the Egyptians* 44 and 66; *Zostrianos* 127.

109. *Greek Magical Papyrus* 3:560–85; 4:945, 960, 1120–25; 12:345–50. David E. Aune thinks that the differences are more important than the similarities, in "Magic in Early Christianity," *ANRW* II.23.2 (1980) 1549–51.

apparently even used babbling speech in public, at least according to the anti-Christian polemicist Celsus, who calls their utterances "without form or meaning."[110]

Arguments from silence are deservedly suspect, but the paucity of evidence for glossolalia in the second 200 years of Christianity suggests that it became an increasingly marginal activity. Most of the occurrences appear in groups rejected by the Orthodox tradition. This is no surprise. As Lewis notes, "the more entrenched the religious authority, the more hostile toward haphazard inspiration."[111] The silence itself, however, can variously be weighed. It may indicate that tongues was practiced rarely and by dissident groups. Or, it may suggest that orthodox writers, suspicious of charismatic activity generally, ignored manifestations of popular religion that did not meet their increasingly high standards of rationality.[112]

In either case, our information comes mainly from the orthodox side, and at our present distance we can only observe that by the late fourth century John Chrysostom confesses himself at a loss interpreting the passage about tongues in 1 Corinthians. He can only guess that Paul was referring to foreign languages.[113] And in the fifth century, Augustine of Hippo dismisses the significance of tongues as a special dispensation of the primitive church, no longer of pertinence to the church in his day.[114] An experience of the Holy Spirit

---

110. Origen, *Against Celsus* 7, 9. Note also Origen's sexualized portrayal of pagan prophecy in *Against Celsus* 7,3.

111. Lewis, *Ecstatic Religion*, 34.

112. See Eusebius, *Ecclesiastical History*, V, 17, 2–4; Lewis, *Ecstatic Religion*, 132.

113. "This whole place is very obscure; but the obscurity is produced by our ignorance of the facts referred to and by their cessation, being such as used to occur but now no longer take place." See John Chrysostom, *Homilies on First Corinthians* 29, 32, 35.

114. Augustine, *Homilies on First John*, 6, 10; see also *On Baptism against the Donatists* 3, 18.

that in the end seemed as embarrassing as it was impressive, glossolalia began its long subterranean life, surfacing only now and then as a form of enthusiasm that inspired some and repelled as many others.[115]

115. It is a fascinating aspect of this history that the gender dimension analyzed by I. M. Lewis remains an important element; see the role of women in enthusiastic movements, described by R. A. Knox, *Enthusiasm*, 30, 55, 68, 162, 319.

5

MEALS ARE WHERE
THE MAGIC IS

Ritual meals of the early Christians pose an even greater challenge to phenomenological description than do baptism and
glossolalia. Sharing meals, after all, is not a practice specifically generated by communal identity, as rituals of initiation
are, nor by personal religious experience, as glossolalia is.
People everywhere eat and drink as a biological necessity.
Meals are the most ordinary of human activities. People eat
and drink *together,* however, out of a combination of economic
and cultural factors. Meals are at once complexly significant
and opaque. They can signify so many things at so many levels
that the disentangling of a meal's precise religious significance would be difficult even if we were in possession of a
complete cultural code within which it took place.[1] In the
case of nascent Christianity, we do not possess a complete

1. See, e.g., A. L. Knudsen, "The Meaning of Food," in *The Individual,
Society, and Behavior* (New York: Russell Sage Foundation, 1965) 132–43. For
a survey of social-scientific literature, see A. Mennell, A. Murcott, A. H. Otter-
loo, *The Sociology of Food: Eating, Diet, and Culture* (London: Sage Publications,
1992) 1–34; and R. C. Wood, *The Sociology of the Meal* (Edinburgh: Edinburgh
University Press, 1995). Among important studies, see M. Douglas, "Decipher-
ing a Meal," in *Implicit Meanings: Essays in Anthropology* (London: Routledge
and Kegan Paul, 1975) 249–75; M. Douglas, "Food as a System of Communication," in *In the Active Voice* (London: Routledge and Kegan Paul, 1982)
82–124; C. Lévi-Strauss, *The Origin of Table Manners,* vol. 3 of *Introduction to a
Science of Mythology,* trans. J. and D. Weightman (New York: Harper and Row,
1968) 471–508.

code. Our phenomenological appreciation of ancient Christian experience is once more complicated by data that are as fragmentary as they are suggestive.

The subject of meals nevertheless provides an appropriate closing test-case. It offers the opportunity to return to conversation with both the historical-critical paradigm and with Jonathan Z. Smith's history-of-religions approach. The way meals are interpreted in each approach, and especially the arguments used to reach such interpretations, enable a more detailed consideration of the issues raised theoretically in the first chapters.

Evidence Concerning Christian Meals

What data need to be taken into account?[2] First are the stories in the Gospels concerning Jesus' presence at meals. During his ministry, Jesus is pictured at meals in the homes of opponents[3] and at table with his followers.[4] In his parables, he images the kingdom of God in terms of meals.[5] Before his death, he shares a last meal with his disciples.[6] And after his resurrection, Jesus appears to his followers in the context of meals.[7] At the heart of each Gospel narrative, moreover, is an account of Jesus sharing an open-air meal (or meals)

---

2. A useful survey of the basic New Testament evidence is J. Delorme, et al., *The Eucharist in the New Testament: A Symposium*, trans. E. M. Stewart (Baltimore: Helicon Press, 1964).

3. Luke 7:36-50; 11:37-52; 14:1-14.

4. Mark 1:31‖Matt 8:13; Luke 5:39; Mark 2:15-17‖Matt 9:10-13; Luke 5:29-32; Mark 7:2-23/Matt 15:1-20; Mark 14:3-9; Luke 10:38-42; 19:1-10 (by implication); John 12:2-8.

5. Matt 22:1-14; 25:1-13; Luke 12:35-48; 13:22-30; 14:15-24; 15:11:31; 16:19-31; 17:7-10; 17:22-37.

6. Mark 14:12-25; Matt 26:17-29; Luke 22:14-38; John 13:2-30.

7. Mark 16:4; Luke 24:13-35; 24:36-49; John 21:9-14.

with thousands,[8] a meal that he himself made possible by a wondrous multiplication of loaves and fishes.[9] These Gospel stories are scarcely flat reportage. Their shaping suggests intricate symbolic links between Jesus' presence at a meal, his fellowship with his followers, and his authority,[10] links that are typically made explicit by John's discourse following the multiplication of the loaves (John 6:26-59). In short, the stories of Jesus at meals during his lifetime are selected and shaped for their significance to the readers of the Gospels many years after his death.

The significance of group meals for followers of Jesus after his death is shown by the references in Acts to the "breaking of bread"[11] and by the importance of table-fellowship in the conversion of the Gentiles.[12] Identity and table-fellowship are linked also in the New Testament epistolary literature.[13] Several times in 1 Corinthians, Paul attaches moral significance to communal eating practices: In 5:6-8, expulsion of the errant member who was practicing incest is explicitly linked to the use of unleavened bread at Passover and is followed by the instruction not to eat or drink with anyone immoral who bears the name of brother (5:11). The warning against the worship of idols in 10:14-22 is cast in terms of opposition between "the cup of demons" and the "table of demons" (10:21) and "the cup of blessing which we

---

8. Mark 8:1-10 and Matt 15:31-39 have a second feeding of the multitude, this time four thousand.

9. Mark 6:35-44; Matt 14:13-21; Luke 9:10-17; John 6:1-14. Apart from the passion accounts, this is the only specific incident concerning Jesus that is found in all four canonical Gospels.

10. Mark 2:18-22||Matt 9:14-17; Luke 5:33-39; Mark 8:14-21/Matt 16:5-12; John 4:31-34.

11. Acts 2:42, 46; 20:7; 27:35. Perhaps one should include as well the "daily *diakonia*" in Acts 6:1-6, since according to Peter's declaration, it was a *diakonia trapezēs* (6:2).

12. See Acts 10:9-16, 41; 11:3; 15:9, 20, 29.

13. See Rom 14:1-23; 1 Cor 8-10; Gal 2:11-14; Rev 2:14, 19.

bless" and the "bread which we break" (10:16). And in a passage that is both the most explicit witness to a "Lord's supper" (*kyriakon deipnon*) among early Christians, as well as the most confusing evidence as to its composition and meaning, Paul rebukes the Corinthians for their neglecting and despising of each other at such meals by reminding them of the tradition concerning the words spoken by "the Lord Jesus on the night when he was betrayed" (11:17-34).[14]

Over the following centuries there is evidence of a complex development of Christian worship that is also structurally related — if ever more loosely — to the sharing of a meal. From the casual reference to the meetings of Christians at meals by pagan observers[15] and the prayer over the bread and wine in the *Didache*,[16] we move through eucharistic references and imagery in second and third century literature,[17] the sa-

---

14. Outside of Paul and the Gospels, evidence for communal meals is sparse: the reference to those who are blemishes at love feasts (*agapais*) in Jude 12 and possibly in 2 Pet 2:14 would be completely obscure if the designation *agapē* for a Christian meal did not occur also in later patristic texts, and the mention of the "marriage feast of the lamb" in Rev 19:9 (see also 19:17) may have only an eschatological referent. Allusions to common meals are only just possible in the expression "tasting the heavenly gift" in Heb 6:4, and "if you have tasted the sweetness of the Lord" in 1 Pet 2:2.

15. Pliny the Younger, *Letter* 10.96, reports on what he learned of Christians in Bithynia: "They would come together to take food, but of an ordinary and harmless kind; this itself they ceased doing after my edict." Lucian of Samosata, in his narrative concerning the charlatan Proteus Peregrinus, recounts his sojourn among the Christians in Palestine: "various meals (*deipna poikila*) were brought in and their sacred *logoi* (words? books?) *elegonto* (were spoken? were read?)" *Peregrinus* 12.

16. The *Didache* (late 1st century?) has instructions *peri tēs eucharistias* (9.1), first over the cup (9.2), and then over the broken bread (*klasma*, 9.3-4), with additional instructions for thanksgiving after the meal (10.1-7). Finally, in 14.1, we find the instruction, "On the Lord's day of the Lord (*kyriakon tou kyriou*) come together, break bread and hold eucharist."

17. See *1 Clement* 40–41; *The Martyrdom of Polycarp*, 13–14; Ignatius of Antioch, *Eph.* 5.2; *Tral.* 2.3; 6.1; *Rom.* 4.1; 7.3; *Phil.* 4.1; *Smyr.* 3.3; 7.1; 8.1; Justin,

cred meals in the Apocryphal Acts of the Apostles,[18] and the ceremonies prescribed by Church Orders.[19] By the time of its imperial cooptation, Christianity had developed a full-blown *cultus* — the Christian Eucharist — that was linked to a meal in only the most formal fashion.

Meals within the Historical Paradigm

Scholars working within the historical paradigm have sifted this great mass of material. Their focus has been almost exclusively on the ritual meal called the Eucharist. Their questions concern origin and dependence. From one end, historians ask how the great liturgies of the fourth and fifth centuries could be traced back to the evidence of the New Testament. Is this a natural development or a bizarre mutation? From the other end, they seek the sources of the New Testament meals themselves. Do they derive from Greco-Roman cultic meals, Jewish ritual meals, or the idiosyncratic practice of Jesus and his followers? At either end, the data are difficult to decipher.

A classic expression of the historical method applied to Christian meals is Hans Lietzmann's 1926 monograph *Mass and Lord's Supper.*[20] Lietzmann was massively erudite and

---

1 Apology, 65–67; *Dialogue with Trypho* 41, 70; Irenaeus, *Against Heresies* 4, 18, 1–6; 5, 1, 1–2; 5, 2, 2–3; Clement of Alexandria, *Pedagogue* 1.6; 2.1–2; *Stromateis* 1.10; 1.19; 4.25; Tertullian, *On the Crown* 3; *Apology,* 39.

18. See *Acts of Paul* 25; *Acts of John* 85, 106–10; *Acts of Thomas* 27–29; 49–50; 120–21; 133; 158; *Acts of Peter* 2, 5 [Vercelli Ms]; *Clementine Homilies* 14:1.

19. See *The Apostolic Tradition* attributed to Hippolytus (early 3rd cent.), the *Didascalia Apostolorum* (early 3rd cent. Syria), the *Euchologion* of Serapion (4th cent. Egypt), and the *Apostolic Constitutions* VII, 33–39 (late 4th cent.).

20. H. Lietzmann, *Mass and Lord's Supper: A Study in the History of the Liturgy,* trans. of *Masse und Herrenmahl — Eine Studie zur Geschichte der Liturgie* (1926), by D. H. G. Reave, with Introduction and Further Inquiry by R. D.

utterly confident that the question of historical development
was the right one to pose. He starts at the upper end with
the fourth- and fifth-century Christian liturgical texts, with
the observation that there are actually different families of
liturgies.[21] Using the method of source criticism, he works his
way backward through time, trying to determine, from seams
in the texts, places where alternative traditions may have in-
truded.[22] He looks for the archetypes lying behind the later
liturgical forms.[23]

Lietzmann's basic argument is that evidence for a later
distinction between a form of ritual meal called the agapē
(that did not contain the words of institution)[24] and the
Eucharist (which did make express remembrance of Jesus'
words over the bread and the cup) point back to the beginning of Christianity, when there were two "primitive types"
of sacred meals.[25] The first was practiced in Jerusalem as a

---

Richardson (Leiden: E. J. Brill, 1979); the basic lines of Lietzmann's inquiry
are anticipated by J. F. Keating, *The Agapē and the Eucharist in the Early Church:
Studies in the History of the Christian Love-Feasts* (London, 1901; New York:
AMS Press, 1969), and R. L. Cole, *Love-Feasts: A History of the Christian Agapē*
(London: Charles H. Kelly, 1916).

21. Lietzmann, *Mass and Lord's Supper,* 142.

22. See in particular his analysis of the *Euchologion* of Serapion in *Mass and
Lord's Supper,* 152–60.

23. In this respect, the method of examination closely resembles that of
textual-criticism, which sorts through variants, seeks families of textual tradition, and tries to find the archetypes of texts. This similarity to textual
criticism is noted by R. D. Richardson and turned about: the presence of New
Testament text variants might give important information on the development
of local liturgical practices (in "A Further Inquiry into Eucharistic Origins,"
Mass and Lord's Supper, 221–86.

24. The main evidence for such a meal is in the *Apostolic Tradition* of Hippolytus, 113.8 (see also the *Canons of Hippolytus* 32); *The Apostolic Constitutions*
2.28; the *Epistula Apostolorum* 15; and Tertullian, *Apology,* 39. The use of *agapē*
and *agapan* in Ignatius, *Rom.* 7.8 and *Smyr.* 7.1 is less decisive. See Lietzmann,
Mass and Lord's Supper, 161–71.

25. Lietzmann, *Mass and Lord's Supper,* 206.

Meals Are Where the Magic Is | 143

simple fellowship meal in direct continuity with those Jesus shared with followers during his ministry. It made no mention of Jesus' death or last meal.[26] The second type was the Lord's Supper, which took its origin in Pauline Christianity.[27] Lietzmann also concluded that although Jesus' last meal with his disciples has some historical basis, its literary depiction in terms similar to those reported by Paul in 1 Cor 11:23-26 is due to an "aetiological cult legend," whereby the practice of the church is retrojected into the story of Jesus.[28]

Lietzmann's excavation of liturgical texts has subsequently been modified either in the direction of a greater harmonization of the sources[29] or an even greater differentiation of them.[30] These later investigations, however, share

26. Ibid., 170–71, 204.

27. Ibid., 205.

28. Ibid., 207.

29. In *The Shape of the Liturgy*, 1945, with additional notes by P. V. Marshall (New York: Seabury Press, 1982), Dom Gregory Dix agrees that there was a difference between the *agapē* = "Lord's Supper" and the Eucharist (81–96), and that Jesus' last meal with his disciples was not a Passover meal, but rather a *"chaburah"* or fellowship meal (50–54). In contrast to Lietzmann, however, Dix insists that Paul's version of the meal was that shared also in Jerusalem, and what Paul means by "I received from the Lord" in 1 Cor 11:23 is the reception of tradition from the Jerusalem community, and not (as in Lietzmann, *Mass and Lord's Supper*, 208), a special revelation from the risen Christ (Dix, 63–72). Louis Bouyer emphasizes the natural development of Christian liturgy out of the piety of Jewish *berakoth* and in some sense does not really address the problem posed by textual discrepancies; see L. Bouyer, *Eucharist: Theology and Spirituality of the Eucharistic Prayer*, trans. C. U. Quinn (Notre Dame: University of Notre Dame Press, 1968); but see his short response to Lietzmann in L. Bouyer, *Liturgical Piety* (Notre Dame: University of Notre Dame, 1954) 81–85. See also the rejection of Lietzmann in J. A. Jungmann, *The Mass: An Historical, Theological, and Pastoral Survey*, trans. J. Fernandez, ed. M. E. Evans (Collegeville, Minn.: Liturgical Press, 1975) 33.

30. See, e.g., Richardson in Lietzmann, *Mass and Lord's Supper*, 286–444. Recently, B. D. Chilton has taken Lietzmann as the incentive to differentiate five different versions of meal, two originating with Jesus and three developed

Lietzmann's preoccupation with the origin and development of the Eucharist.[31] They also display the apologetic interest that Jonathan Z. Smith has identified in other Christian historiography.[32] There is obvious anxiety concerning the connection between Jesus and the church: how can later developments be legitimate if they do not go back to Jesus?[33] But there is equally concern for the uniqueness of Christian origins, most evident in discussions of resemblances between early Christian meals and Greco-Roman or Jewish ritual meals.[34] We are startled to find in the middle of the

respectively by Peter, James, and Paul; see B. D. Chilton, *A Feast of Meanings: Eucharistic Theologies from Jesus through Johannine Circles* (NovTestSup 72; Leiden: E. J. Brill, 1994) 7–11, 146–49; see also J. W. Riggs, "The Sacred Food of Didache 9-10 and Second Century Ecclesiologies," in *The Didache in Context: Essays on Its Text, History, and Transmission,* ed. C. N. Jefford (NovTestSup 77; Leiden: E. J. Brill, 1995) 257–83.

31. See also W. Marxsen, *The Lord's Supper as a Christological Problem,* trans. L. Nieting (Facet Books, Biblical Series 25; Philadelphia: Fortress Press, 1970).

32. See J. Z. Smith, *Drudgery Divine: On the Comparisons of Early Christianities and the Religions of Late Antiquity* (Jordan Lectures in Comparative Religion 14; Chicago Studies in the History of Judaism; Chicago: University of Chicago Press, 1990) 1–35.

33. Richardson in his supplementary essay to *Mass and Lord's Supper,* 221, comments on Lietzmann, "His most debatable conclusions are those on eucharistic origins. The matter is one which affects all Christian people, *for it lies at the heart of their religious practice*" (emphasis added). Likewise, J. Jeremias's argument in *The Eucharistic Words of Jesus,* trans. N. Perrin (Philadelphia: Fortress Press, 1964), that Jesus' last meal actually was a Passover celebration: "In all of this we are not concerned, as is often claimed, with questions of only archaeological or chronological interest. It is much more a question of setting the Last Supper within the context of the *Heilsgeschichte*" (88). The same argument occurs in I. H. Marshall, *Last Supper and Lord's Supper* (Grand Rapids: Eerdmans, 1980): "Although the exercise has been academic and exegetical, we would hope that the theological significance of the Last Supper and Lord's Supper for today has been apparent from time to time in the discussion" (155).

34. On one side is the typical nervousness concerning the possible influence of pagan mysteries. Lietzmann is palpably relieved to conclude that the earliest community shared only the simple meals inherited from Jesus (*Mass and Lord's Supper,* 204). Notions of sacrifice and mystical commu-

discussion of some technical point the declaration that Jesus could not have said or meant something on the basis of an appeal to Jesus' self-understanding![35] Supposedly disinterested scholarship is directed by theological predispositions and commitments.[36]

More distressing than the mixture of historical and apologetic interests is the fact that an exclusive preoccupation with origin and development means that other questions remain unasked, especially the most critical one: what might these meals have meant religiously to those who practiced them? The obsessive concentration on the so-called words of institution is demanded not by the weight of the data but by concern for theological legitimacy.

nion come from Paul and flourish in a "Hellenistic" context (ibid., 207). Jesus and "original" Christianity are thereby kept untainted by the Catholic magic of sacraments. On the other side is also skittishness concerning the links between Christian meals and Judaism. That there is a Jewish influence on the prayers found in later anaphoras is undeniable; the formal resemblance between the Christian *eucharistia* and the Jewish *berakah* cannot be missed (see esp. Bouyer, *Eucharist*). But where did the influence enter in? Here scholars flail about in the awesome difficulties of dating Jewish traditions. The appeal of a *chaburah* meal shared with Jesus' companions is diminished by the appreciation that the sources for Pharisaic practice are less reliable than those for the Christian! Jewish sources more contemporary to Jesus (like the Dead Sea Scrolls or *Joseph and Aseneth*) generate other anxieties. Some of the striking resemblances may be due to Christian interpolations; or the parallels are incidental or irrelevant because they are found within a different overall ideology (Richardson, in *Mass and Lord's Supper,* 336–56.

35. Richardson in *Mass and Lord's Supper,* 356–63; Chilton's *A Feast of Meanings* is even more confident in its appeal to "Jesus' Theory of Purity" and his intentions at his last meals in Jerusalem, as though there were no difficulty reading history off the pages of the Gospels (46–74).

36. For an analysis of the way historical and theological issues became intertwined in the study of the Eucharist, see R. Feneberg, *Christliche Passafeier und Abendmahl: Eine biblische-hermeneutische Untersuchung der neutestamentlichen Einsetzungsberichte* (SANT 27; Munich: Kösel-Verlag, 1971).

Meals in Revisionist History

In *Drudgery Divine,* Jonathan Z. Smith gives brief but provocative attention to Christian meals.[37] Presenting Smith's position fairly requires placing it within his larger argument and the argument of those scholars whose work he utilizes.

Smith's criticism of previous scholarship and statement of theoretical principles are typically trenchant. He shows how comparison between Christianity and other religions in its "environment" has been distorted by a preoccupation with uniqueness.[38] Indeed, he considers assumptive distinctions between the "Jewish" or "Greco-Roman" or "Christian" traditions to be misleading since internal variations within such broad traditions may be more decisive (and distinguishing) than differences between them.[39] Comparison in religions, he says, should follow the example of the sciences, where "difference rather than identity governs the comparisons; the language of 'uniqueness' is increasingly eschewed; and analogy rather than genealogy is the goal."[40]

Smith's example is soteriology. He complains that a uni-

---

37. The chapter is entitled "On Comparing Settings," and concludes the book (116–43).

38. *Drudgery Divine,* 116–17.

39. Ibid., 117–18. Smith's point here is similar to his effort to distinguish monothetic and polythetic approaches to "naming the differential quality" in early Judaism, in "Fences and Neighbors: Some Contours of Early Judaism," in *Imagining Religion: From Babylon to Jamestown* (Chicago Studies in the History of Judaism; Chicago: University of Chicago Press, 1982) 1–18. It is a useful reminder but one that should not obscure the obvious ways in which larger traditions *can* be distinguished and *were* distinguished in antiquity. Philo and Plato share much of their worldview, but Plato never cites the Septuagint.

40. Ibid., 118; Smith's major point must be granted, which is that comparisons between Christianity and other traditions, especially in the period of Christian nascence, are distorted when it is simply assumed that Christianity is monolithic and the same in all its manifestations. His remarks here would seem to move in the direction of privileging attention to specific phenomena for the sake of precise comparison.

vocal understanding of Christian soteriology shaped by Paul's understanding of death and resurrection has distorted comparison between traditions. Because triumph over death is taken as the standard form of Christian soteriology, for example, the presence or absence of "dying and rising" motifs becomes the criterion for affirming or denying the "influence" of the mysteries on Christianity.[41] Smith argues for an alternative approach, using his own distinction between "locative" and "utopian" cults in antiquity.[42] Locative cults are rooted in local cult places. They serve to celebrate and cement the regular patterns of nature and society — they are stabilizing traditions. In contrast, utopian cults are diasporic and mobile, and serve to challenge both social and cosmological boundaries. Using this typology, we would expect to find in locative cults cultic expressions of "salvation" that do not challenge death but enable a life harmoniously ordered to death's natural inevitability. It is in utopian cults that rituals would express triumph over death in resurrection or immortality.

Starting from the Greco-Roman side, Smith declares that recent work on the Attis cult shows that even in its "diasporic" form this mystery is thoroughly locative in its religious character, that is, the dying god Attis is not "resurrected" yet survives in a sort of presence in the cult that Smith designates as "subsistence 'in death.'"[43] Smith concludes that "it

---

41. Ibid., 119–20.

42. Smith first elaborates the distinction in several of the essays in *Map Is Not Territory: Studies in the History of Religions* (Studies in Judaism in Late Antiquity 23; Leiden: E. J. Brill, 1978) xi–xv, 67–207; see also idem, "Native Cults in the Hellenistic Period," *History of Religions* 11 (1971) 236–49. Much the same sort of distinction is adumbrated by A. Loisy, "Religions nationales et cultes de mystères," in *Les Mystères Païens et le Mystère Chrétien* (Paris: Emile Nourry, 1930) 9–50.

43. *Drudgery Divine,* 126–27; Smith is using the work of G. S. Gasparro, *Soteriology and Mystic Aspects in the Cult of Attis and Cybele* (EPRO 103; Leiden: E. J. Brill, 1985).

is possible to have a satisfying formulation of a soteriological dimension to the death of a cult figure without invoking the notion of resurrection or 'rising.' "[44]

Having identified to his own satisfaction a mystery cult whose ritual meal suggests communion with a dead deity but no real resurrection,[45] Smith takes up the other pole of comparison, found not in a coherent religion called Christianity but in "a heterogeneous collection of relatively small groups, marked off from their neighbors by a rite of initiation (chiefly, adult baptism), with their most conspicuous cultic act a common meal, and a variety of other activities that would lead a scholar to classify these groups as being highly focused on a cult of the dead."[46]

Is there amid such heterogeneity a group equally "locative" in its soteriology, or did all varieties of nascent Chris-

---

44. *Drudgery Divine*, 128. Smith continues, "While the death, appropriately, cannot be overcome, its effects are [by the cult] ameliorated. The land of the dead remains other than the realm of the living, but it is not entirely alienated from life. There is growth and movement, albeit in an attenuated fashion. And, there is a memory which if undertaken in a ritualized context guarantees a sort of *presence* and, above all, a *confidence* in the face of inescapable death" (129, emphasis original).

45. For the sake of this argument I am taking his reading of Gasparro as accurate and Gasparro's reading of the pertinent data as adequate, although my working through of the other sources used by Smith suggests that analysis might be appropriate (see, e.g., the review of *Drudgery Divine* by R. M. Price in *The Journal of Higher Criticism* 3 (1996) 137–45). When Smith finds conclusions congenial to his own, he is less precise and critical in his reading than when he is dealing with positions he finds unacceptable.

46. *Drudgery Divine*, 129–30. It is patent that definition and description exercise considerable interpretive force. In the present case it is worth pointing out that Smith does not use the name "Jesus" or the title "Christ" as a unifying element for this collection of groups, nor does he connect it to Torah or Judaism. He does not, furthermore, identify the "variety of other activities" that he suggests point to a cult of the dead: what is there besides baptism and the meal? As for the meal itself, is it not a begging of the question to identify it from the start as evidence for a cult of the dead? Presumably it is precisely the character of the meal which is here under investigation.

tianity share the "utopian" Pauline soteriology of death and resurrection? That depends on finding evidence, first for manifestations of Christianity that are completely distinct from Paul, and second for rituals that relate "locatively" rather than "utopianly" to death. For this part of his argument, Smith relies heavily on scholarship he considers authoritative, namely, Graydon Snyder's collection of early Christian funerary art and Burton Mack's multistrand unraveling of earliest Christianity.

Snyder's contribution is a valuable collection of archaeological evidence connected to Christianity before specifically Christian art and architecture went public in the fourth century.[47] His book is slender for good reason: before 180 there is no certain archaeological evidence for Christianity's existence, and even after that period only bits and pieces are found in a few locations (mainly Rome) and settings (mainly burial). At the very best, then, the value of archaeological data for understanding nascent Christianity is severely restricted. Large inferences drawn from such meager data are rightly resisted.[48]

Two theoretical perspectives affect Snyder's interpretation of the data. First, he opposes the work of the dominant "Roman School" of archaeologists, which contextualized fragmentary evidence with literary evidence. Snyder thinks the archaeological evidence must be read on its own.[49] In some circumstances this approach makes sense, but not in this

---

47. *Ante Pacem: Archaeological Evidence of Church Life before Constantine* (Macon, Ga.: Mercer University Press, 1985).

48. The data are too little, too late, too local, and too limited to support grand hypotheses. For supplementary (Montanist) evidence from Phrygia and North Africa, see now William Tabberne, *Montanist Inscriptions and Testimonia: Epigraphic Sources Illustrating the History of Montanism* (North American Patristic Society Patristic Monograph Series 16; Macon, Ga.: Mercer University Press, 1997).

49. Snyder, *Ante Pacem*, 5–7.

one.[50] The New Testament and a library of Christian literature precedes even the smallest hint of archaeological evidence; interpreting depictions of meals on sarcophagi in complete isolation from such literary evidence is misguided, for the simple reason that without an explicit Christian code for interpreting symbols they inevitably must be read within the only other available code, which is that of Greco-Roman myth and ritual.[51] Christianity simply disappears into its environment.

Snyder also contextualizes the data by means of class analysis:[52] Upper-class people (wealthy, urban, educated) prefer the distinctive revelation found in the texts of the "great tradition"; lower-class people (poor, artisan, rural) privilege the ancient local traditions, assimilating new revelations into those older patterns.[53] There's a certain broad legitimacy to

50. See, e.g., the work of G. Schopen on earliest Indian Buddhism, "Archaeology and Protestant Presuppositions in the Study of Indian Buddhism," *History of Religions* 31 (1991) 1–23. In that case, the earliest written evidence is found in manuscripts no earlier than the seventeenth century C.E., whereas the archaeological evidence comes from the earliest centuries C.E. Interestingly enough, Schopen himself criticizes Snyder (pp. 17–18) for not going far enough in the direction of asserting archaeology's claims over against literary evidence. It is not clear, however, whether Schopen has any knowledge of Christian origins or the literature pertaining to it.

51. Even in this case, preservation of the myths through literary renderings is far more substantial and coherent than the remaining archaeological evidence, which is one of the reasons why we remain so much in the dark concerning such basic information as what was done in pagan rituals. The issues here are not unlike the debate concerning the interpretation of Jewish symbols; see, for example, M. Smith, "Goodenough's *Jewish Symbols* in Retrospect," *Journal of Biblical Literature* 86 (1967) 53–68.

52. Snyder, *Ante Pacem*, 8–11, makes use specifically of R. Thouless, *Conventionalization and Assimilation in Religious Movements as Problems in Social Psychology* (Oxford: Oxford University Press, 1940); R. Redfield, *Peasant Society and Culture* (Chicago: University of Chicago Press, 1956); and M. Marriott, "Little Communities in an Indigenous Civilization," in *Village India*, ed. M. Marriott (Chicago: University of Chicago Press, 1955) 197–200.

53. Snyder, *Ante Pacem*, 9–10.

this distinction. People who read do tend to pay more attention to texts. But Snyder uses it to give greater leverage to his relatively unimpressive data. These bits and pieces from burial sites are now tokens of a "cemetery" form of Christianity in tension with the "city" form associated with book-learned bishops like Irenaeus. They therefore are better evidence for "what the simple folk did" in early Christianity.[54]

Theoretical sophistication cannot compensate for lack of real data or sound judgment. Because Snyder insists that funerary art cannot in principle derive from New Testament narratives, for example, he will not identify the dove in the depiction of Jesus' baptism by John as the Holy Spirit,[55] even though without such narratives, we would wonder why there would be depictions of Jesus' baptism by John in the first place![56] Snyder consistently suppresses any distinctively Christian symbolism. Take the depiction of the raising of Lazarus[57] appearing on the same sarcophagus with a cycle of scenes showing Jonah falling overboard, being swallowed by the whale, being spewn out, and then reclining on land.[58] Snyder concedes that this expresses "the

54. Ibid., 164. But does not the production of sarcophagi with such ornamentation presuppose a fairly substantial degree of wealth? And if the sarcophagi make reference (as I will argue) to biblical traditions, does not the cemetery version of Christianity also appear as literate?

55. See ibid., 16–17.

56. Ibid., 17, 36, 57.

57. Not only is the scene unmistakable, it is one that could only be generated by a specific narrative text of the New Testament, namely, John 11:33-44. By designating it as "the raising of Lazarus," therefore, Snyder is relying in an unacknowledged way on the literary contextualization he has explicitly rejected.

58. See C. Museo Pio cristiano #119, represented by plate 14, Snyder, *Ante Pacem*, 37. The Jonah-cycle is one of the most frequent pictorial representations in this funerary art (see the chart in Snyder, 43). There is, of course, no other source for this particular sequence of incidents other than the biblical book of Jonah. But Snyder asserts, "There is little in these three scenes to indicate that the biblical story of Jonah is being told. To be sure, if one

resurrection hope of the dead buried in the catacombs," but then, for whatever reason, he contrasts this to a "view of otherworldly immortality...end-time judgment and resurrection." He then offers a flat-footed and unsubstantiated interpretation, arguing that "in the social matrix the people believed the dead remained in the houses of places prepared for them.... These resurrected dead then were part of the extended Christian family."[59] Despite the fact that a depiction of *sol invictus* appears immediately beside Lazarus and Jonah[60] and despite the fact that Jonah is specifically connected to the

knows the biblical story, one recognizes the boat, the ketos, and the vine. But there is no call of God, no refusal, no Nineveh, no preaching and no pouting of Jonah under the vine" (46). This is a truly remarkable statement, to which three responses should be made: (1) the fact is the reverse: without the biblical narrative the three elements would not be recognizable as representing Jonah; (2) the selection of these three elements is obviously deliberate and pertinent to the placement on a sarcophagus: life, death, new life — not all the elements of the Jonah story but those that form a certain pattern are represented consistently; (3) these are the elements that are appropriated by the use of the Jonah story in the Gospel of Matthew 12:28-34 with specific reference to the resurrection!

59. Snyder, *Ante Pacem*, 61. Snyder consistently creates false oppositions in order to secure his interpretations. He does not state why "otherwordly immortality" should be the category for comparison. Nor does he suggest how that might pictorially be represented. As for "end-time judgment," why should it necessarily be included?

60. The identification of the *sol invictus* figure is tentative (37). In his discussion of the only unquestioned example of the *sol invictus* in pre-Constantinian art (ibid., plate 31, pp. 62–63) Snyder grants that the *sol invictus* points to Jesus (in a fashion similar to the representation of the ascension of Elijah in the synagogue at Dura Europas). But he inexplicably does not see that such a representation would suggest the equivalent reality for Christians, namely, the resurrection of Jesus. This is at least partly because Snyder works with a notion of resurrection that is roughly equivalent to resuscitation; whereas in Luke-Acts, where Christ's ascension is described, the event is part of Luke's larger resurrection narrative dialectic of absence and presence of Jesus after his death: empty-tomb = absence; appearances = presence in a new mode; ascension = absence as physical presence; Pentecost = presence in a new mode.

resurrection of Christ by Matt 12:28-34, the intertextual connections concerning the resurrection in the "great tradition" are suppressed in favor of entirely hypothetical suggestions derived from the circumambient culture.[61]

When we turn to Snyder's interpretation of meal iconography, his tendency is immediately evident. His reason for denying that depictions of a "vase" could also be a chalice is, "the art and symbols of third century Christianity simply do not reflect the *anamnēsis* eucharist," a splendid example of the logical fallacy of *petitio principii* or assuming what needs proving.[62] As for the meals at which the vase appears, they "probably refer to the feeding of the five thousand,"[63] which Snyder immediately assimilates to the "general cultural practice of eating with the dead."[64] Acknowledging that the vase could sometimes be a pitcher, holding wine, and that in some representations there is a dove involved,[65] Snyder is unable to see the dove as symbol of the Holy Spirit, but only a symbol for peace.[66] He cannot make the obvious link with Paul's statement in 1 Cor 12:13, "We have all been made to drink of the one Spirit." Such scenes therefore cannot depict the Eucharist but only a *refrigerium,* a meal celebrated in fellowship with the dead.[67]

61. Ibid., 46–49.

62. Ibid., 16.

63. This identification also contradicts Snyder's principle of not contextualizing such symbols by biblical stories. In this case, however, it is apparently better to choose the feeding over, let's say, the last supper narrative. The determinative iconographic reason seems to be the presence of fish on the table.

64. The only support possible for this identification is the location of such depictions at burial sites. But that they should represent "eating with the dead" is not thereby warranted. Once more a theoretical assumption dictates the interpretation.

65. Ibid., 16.

66. Ibid., 16–18.

67. Ibid., 16. For the way in which the pagan meal for the dead was carried on, especially in North Africa, in *refrigeria* for the Christian dead,

What about bread as an iconographic symbol? When it
appears with fish, Snyder thinks the meals "reflect much
more the eschatological meal, or agapē, than the Christian-
ized passover meal, or *anamnēsis*."[68] We are not surprised that
when discussing fish as a symbol he flatly denies any reference to Christ, despite his recognition that the acrostic *ichthys*
is very early and already applied directly to Christ by Tertullian.[69] We begin to suspect that Snyder will go to any length
to interpret symbols in a manner other than what the "great
tradition" understood them to be.

The analysis of the individual elements prepares us for
Snyder's interpretation of the meal. His sweeping generalization that all such representations refer to "the multiplication
of the loaves" is questionable.[70] Some of the plates do suggest
the Gospel story of the feeding,[71] but others are less certain.
One sarcophagus, for example, has a meal scene immediately

---

see F. Van der Meer, *Augustine the Bishop,* trans. B. Battershaw and G. R.
Lamb (London: Sheed and Ward, 1961) 498–526; for the celebrations at
the burial place of martyrs, see ibid., 471–97; and P. Brown, *The Cult of
the Saints: Its Rise and Function in Latin Christianity* (The Haskell Lectures
on the History of Religions, n.s. 2; Chicago: University of Chicago Press,
1981).

68. Snyder, *Ante Pacem,* 22; he offers no evidence for this opinion, for
there is none possible to offer.

69. "But we little fishes, after the example of our *ichthys,* Jesus Christ, are
born in water...." Tertullian, *De Baptismo,* 1. Furthermore, as Snyder notes,
the phrase *ichthys zōntōn* appears iconographically with an anchor on the
(probably early) stela of Licinia (*Ante Pacem,* 24). Ignoring the obvious, Snyder suggests a "two fish hypothesis," in which an earlier symbolism of the
fish as pointing to Christians in an alien environment was later (after the
peace) joined to another early symbol of the fish at the multiplication story,
to gain prominence as a christological symbol (Ibid., 24–26). This is indeed
convoluted as well as unnecessary.

70. As is his flat declaration, "Unquestionably the early Christians celebrated a meal together that was based on the multiplication of the loaves"
(Snyder, *Ante Pacem,* 64).

71. See, e.g., plate 17, ibid., 40.

adjacent to Jesus' baptism.[72] The celebrants are reclining at a table holding seven loaves of bread and a single fish. One of the celebrants holds a chalice, while another is either drinking from one or eating bread. The figure holding the chalice, furthermore, is gesturing across the table with his first two fingers extended.[73] These iconographic details[74] can support an argument that this scene represents the Last Supper,[75] appearing in tandem with Jesus' baptism for obvious reasons.[76] Snyder's reading of the iconography itself is neither careful nor precise.

Nevertheless, he quickly reaches the predictable conclu-

---

72. Plate 33, showing a sarcophagus located in the Museo Pio Christiano, #123, in ibid., 64.

73. The two fingers extended, with the thumb apparently touching the other two fingers behind those extended, suggests the traditional hieratic gesture of blessing.

74. Namely: one fish with baskets of bread, the presence of wine and chalice, the gesture of blessing. The only details I have omitted are the presence of a figure carrying bread to the table (despite the loaves already arranged on it) and the depiction of a tree or vine slightly behind and to the left of the recumbent figures. The figure could be the boy from the multiplication accounts or a server at a meal. The vine may be only decorative or may represent a merging of the symbolism of the multiplication of the loaves (held outside) and the last supper (at table), a link already established literarily by the Gospels themselves.

75. The presence of the fish obviously argues against this identification, but the presence of wine argues just as strongly against the multiplication! As I suggested in the previous note, it may well be that the iconography accomplishes the same merging of the meals as is suggested by the literary signals in the Gospels themselves.

76. For the symbolism of death and resurrection attached to baptism, see chap. 3 n. 36. The connection between Jesus' suffering and the cup at his last meal is established not only by the words, "This is my blood of the covenant, which is poured out for many" (Mark 14:24), but also by the words shortly thereafter in the garden, "Father, for you all things are possible; remove this cup from me; yet, not what I want, but what you want" (Mark 14:36, NRSV). The literary link between baptism and the last meal is found in the question posed to the disciples in Mark 10:38, "Are you able to drink the cup that I drink, or be baptized with the baptism that I am baptized with?"

sions: Using Lietzmann, he refers to the two different meals at the start of Christianity,[77] then connects the multiplication of the loaves to the Agapē meal of the New Testament (!), which is in turn coalesced with the meal for the dead in the social matrix: "The meal can be seen as a continuation of the non-Christian meal for the dead in light of the New Testament paradigm of the Feeding of the Five Thousand."[78]

With such fragmentary evidence, theoretical bias, and clumsy readings, Snyder's assertion that one of the most central cultic activities before the time of Constantine was an act of eating together with the dead in an extended "kinship meal," a "*koinonia* meal that did not recall the sacrifice of Jesus Christ," is nothing more than baseless speculation.[79] Nor has he provided the support for his evaluation of the funerary data: "There is no sign of a more sophisticated immortality, nor does resurrection, at least as revivification or resuscitation play any role."[80]

We can understand why Smith would be predisposed toward Snyder's book, for it dovetails with Smith's interest in non-literary indices of identity[81] and his typology of locative

77. Again, I note the methodological inconsistency in Snyder's reliance on literary sources for interpretation.

78. Snyder, *Ante Pacem*, 65.

79. See ibid., 16, 22, 65, and the citation of him in Smith, *Drudgery Divine*, 131. Even if everything that Snyder asserted about the meals at burial sites were accurate, he could not on that basis deny a connection to the resurrection for the obvious reason that one cannot argue from silence to a negative conclusion.

80. Snyder, *Ante Pacem*, 167. Once more, Snyder's language is imprecise. In the first place, the recumbent Jonah figure *would* be compatible with an understanding of resurrection as resuscitation — indeed, that would be its most obvious reading. But more significantly, what could possibly be meant by a "more sophisticated immortality," and how could it have been represented iconographically? Moreover, as I have noted, the image of Jesus as *sol invictus* comes closer to the literary understanding of resurrection than Snyder's resuscitation or revivification.

81. See Smith, *Imagining Religion*, 1–18.

versus utopian traditions. But how can a scholar otherwise so critical take as the basis for further inferences this confused line of reasoning and skewed reading of evidence?[82] Undoubtedly it is because Smith gets from it a version of Christian practice in which "the dead remain dead, in a sphere other than the living; but there is contact, there is continuity of relationship, there is memorialization, there is presence."[83] The presence, we note, is not to a risen and powerful Lord, but only of worshippers to each other among the tombs.[84]

The second source for Smith's argument is Burton Mack's dissection of earliest Christianity into separate strands, based on discrete textual traditions: five forms of the Jesus movement in Palestine, a diasporic Christ cult, and the Pauline variation of the Hellenistic Christ cult.[85] Smith recognizes

82. Snyder's analysis can usefully be compared to that of two other art historians, who do not share his ideological preoccupations. F. Gerke, *Die christlichen Sarkophage der vorkonstantinischen Zeit* (Studien zur spätantiken Kunstgeschichte 11; Berlin: Walter de Gruyter, 1940), recognizes the ways in which Christian art emerges from and employs pagan elements (37) but has no difficulty recognizing the distinctive character of the depiction of meals on the pre-Constantinian sarcophagi (112–50), finding them to be representations of the Eucharist (316). The dominant theme of the sarcophagus art Gerke finds to be victory over death (317), and in the depiction of the raising of Lazarus he sees an allusion to the resurrection of the flesh (318). Similarly, A. Grabar, *Christian Iconography: A Study of Its Origins* (A. W. Mellen Lectures in the Fine Arts, 1961. Bollingen Series 34/10; Princeton: Princeton University Press, 1968), sees the ambiguity in the meals scenes (8–9) but ultimately sees them as representations of Christian meals that celebrate Christ's victory over death (15). He notes, "Image signs, as found in the catacombs, fulfill their purpose successfully only insofar as they are clear, but the concept of clarity is a function of the training of the viewer" (9).

83. Smith, *Drudgery Divine*, 132.

84. It is important to stress this point, for the language used by Smith is sufficiently evocative to mislead: the only "presence" of the dead, for Smith, is through the sociopsychological mechanisms of memory. They stay dead and gone. There is no "other" than that of the cultists to each other.

85. B. Mack, *A Myth of Innocence: Mark and Christian Origins* (Philadel-

in Mack's Palestinian forms of the Jesus movement his own "locative" type of tradition: the basic framework of the ancient Judaism is not fundamentally challenged, only modified. There is no significance given to Jesus' death and resurrection. Whatever meals were celebrated by these followers would be the sort of *agapē* meals shared with Jesus before his death.[86]

Mack's "synagogue Reform" group, in turn, "staked out a claim for table-fellowship in close proximity to the synagogue and Pharisaic groups."[87] In his closest approximation to Snyder's analysis, Smith remarks of the Q community in its later phases, "such traditions would have led, eventually, to a cult of the powerful dead, the 'tombs of the prophets' (Matt 23:29/Lk 20:47), the Jewish and Christian *martyria,* which are thoroughly locative structures."[88] Smith has found a form of

---

phia: Fortress Press, 1988). Earlier in the book, Smith had already designated Mack's work "the first study of 'Christian Origins' which may be taken up, with profit, by the general student of *religion*" (*Drudgery Divine,* 110 n. 43, emphasis in original). The level of praise is particularly puzzling when placed, for example, against Smith's appreciation of Reitzenstein, 76–77 n. 35.

86. If, however, one were to accept the reconstruction of the Q community in B. Mack, *The Lost Gospel: The Book of Q and Christian Origins* (San Francisco: Harper San Francisco, 1993), as a basically countercultural and (at least ideologically) itinerant movement, it is difficult to see how this would fit Smith's locative type, which ordinarily situates itself around a "sacred place." The putative placement of the movement in Galilee would only make it "locative" because it inhabited a particular place, and thereby presumably less "diasporic" in character than the hypothesized Hellenistic Christ cult.

87. Smith, *Drudgery Divine,* 135, referring to Mack, *Myth of Innocence,* 94–96. It may be worth noting again that the synagogue was scarcely a "sacred space" in the way that the Jerusalem temple was and that the pharisaic tendency in formative Judaism was remarkably portable as it made its transition into the Diaspora. It was precisely this form of Judaism, furthermore, that most cultivated belief in the resurrection of the righteous, which, if I understand Smith's typology correctly, ought to be a characteristic of utopian cults rather than locative ones.

88. Smith, *Drudgery Divine,* 138. Here Smith reverts to the full typology, with an emphasis on the *place* as defining the locative cult.

"Christianity" or "Jesus Movement" that goes back to Jesus himself, that supposedly has no myth of death or resurrection, and whose meals are simple acts of communion with the dead.

Still following Mack, Smith moves to the three putative varieties of the "pre-Pauline or non-Pauline Christ cult," one of which supposedly focused on Jesus' death but not his resurrection, a second that focused on Jesus' death and resurrection, but only as it applied to him, and a third that focused on the salvific effect of the resurrection on the community but minimized the death. Each of these separate strands of the "Christ cult," in turn, had its own symbolization, still detectable in the strata of Paul's letters.[89] Paul, in turn, appears as a creative manipulator of these prior cult traditions, with his soteriological emphasis on both the death and resurrection of Jesus seen as a corrective to what Smith calls "the presence of '[dying] and rising' motifs within some early Hellenistic Christ-cults with which Paul had a problematic relationship."[90] What makes Paul distinctive is his aggressive extension of Jesus' death and resurrection into what Smith considers "a thoroughly utopian understanding... instituting radical dualism at all levels of the system."[91]

Since the title of his chapter is "On Comparing Settings" and since the topic of meals was critical for the establishment of supposedly locative traditions within Christianity, we would expect Smith at this stage in his argument to turn to Paul's account of the Lord's Supper in 1 Cor 11:23-26, with its distinctive *anamnēsis* or memory of Jesus' death, and draw out the contrast with the *koinonia*, meals of the Jesus movement.

89. Ibid., 138–39, using Mack, *Myth of Innocence*, 100–113.

90. Smith, *Drudgery Divine*, 140; we can recognize here the standard view purveyed already by W. Bousset in *Kyrios Christos: A History of the Belief in Christ from the Beginnings of Christianity to Irenaeus*, trans. of the fifth German ed. by J. Steely (1913; Nashville: Abingdon Press, 1970).

91. Smith, *Drudgery Divine*, 141.

But the Pauline *meal* is simply not discussed. Instead, Smith draws on the "dying and rising" text in Rom 6:1-11, which deals with baptism. Presumably, given the logic of his analysis, Smith would agree with Hans Lietzmann that the form of the Lord's Supper found in 1 Cor 11:23-26 was distinct from the *agapē* meals of the Jesus movement. But he does not carry this analysis through, wandering instead into a characterization not of the Pauline meal but of the Pauline ideology.[92]

Smith reads Mack as uncritically as he does Snyder. In fact, there is no positive evidence for most of these "original" strands of the Jesus movement.[93] Mack's efforts to derive both "communities" and their "ideologies" from supposed strata of literary compositions are deeply problematic.[94] Be-

---

92. Smith, *Drudgery Divine*, 141. Smith's tendency to shift focus in the middle of an argument has been noted earlier.

93. Mack places the "Q community" in Galilee. But there is no positive evidence for any form of Christianity (or "Jesus movement") in Galilee in the first generations (apart from Acts 9:31). As a result, Galilee has become a favorite dumping ground for scholars who want to provide a specific provenance for compositions. Thus, Mark is supposed to be "Galilean" on the basis of Mark 14:28 and 16:7, as in W. Kelber, *The Kingdom in Mark: A New Place and a New Time* (Philadelphia: Fortress Press, 1974); and the Letter of James has been proposed as "Galilean" on the basis of its social teaching, as in L. Elliott-Binns, *Galilean Christianity* (Studies in Biblical Theology; London: SCM Press, 1956). Given the use of Jesus traditions in James, in fact, the traditional understanding that the "sayings of Jesus" were transmitted in the Jerusalem church, which was at least partially made up of "those from Galilee" (Acts 1:11-26), has much to recommend it.

94. Smith seems unaware of the tenuous character of Mack's distinctions between literary strands and their attachment to proposed social groups. The entire enterprise represents an extension of source and form criticism beyond the bounds of probability and is based on simplistic theories concerning the relationship between literary compositions and communities. There exists no reliable textual evidence for "the Trans-Jordanian 'Family of Jesus'" as an ideologically distinct movement (Mack, *Myth of Innocence*, 90–91). The proposed "Congregation of Israel" (91–93) is a hypothetical entity made up to fit a selection of material that, so far as the evidence goes, never existed in any form apart from the one it now inhabits in the Synoptic Gospels. Even more bizarre are the efforts to dissect layers in Paul. When Smith characterizes the

sides inventing evidence for phantom communities, Mack also suppresses evidence suggesting deep levels of intercommunication across the undoubtedly diverse realizations of early Christianity.[95]

Smith likes Mack for two reasons. The postulation of Jesus movements completely out of contact with the Christ cult and with Paul enables Smith to advance his own thesis that some forms of early Christianity were locative in character and that, "measured in this way, most of the 'mystery' cults and the non-Pauline forms of Christian tradition have more in common with each other."[96] With this shaky conclusion reached, Smith

enterprise as one "drawing upon a variety of scholarly constructions" (*Drudgery Divine,* 139), he perhaps speaks more strictly and accurately than he appreciates. In the end, Mack simply extends beyond the bounds of the evidence the classic but already flawed tripartite version of early Christian development sketched by the *religionsgeschichtliche Schule* and used already by Lietzmann.

95. The sort of historiography represented in an extreme form by Mack proceeds by ignoring three kinds of evidence that always constrained earlier historians and replacing them with a purely form-critical approach to literature: every seam in a text points to a source, and every source has its separate setting. First, the evidence of Acts is ignored or rejected in a manner far exceeding the relatively restrained evaluation of its *tendenz* by F. C. Baur. In complete disregard of recent scholarship on Acts, which tends to give much more credit to the essential historicity of the account, this narrative is considered irrelevant, a "myth of origins" not worth taking seriously. Second, the evidence of Paul's letters concerning his relationship to tradition and to the Jerusalem church is simply ignored. Third, the evidence of other "Hellenistic" Christian literature of the first century, above all James, Hebrews, and 1 Peter, is not taken into account. As a result, assertions are made in clear contradiction to the information contained in this literature. On the matter of Paul's sharing wider church traditions, for example, or being in fellowship not only with the pillars of the Jerusalem church politically but also "preaching the same Gospel" as them (see Rom 15:18-29; 1 Cor 1:2; 4:17; 9:5-6; 11:2, 16; 14:33, 36; 15:3-11; Gal 1:18-20; 2:7-10), the evidence cannot be ignored. One must either acknowledge that Paul and Jerusalem had — at least in Paul's view — such fellowship or one must clearly state that Paul was deceived or lying. Mack does not go to the trouble to consider the evidence. But this is not history. It is creative writing.

96. Smith, *Drudgery Divine,* 142.

can in turn scold scholars who have been so preoccupied with the Pauline form of Christianity as to miss these subtler links to "other forms of Christianity." This leads Smith to conclude, "The entire enterprise of comparison between the 'mystery' cults and early Christianity needs to be looked at again."[97] Because Smith has not subjected Mack or antecedent historical scholarship to rigorous criticism, he mistakenly thinks Mack's position superior to those who understand earliest Christianity as a diverse movement that had genuine intercommunication and sharing of traditions.

Mack's dissecting of Christianity into multiple ideological strands with no shared point of origin, much less shared originative experience, also suits Smith's predilection for a history in which there is no "other" and no *novum,* but only "that which happens in Europe every day."[98] If Christianity is reduced to a loose assemblage of social groups mapping reality through the play of power, then there really is nothing to explain, only data to describe. Smith therefore launches a final attack on Christian scholars who focus on Paul, as people engaged in "an enterprise undertaken in bad faith."[99] Not inadequate method, or deficient data, or limited insight, notice, but "bad faith." Why? Because the supposition of "the centre, the fabled Pauline seizure by the 'Christ-event' or some other construction of an originary moment, has been declared, *a priori,* to be unique, to be *sui generis,* and hence, by definition, incomparable."[100] By using Paul as the measure of what

---

97. Ibid., 143.

98. Smith, *Imagining Religion,* xiii.

99. Smith, *Drudgery Divine,* 143.

100. As I have pointed out before in these pages, Smith's anxiety concerning illegitimate claims to "transcendental origin" and "revelation" and therefore "uniqueness," have led him to an impossible stance for a historian. Would he likewise be unwilling to grant a historical point of origin to Manichaeism or Mormonism? Is he unwilling to grant that these founders had some sort of religious proclivity if not experience that, while possibly deluded, might also have been sincere? Does he truly want to collapse Buddhism back

is authentically Christian, Smith asserts, other forms have been "subjected to procedures of therapeutic comparison. This is exorcism or purgation, not scholarship."[101]

Smith concludes his book preaching. He blasts "the Protestant hegemony over the enterprise of comparing the religions of Late Antiquity and early Christianities" and expresses the hope that when the academy can truly control this enterprise it will bring about a "radical reformulation" — (I almost wrote "reformation") — "of the generative questions and a thorough reevaluation of the purposes of comparison." What will result? "A phenomenon will be privileged only with respect to its utility for answering a theoretical issue concerning the scholarly imagination of religion. 'Let him who has ears, hear.'"[102] I leave the reader to ponder the remarkably religious and hegemonic language. Smith's concern ultimately seems to be who gets to be priest and control the *arcana*.[103]

Fellowship with the Dead
or the Living (One)?

The practice of dissecting nascent Christianity into separate ideological strands ends with the disappearance of Christianity. And with the dismissal of a distinctive religious ex-

into the Vedic system, because Siddhartha could not have had convictions or experiences that were distinctive and which created a world movement? Does he really consider history to be nothing more than a set of variations on (always pre-existing) themes?

101. Ibid.

102. Ibid.

103. More to the point, Smith's new history, dependent in large part on the flawed work of Snyder and Mack, turns out to be not much more helpful than the old history in getting at what was going on in ancient Christian meals. Although driven by a different ideological engine, it is still preoccupied by issues of origin, dependence, and development, in which the religious significance of specific events and experiences is suppressed when not ignored.

perience, Christian meals also lose any particular character and must be understood within the context of the circum-ambient culture. But an alternative approach is possible. If we shift from a preoccupation with questions of origin, de-pendence, and development, to a phenomenological reading of the available evidence, we can consider not only the social, historical, and ideological register of language but also its ex-periential dimension. Whether we ourselves want to declare in favor of transcendence, we can entertain the notion that participants at such meals considered themselves engaged by a power that was truly Other. These six steps toward a new way of reading ancient meals can be taken.[104]

1. Such a reading would begin with a phenomenology of meals, especially those celebrated by intentional communi-ties.[105] What are the implications of gathering under a certain

---

104. In the framework of this programmatic effort, only a sketch is possible and appropriate.

105. The analysis can take clues from the remarkable upsurge in attention paid to food, diet, and meals within social-scientific literature over the past thirty years. In addition to the literature listed in n. 1, above, see such spe-cific studies as M. Douglas, "Social and Religious Symbolism of the Lele," in *Implicit Meanings: Essays in Anthropology* (London: Routledge and Kegan Paul, 1975) 9–26; R. Barthes, "Towards a Psychosociology of Contemporary Food Consumption," in *Food and Drink in History,* ed. R. Foster and O. Ranum (Bal-timore: Johns Hopkins University Press, 1979) 166–73; P. Atkinson, "Eating Virtue," in A Murcott, ed., *The Sociology of Food and Eating: Essays in the Soci-ological Significance of Food* (Hants., England: Gower Publishing, 1983) 9–17; M. Douglas, ed., *Food in the Social Order: Studies of Food and Festivals in Three American Communities* (New York: Russell Sage Foundation, 1984); S. Kan, *Sym-bolic Immortality: The Tlingit Potlatch of the Nineteenth Century* (Washington, D.C.: Smithsonian Institution Press, 1989) 181–254; P. Farb and G. Armelagos, *Con-suming Passions: The Anthropology of Eating* (Boston: Houghton Mifflin, 1980). For studies that begin to apply anthropological perspectives to ancient meals, see G. Feely-Hanick, *The Lord's Table: The Meaning of Food in Early Judaism and Christianity* (Washington, D.C.: Smithsonian Institute Press, 1994), and esp. the literature provided by J. H. Neyrey, "Meals, Food, and Table Fellow-ship," in *The Social Sciences and New Testament Interpretation,* ed. R. Rohrbaugh (Peabody, Mass.: Hendrickson Publishers, 1996) 159–82.

"name," of eating the same food and drink, and of speaking ritual words while food and drink are being shared? We find that the sense of *koinonia*, or fellowship, is built into the very *actus* of sharing food, a sense of participation in a reality larger than the individual self. Individuality is not lost but is located within a power field that encompasses all participants.[106] This sense of participation in a greater energy field marks off the time and space dedicated to such meals as distinctive, heightening the sense of boundaries around the group.[107] Increased awareness of boundary, in turn, means access to the meal requires qualification[108] and gestures of transition.[109] Rudeness or inhospitality is

106. See the examples provided by G. Van der Leeuw, *Religion in Essence and Manifestation: A Study in Phenomenology*, 2 vols., trans. J. E. Turner (New York: Harper and Row, 1963) 1:201; 2:350–63; J. Wach, *Sociology of Religion* (Chicago: University of Chicago Press, 1944) 42, 79, 84, 141, 182.

107. The communal meal represents the most concentrated expression of the social group as such. As it eats and drinks together, it quite literally is enlivened and grows *as a group*. All of the issues of unity and separation that go with group identity are thereby naturally equally concentrated, which means that the otherwise perhaps diffuse dangers to the system are here brought to specific and concrete focus through the medium of food and drink. See, e.g., M. Douglas, *Purity and Danger: An Analysis of the Concepts of Pollution and Taboo* (London: Routledge and Kegan Paul, 1966) 94–128.

108. This is precisely the issue for Jewish messianists when Gentiles are first converted. Note the way that making distinctions between unclean and clean foods is established as a theme by Peter's opening vision (Acts 10:9-17); and although the author of Acts has Peter progressively understand this in terms of God's choice of a people (15:7-11), his Jewish Christian colleagues continue to see it as a matter of polluted table fellowship: "Why did you go to uncircumcised men and eat with them?" a pollution that could only be resisted by the assurance that all gentile converts themselves be circumcised (15:1-5).

109. The "table etiquette" by which one negotiates the space between the realm of ordinary endeavors and the space of the sacred meal varies from culture to culture. It is worth noting that the ritual of *washing* is not connected to hygiene but is a miniature *rite de passage;* when a Pharisee invites Jesus to dine, he is "astonished to see that he did not wash first before dinner" (Luke 11:37). In the case of Christianity, use of water mimics the ritual of baptism

intolerable,[110] unexcused departure a rupture of unity,[111] and exclusion a kind of death.[112] Phenomenological analysis shows meals in such intentional communities truly to have a magical quality.[113]

2. A phenomenologically informed analysis can next be turned to meals in Greco-Roman contexts. Once more, the starting point should not be those meals that are recognizably cultic but the broader phenomenon of meals shared

by which a person was made part of the fellowship in the first place. This symbolism is still attached to the holy water font in Roman Catholic churches and the ritual of signing oneself with the water "in the name of the Father and of the Son and of the Holy Spirit." The specific reason for entering the church, of course, is to join the meal of the sanctified. This point is missed by G. Van der Leeuw, *Religion in Essence and Manifestation,* 1:59–60.

110. For hospitality as a way of negotiating dangerous power, see G. Van der Leeuw, *Religion in Essence and Manifestation,* 1:43-47. Luke gains considerable literary leverage from the inhospitality of Jesus' opponents at meals, precisely because of the cultural conventions involved; see esp. Luke 7:36-50 and 14:1-6, as well as the culturally shocking examples offered by Jesus in Luke 12:41-48 and 17:7-10.

111. John's depiction of Judas's departure from the Last Supper has unparalleled force, with the morsel of food given him by Jesus carrying the symbolism of apostasy and betrayal: "Then, after the morsel, Satan entered into him. Jesus said to him, 'What you are going to do, do quickly.' . . . So, after receiving the morsel, he immediately went out; and it was night" (John 13:26-30). In the Synoptics, the same reality is conveyed by Jesus' noting that "the hand of him who betrays me is with me on the table" (Luke 22:21), or "it is one of the twelve, one who is dipping bread into the dish with me" (Mark 14:20; Matt 26:23). The weight of these characterizations can only be felt if the significance of meal *koinonia* is recognized.

112. See Josephus's account of the Essenes: "Those who are convicted of serious crimes they expel from the order; and the ejected individual often comes to a most miserable end. For, being bound by their oaths and usages, he is not at liberty to partake of other men's food, and so falls to eating grass and wastes away and dies of starvation." *Jewish War* 2:143.

113. This quality of the Potlatch is effectively captured by M. Mauss, *The Gift: The Form and Reason for Exchanges in Archaic Societies* (1950), trans. W. D. Halls (New York: W. W. Norton, 1990) 32–44; see also the discussion of *mana* (power) as a social reality in groups, in *A General Theory of Magic,* trans. R. Brain (1950; London: Routledge and Paul Kegan, 1972) 108–44.

by groups.[114] What symbolic values are attached to eating and drinking and discoursing together?[115] The data on cult meals are typically fragmentary, but the extant evidence can be meaningfully placed within this larger cultural matrix.[116] If

114. One must include here, of course, those *symposia* whose tutelar spirit was Dionysius: see, e.g., Plato, *Symposium;* Xenophon, *Memorabilia* and *Symposium;* Plutarch, *Table-Talk;* see, e.g., D. E. Smith, "Greco-Roman Meal Customs," *Anchor Bible Dictionary,* ed. D. N. Freedman (New York: Doubleday, 1992) 4:650–55.

115. Three kinds of meals come under consideration: those practiced by associations such as the *collegia,* those held in honor of the dead, and those held as cultic meals in honor of a specific deity. The categories are not mutually exclusive, and all have some religious component. The pertinence of the *collegia* was advanced by E. Hatch, *The Organization of the Early Christian Churches: Eight Lectures* (London: Rivingtons, 1881); and picked up by Keating, *Agapē and Eucharist,* 1–19; and Cole, *Love-Feasts,* 17–34; for a recent appreciation and updating of Hatch, see J. S. Kloppenborg, "Edwin Hatch, Churches and *Collegia,*" in *Origins and Method: Towards a New Understanding of Judaism and Christianity* (Essays in Honor of John C. Hurd), ed. B. H. McLean (JSNTSup 86; Sheffield: JSOT Press, 1993) 212–38. For cultic meals, see R. K. Yerkes, *Sacrifice in Greek and Roman Religions and Early Judaism* (New York: Charles Scribner's Sons, 1952) 51–114; M. Detienne and J.-P. Vernant, eds., *The Cuisine of Sacrifice among the Greeks,* trans. P. Wissig (Chicago: University of Chicago Press, 1989); and P. F. Foucart, *Des Associations Religieuses chez les Grecs: Thiases, Eranes, Orgéons* (Paris, 1873; New York: Arno Press, 1975). On memorial meals for the dead, see the references given by H. Lietzmann, *An die Korinther I,* 2nd ed. (Tübingen, 1931) 58; and the discussion in Jeremias, *Eucharistic Words,* 238–43.

116. The positions concerning the possible influence of mystery religions on Christian meals correspond to those taken on baptism. Among those seeing a positive influence are R. Reitzenstein, *The Hellenistic Mystery Religions: Their Basic Ideas and Significance,* trans. J. E. Steely (Pittsburgh: Pickwick Press, 1978) 73–80; A. Loisy, *Les Mystères Païens et le Mystère Chrétien* (Paris: E. Nourry, 1934) 272–92; O. Casel, *The Mystery of Christian Worship* (Westminster, Md.: Newman Press, 1962). A more neutral position is adopted by W. Burkert, *Ancient Mystery Cults* (Cambridge: Harvard University Press, 1987) 107–14. Those rejecting any real influence include J. F. McConnell, "The Eucharist and the Mystery Religions," *Catholic Biblical Quarterly* 10 (1948) 29–41; H. A. A. Kennedy, *St. Paul and the Mystery Religions* (London: Hodder and Stoughton, 1913) 256–79; A. D. Nock, "Hellenistic Mysteries and Christian Sacraments," in *Essays on Religion in the Ancient World,* ed. Z. Stewart (Oxford: Clarendon

koinonia is a feature of all meals held by intentional groups, the key question is the specific character of that fellowship for meals honoring a deity.[117] Although Paul follows Jewish practice in denying divinity to pagan gods, calling them *daimonia* instead,[118] he clearly asserts the reality of the power connected to such spiritual entities at cultic meals: "You are not able to drink the cup of the Lord and the cup of demons. You are not able to share the table of the Lord and the table of demons" (1 Cor 10:21). Paul casts this opposition in terms of competing realms of power: "Or are we stirring up the Lord's jealousy? Are we more powerful than him?" (1 Cor 10:22).[119]

Press, 1972) 2:790–820. For a full review of options and of primary sources, see H.-J. Klauck, *Herrenmahl und Hellenisticher Kult: Eine religionsgeschichtliche Untersuchung zum ersten Korintherbrief* (Neutestamentliche Abhandlungen 15; Münster: Aschendorff, 1982).

117. The case of the Mithras cult is particularly interesting, since Justin in *First Apology* 66 makes an explicit allusion to the similarity between "the mysteries of Mithra" and the Christian Eucharist: "Bread and a cup of water are given in the rites of initiation, and certain words are said." A more obscure reference is found also in Tertullian, *On the Prescription of Heretics* 40. The similarity is exploited by F. Cumont, *The Mysteries of Mithra*, trans. T. J. McCormack (Chicago: Open Court Publishing, 1910); but is evaluated more modestly by R. Merkelbach, *Mithras* (Königstein: Verlag Anton Hain, 1984) 132–39; and esp. J. P. Kane, "The Mithraic Cult Meal in Its Greek and Roman Environment," *Mithraic Studies*, ed. J. R. Hinnells (Proceedings of the First International Congress of Mithraic Studies; Manchester: Manchester University Press, 1975) 2:313–51, which provides a splendid survey of the current evidence concerning other cult meals as well.

118. 1 Cor 10:15-22, following the lead of the Septuagint of Psalm 95:5, which declares *pantes hoi theoi tōn ethnōn daimonia*.

119. The critical point here is not whether Paul has been influenced by the mysteries in this perception or is projecting on the mysteries his own perception. The critical point is that the comparison itself so profoundly reveals the experiential perception of a first-century participant at cultic meals. Paul is talking to them as "people who are perceptive" (*hōs phronimois*, 10:14), and he follows with questions introduced with *ouk* or *ouchi* (10:16, 18) that must be answered, "Yes, of course." Paul is therefore appealing to broad cultural perceptions. This is indicated further by the fact that he claims the same

3. The same questions can be directed to Jewish meals.[120] Since the point is not which types of meals preceded others or what the constitutive elements of a *chaburah* meal as opposed to a *pesach* meal might be, we are free to gather evidence from all available sources concerning the same range of questions.[121] What are the requirements for joining

koinonia for the participants in the cult of Israel "according to the flesh" (10:18).

120. The data here include: (1) Evidence for fellowship meals among Pharisaic associates, which phenomenologically resemble Greco-Roman *collegia;* for what sparse evidence there is apart from the Gospels, see E. P. Sanders, *Jewish Law from Jesus to the Mishnah* (London: SCM Press, 1990) 131–242. (2) Evidence for the *seder* of festivals, above all Passover; see B. M. Bokser, *The Origins of the Seder: The Passover Meal and Early Rabbinic Judaism* (Berkeley: University of California Press, 1984) esp. 14–28 and 50–66; J. Jeremias, *The Eucharistic Words of Jesus,* trans. N. Perrin (Philadelphia: Fortress Press, 1964). (3) Evidence for *berakoth* at synagogal services which bear strong resemblance to the Christian anaphora in *The Apostolic Constitutions;* see L. Bouyer, *Eucharist: Theology and Spirituality of the Eucharistic Prayer,* trans. C. U. Quinn (Notre Dame: University of Notre Dame Press, 1968). (4) Evidence for meals and prayers at Qumran in the Dead Sea Scrolls, in particular 1Qs 6:1-6 and 1Qsa 2:17-22; see K. G. Kuhn, "The Lord's Supper and the Communal Meal at Qumran," in *The Scrolls and the New Testament,* ed. K. Stendahl (New York: Crossroad, 1992) 65–93. (5) Evidence for meals among the Essenes (Josephus, *War* 2:129–43; Philo, *Every Good Man Is Free* 75–92; *Hypothetica* 11.1–11) — Philo says the Essenes "live together formed into clubs, bands of comradeship with common meals" (11.5) — and Therapeutae (Philo, *On the Contemplative Life* 30–89). (6) Evidence for meals or prayers in other Jewish literature, such as *Joseph and Aseneth;* for the evidence from the last categories, see R. D. Richardson, "Supplementary Essay: A Further Inquiry into Eucharistic Origins with Special Reference to New Testament Problems," in Lietzmann's *Mass and Lord's Supper,* 335–53. For the basic problems in dating Jewish liturgical materials, see N. Mitchell, "Jewish Liturgy in the Talmudic Period," *Resonance* 4 (1969) 18–44.

121. The search for influence and origins leads to a false focus on either the elements of a meal or the ideology of a meal. The approach taken by L. Bouyer in *Eucharist* is fundamentally sounder: rather than focus on the specific differences in ritual (which, so far as we can tell, are not so very great anyway), he concentrates on the common theme of blessing/thanksgiving that links all such Jewish meals.

meals[122] and the implications for being banned from the meal?[123] How are words and gestures complicit in weaving interpretation?[124] What is the function of memory in establishing fellowship between the living God and the people?[125] How do prayers of blessing relate the *koinonia* of the meal participants to the power of the living God?[126] We seek not

122. The main qualification is purity, as it is defined by each of the groups in question: see M. Smith, "The Dead Sea Sect in Relation to Ancient Judaism," *New Testament Studies* 7 (1960-61) 347–60, esp. 352; B. M. Bokser, *The Origins of the Seder,* 10–13, 53–62. Rituals of cleansing were therefore paramount: for the Pharisees, see Sanders, *Jewish Law,* 213–36; for the Essenes, a period of probation was also required before sharing in the common meal (Josephus, *War* 2:138–39); 1Qs 6:20-23 makes clear that knowledge of the teachings is a requirement at Qumran. The Essenes also made use of water for purification before meals according to Josephus, *War* 2:129, and 1Qs 3:4, 9.

123. I have already cited the passage in Josephus, *War* 2:143, which suggests that those excommunicated by the Essenes sometimes starved; note the exclusion from the meal for shorter periods as a means of correction in 1Qs 7:2-3, 16-17.

124. Jeremias, *Eucharistic Words,* 218–38, correctly emphasizes the coincidence of action and words in the Passover seder. But the same must also be the case with the meals of the Therapeutae, which involved teaching and hymn-singing as well as prayers (Philo, *Contemplative Life* 66, 75–78, 80, 84–89), and the Essenes, whose meals included prayers before and after the main meal (Josephus, *War* 2:131) and perhaps reading and teaching (Philo, *Every Good Man Is Free,* 81). This suggests that the meal described in *Joseph and Aseneth* 14–17 should not be disconnected from the prayers in 11–13. Likewise, analysis of meals in the Dead Sea Scrolls needs to include as well prayer such material as the "Songs for Sabbath Sacrifice" (4Q400-407; 11Q 5-6), the prayer fragments in 1Q34, 4Q507-9, 4Q503, and perhaps 1QSb.

125. The clarification of this point is particularly important, if one is not to mistake the language of "in memory of me" as though it were the memorial of a dead person, rather than the actualization of a living presence; see Jeremias, *Eucharistic Words,* 244–62; Bouyer, *Eucharist,* 84–90; W. R. Crockett, *Eucharist: Symbol of Transformation* (New York: Pueblo Publishing Company, 1989) 9–28.

126. As in the *berakah* over the cup in the Passover Haggadah, "Blessed art thou, O Lord, our God, King of the universe, who redeemed us and who redeemed our fathers from Egypt, and has brought us to this night, to eat thereon unleavened bread and bitter herbs. So, O Lord our God and God of

the distinctive shadings that divide Jews into sects but the shared meanings that enable them to see themselves and each other as members of a common people.

4. Analysis of meals in the New Testament, then, asks not which meal was earliest but rather what interconnections of meaning were available to the celebrants of meals and the readers of these compositions. Granting diversity of practice and wording in the beginning (it could scarcely be otherwise),[127] we can observe in our earliest sources the emergence of a shared range of symbols that point toward some significant degree of common experience and conviction already in the middle and late first century.[128]

The overwhelming impression given is that these meals involve a fellowship, not with dead kinfolk, but with the risen and living Lord Jesus.[129] Take the multiplication of the loaves:

our fathers, bring us to other festivals and holy days that come toward us in peace, happy in the building of thy city and joyous in thy service. And there may we eat of the sacrifices and paschal offerings, whose blood will come onto the walls of thy altar for acceptance. Then shall we give thanks to thee with a new song, for our redemption and the liberation of our soul. Blessed art thou, O Lord, Redeemer of Israel." The blessing contains: (1) memory of the past actions of God (2) actualized in the present company, (3) with hope for the future.

127. My complaint about the dissections of Lietzmann, Mack, and Chilton is not the premise of a plurality of practice — which makes good sense, given the circumstances of Christianity's expansion — but the pretense that (1) these strands can now adequately be distinguished, and that (2) the diversity represented fundamental disagreement among the parties. There is simply no basis in the sources for either premise.

128. See, e.g., the way that B. Reicke develops, in connection with these meals, the themes of service, joy (*hagaliasis*), and unity, in *Diakonie, Festfreude und Zelos in Verbindung mit der altchristlichen Agapenfeier* (Uppsala Universitets Arsskrift 1951:5; Uppsala: A. B. Lundesquistska, 1951). The method I suggest resembles that found in X. Leon-Dufour, *Sharing the Eucharistic Bread: The Witness of the New Testament,* trans. M. J. O'Connell (New York: Paulist Press, 1982) 281–302.

129. This is effectively argued by W. Elert, *Eucharist and Church Fellowship in the First Four Centuries,* trans. N. E. Nagel (St. Louis, Mo.: Concordia Publishing

Jesus is portrayed as the powerful Lord of creation in the midst of the people.[130] The language of the account, in turn, deliberately foreshadows that of the Last Supper: the gestures of breaking bread and blessing and giving to others are identical.[131] Read bifocally, as they are surely meant to be read, the stories convey the complex paschal mystery of death and resurrection, of a human life given for others so that they live more abundantly.[132] The discourse on the bread of life in John's gospel gives perfect expression to the conviction that "eating the flesh of the son of man" is a source of eternal life to those who so eat, precisely because Jesus is "the living bread that has come down from heaven."[133] The same conviction that the risen Jesus was present to his followers at shared meals after his death, not as a vague memory

House, 1966) 1–42; and it is seen clearly by O. Cullmann, "The Meaning of the Lord's Supper in Primitive Christianity," *Essays on the Lord's Supper*, trans. J. G. Davies (Ecumenical Studies in Worship 1; Richmond Va.: John Knox Press, 1958) 5–23.

130. The linking of the first feeding to the walking on the water in three of the Gospels (Matt 14:13-33; Mark 6:30-50; John 6:1-21) not only alludes to the Exodus story but also portrays Jesus himself as the one with power over the elements of creation: bread, fish, water. In Luke, the feeding is most closely attached to the revelation of Jesus as God's son in the transfiguration (9:10-17, 28-38).

131. Matt 14:19: *labōn . . . eulogēsen . . . klasas . . . edoken tois mathētais tous artous;* Matt 26: *labōn . . . arton . . . eulogēsas kai dous tois mathētais.* See also Mark 6:41 and 14:22, Luke 9:16 and 22:19 (with *eucharistēsas*).

132. For the way in which the Markan account in particular is crafted so as to link the mystery of Jesus identity with the drama of discipleship, see R. M. Fowler, *Loaves and Fishes: The Function of the Feeding Stories in the Gospel of Mark* (SBLDS 54; Chico, Calif.: Scholars Press, 1981).

133. Without taking up the vexed question of when or how this sensibility entered the Johannine tradition, it is obvious that the final redaction of this Gospel reflects what Bruce Vawter suggestively called "The Johannine Sacramentary," *Theological Studies* 17 (1956) 151–66. In an extraordinarily complex amalgam, the figure of Jesus is portrayed both as the fulfillment of Jewish feasts (especially Passover and Booths) and as the source of Christian initiation and meal rituals.

but as a present and commanding presence, is stated explicitly by Peter in Acts 10:41-42[134] and is vividly demonstrated in two Lukan appearance accounts and John's epilogue.[135] In short, the Gospel stories support the position that Christians gathered at meals in the name of Jesus would truly have considered him present as powerful Lord (see Matt 18:20).[136]

Examination of meals in 1 Corinthians, in turn, must

134. "They put him to death by hanging him on a tree; but God raised him on the third day and made him manifest, not to all the people but to us who were chosen by God as witnesses, who ate and drank with him after he rose from the dead. And he commanded us to preach to the people, and to testify that he is the one ordained by God to be the judge of the living and the dead" (Acts 10:39-42). The point here is not the form of the meal but the fact that it was in the presence of one who is alive and available to judge the living and the dead.

135. In Luke 24:30 we find: "When he was at table with them, he took the bread, and blessed, and broke it, and gave it to them. And their eyes were opened and they recognized him; and he vanished out of their sight," and the men later report how "he was known to them in the breaking of the bread." There is no mistaking in this account that Jesus is present at meals of followers not as a fond memory but as a living presence. Likewise, he joins the disciples as they eat in Luke 24:42-43, not only interpreting the scriptures but commanding them (24:49). Similarly in John 21:12-14, where Jesus shares with his disciples the bread and fish that they miraculously caught on his command (21:6): this Jesus is vividly alive and powerfully directive of their lives (21:15-23). Note that the issue here is not the historicity of the event nor the development of ritual; it is, rather, the symbolism of meals: these stories state unequivocally that those gathered after Jesus' death regarded him as more powerfully alive than before.

136. The same inference can be drawn from the transformative wonder Jesus performs at the wedding feast at Cana (John 2:1-11); the odd dissonance on this point in the Synoptic saying about fasting after the departure of the bridegroom (Mark 3:18-22) is perhaps one of the clearest examples of "the criterion of dissimilarity," for the overwhelming testimony otherwise is that the bridegroom is very much present in the meals celebrated after the resurrection. I have been emphasizing in this argument the presence of the risen Lord. Note must be taken as well of the element of eschatological expectation, found in the statement of Jesus at his last meal (Matt 26:29; Mark 14:25; Luke 22:18), as well as in 1 Cor 11:26: "For as often as you eat the bread and drink the cup, you proclaim the Lord's death until he comes," which is

include evidence from every part of the letter.[137] To evaluate Paul's statements in 11:23-26 without placing them within the implicit symbolization of meals embedded in the entire discussion of chapters 8-11, and above all without correlating them with 10:1-5, 10:14-22 and 5:3-13, is simply irresponsible. Nor should we assess 11:23-26 without showing how Paul's language about "discerning the body" at the meal (11:29) gets extended into an exposition of the church as the "body of Christ" in which all have "drunk the one Spirit" (12:13).

When these passages are read as clues to the understanding of communal meals, it becomes clear that Paul and his readers shared certain convictions and did not share others. They believed that when the church gathered "in the name of the Lord Jesus" (1 Cor 5:4), it was also in the presence of "the power of the Lord Jesus" (5:4); that the cup of blessing that they shared at meals in this name was a *koinonia* in the body of Christ, just as the cup of blessing was a *koinonia* in the blood of Christ (10:16); that, therefore, just as sharing the table of demons was a participation in the power of demons, so also was sharing at this meal a participation in the power of Christ (see 10:22). For Paul and his readers, when they came together to eat (11:33) a meal in the name of Jesus (5:4), or the "Lord's Supper" (11:21), the power of the resurrected one was present, just as it was when they "spoke by the Spirit of God" (12:3) in glossolalia. Their eating and drinking was, therefore, of "supernatural food and supernatural drink" (10:3-4).[138]

probably to be understood together with the acclamation, *maranatha* (1 Cor 16:22; see *Didache* 10:6).

137. Remarkably, 1 Cor 5:1-8 is usually left out of such discussions, despite the obvious presence of the theme of eating with the immoral (5:11), which connects to the discussion of chaps. 8-10 as well as to 15:32-34, and the statement "Christ our pasch has been sacrificed (*pascha hēmōn etythē christos*), therefore let us celebrate the festival," which connects to the discussion in the participation in sacrifices in 9:13-14 and 10:18.

138. If Paul is capable of saying of the wilderness generation, *pantes de auto*

It was the awareness of this present power that made convincing the expectation of Jesus's future coming (5:5; 11:26) and role in God's final triumph (15:20-29). It was this present power that made exclusion from the meal so threatening.[139] It was this present power that made behavior diminishing of the fellowship a source of threat to the well-being of the community.[140] Paul and his readers also presumably shared the conviction that the meals celebrating the presence of the living one were at the same time an *anamnēsis* of his gift of self-donation, so that Paul can refer to the words said by Jesus over the bread and cup "on the night he was betrayed" as a part of the tradition that he received from the Lord and in turn handed on to them (11:23).

When read with literary unity, in other words, 1 Corinthians suggests that the meals of the church gathered at Corinth in the name of Jesus symbolized *both* the death and resurrection of Jesus as part of the same paschal mystery and placed those celebrating such meals into "fellowship with [God's] son, Jesus Christ [the] Lord" (1 Cor 1:9). I speak deliberately of the paschal mystery because of the unmistakable implication of 1 Cor 5:7, which, in the context of eating (5:12) in the gathered assembly (5:4), says, "For Christ our Pasch has been sacrificed. Let us therefore celebrate the festival, not with the old leaven, the leaven of malice and evil, but with the unleavened bread of sincerity and truth" (5:8).

Here is the point at which Paul and his readers seem to diverge, namely, the *moral* implications of sharing a meal

---

pneumatikon brōma ephagon, kai pantes to auto pneumatikon epion pōma. epinon gar ek pneumatikēs akolouthousēs petras, hē de petra de ēn ho christos, then how much the more would he understand it of his own church?

139. It was a handing over to satan "for the destruction of the flesh, that his spirit may be saved in the day of the Lord Jesus" (5:5); compare 1 Tim 1:20.

140. "That is why many of you are weak and ill and some have died" (11:33).

in the presence of One who gave himself as a sacrifice for others. Paul's readers seem to think that there is no link between the power and a moral imperative. Paul insists that there is. To disregard the "body" that is the community by disregarding and acting contemptuously toward the poor brings judgment on the community in the form of illness and death, precisely because the magic at this meal is mediated through a gift of bread and wine imprinted with the Messiah's own self-donation for the sake of others. Although Paul agrees therefore that "food does not commend us to God" (8:8) and allows for some flexibility on the issue of eating foods associated with idolatry (10:25), he is adamant on the point that immoral behavior — and in particular behavior that is self-aggrandizing or selfish and therefore destructive of community identity — must be ruthlessly banished from the common meals. They are to "cast out the old leaven" (5:7), that is, excommunicate a brother living at a level below that even of pagans. They are "not even to eat with such a person" (5:11), for such behavior negatively affects the entire community ("a little leaven leavens the whole lump" [5:7]).

Paul's point is that the mystery of death and resurrection celebrated in the meal means that they are to die to an old way of life and rise to a new way of living (Rom 6:1-11). It is measured by the "law of Christ," that is, the messianic pattern of "bearing one another's burdens" (Gal 6:2). The "Lord's Supper," if it is really to be the Lord's Supper (11:20), must demonstrate this new way of living, which involves respecting the needs of others more than one's own (11:21). Note the pertinence of 15:32 in this connection: "If the dead are not raised, 'let us eat and drink, for tomorrow we die.' Do not be deceived: 'Bad company ruins good morals.'"

In sum, the writings of the New Testament emphatically support the understanding of Christian meals not as a fellowship with the dead in general or the dead in a kinship group but specifically as a fellowship in the powerful life of

God mediated through the resurrected Jesus and proleptic of his future triumph.[141]

5. The multiple meals reported in apocryphal writings can then be assessed from the same perspective. The operative question is not what the formal elements of the meal might be,[142] but within what sort of symbolic structure (provided by the respective literary compositions describing them) are these meals to be understood?[143] The same

141. The "joy" that characterized such meals was not that of simple good fellowship or of the memory of a comrade but the specifically eschatological joy connected to God's triumph in the resurrection of Jesus. See A. B. Du Toit, *Der Aspekt der Freude im urchristlichen Abendmahl* (Winterthur: Verlag P. G. Keller, 1965); see also Klauck, *Herrenmahl und Hellenisticher Kult*, 365–74.

142. Once more, the supposition of ritual diversity is not only appropriate but demanded by the evidence. Justin, for example, says that when bread and wine and water are brought, "the president in like manner offers prayers and thanksgivings, according to his ability" (*Apology* 67).

143. In the *Acts of John* 84, for example, Satan is driven from all the Christian realities, including "eucharists" and "love-feasts," and in 85, John, in the sepulchre, pronounces a blessing over the bread addressed to "thee Lord Jesus Christ" as "God now and forever," whereas "we thy servants, that are assembled and gathered with good cause, give thanks to thee, O Holy One." He then gives all the brethren the Lord's Eucharist (86). Similarly, in *Acts of John*, 108, Jesus is addressed as the living one, "who ever seest the deeds of all and dwellest in all and art everywhere present, encompassing all things and filling all things; Christ Jesus, God, Lord, that with thy gifts and thy mercy protectest those that hope in thee." This prayer precedes the thanksgiving over the bread, which includes these words, "We glorify thy resurrection, that is shown us through thee.... Thou alone, O Lord, art the root of immortality and the fount of incorruption..." (109). Jesus is likewise addressed in the eucharistic prayer of the *Acts of Thomas* 27. In *Acts of Thomas* 49, we read, "Jesus who hast made us worthy to partake of the Eucharist of thy holy body and blood, behold we make bold to approach the eucharist, and to call upon thy holy name; come thou and have fellowship with us!" The prayer continues, "Come and partake with us in this eucharist, which we celebrate in thy name, and in the love-feast in which we are gathered together at thy call" (50) and after the prayer, the mark of the cross is inscribed on the bread. Compare also the eucharistic prayers of *Acts of Thomas* 124, 133, and finally, 158, which concludes, "Because thou didst rise and come to life again let us come to life again, and live and stand before thee in righteous judgment." There can be

questions can to be asked of material in other narrative,[144] epistolary,[145] catechetical[146] and apologetic compositions[147]

no question that the fellowship here celebrated at a meal is a fellowship with the living Lord, not a fond remembrance of the dead.

144. It is obvious, for example, that the *Martyrdom of Polycarp* (ca. 160?) not only conforms the bishop's death to the passion of Jesus but does so in explicitly eucharistic terms, so that he is perceived in the fire as "bread that is being baked" (15:2). Polycarp's "eucharistic prayer" at the moment of his execution therefore deserves special attention: "I bless thee, that thou hast granted me this day an hour, that I may share, among the number of the martyrs, *in the cup of thy Christ, for the resurrection to everlasting life, both of soul and body in the immortality of the Holy Spirit . . .*" (14:2, emphasis added).

145. Like Polycarp, Ignatius of Antioch expresses his martyr piety in eucharistic terms, as he longs to become "the pure bread of Christ" (*Rom.* 4:1-2). What is too seldom noted is the way in which his language about the Eucharist in *Smyrneans* 7:1-2 (those who avoid the Eucharist are those who deny the flesh of the savior in his death and resurrection) is consistent with the emphasis throughout *Smyrneans* on the reality of both Jesus' passion and resurrection: "He ate and drank with them as a being of flesh though he was united in spirit with the father" (3:3; see also 1:1; 2:1; 5:1). It is out of this concern for the integrity of the mystery that he insists that the only valid Eucharist is one celebrated by the bishop (8:1).

146. The *Didache* has a eucharistic prayer that has no mention of the "words of institution," but it is far from a simple fellowship meal. The "broken bread scattered on the mountains" (9:4) may be the only evocation of the death of Jesus (melded with the imagery of the feeding of the multitude), but the thanks for "life and knowledge" (9:2; 9:3) and "knowledge, faith and immortality (*athanasia*)" (10:2) suggest the resurrection of Jesus, as does the reference to "spiritual food and drink" and "eternal light" that come through Jesus (10:4), and the use of *marana tha* (10:6). Note furthermore that the Eucharist is to be celebrated on "the Lord's day of the Lord" (14:1), with only baptized persons present (10:5) and after the confession of sins (14:1). The meal, furthermore, is referred to as a "sacrifice" (*thysia*) in 14:1-2.

147. The eucharistic account in Justin Martyr's *First Apology* is usually singled out because it contains the "words of institution." Equally significant is his comment, "For not as common bread and common drink do we receive these, but in like manner as Jesus Christ our Savior, having been made flesh by the Word of God, had both flesh and blood for our salvation, so likewise have we been taught that the food which is blessed by the prayer of his word, and from which our blood and flesh by transmutation are nourished, is the flesh and blood of that Jesus who was made flesh" (66). And later, "Sunday is

that has significance for understanding eucharistic symbolism, even if not containing a ritual. Within what symbolic framework do these respective accounts demand to be read? Specifically, in what sense is *koinonia* to be understood?[148]

6. Finally, the archeological evidence can be read, now not simply within a complex code of cultural meanings given by Greco-Roman myths and symbols, but as well within the increasingly complex world of specifically Christian symbols.[149]

This sort of study will not determine what a specific group of Christians did at specific meals or what they might have meant by what they did. Nor will it be able to delineate how one liturgical form developed into another. What it can do is contextualize Christian language about meals in a more adequate fashion than that provided by the historical accounts we have surveyed, so that at the very least we might begin to understand how such meals and the elaborate liturgical forms based upon those meals never ceased, from those days to these, to spell magic for those who passed broken bread from hand to hand and whispered the name of the One in whose powerful presence they ate.

the day on which we all hold our common assembly, because it is the first day on which God, having wrought a change in the darkness and matter, made the world; and Jesus Christ our savior on the same day rose from the dead" (67).

148. These citations make clear that, with whatever variations in form and expression, the *religious conviction* underlying all the common meals of the Christians concerned the presence of the Risen Lord Jesus and that therefore the *religious experience* which they expressed was not one of fellowship simply with other believers, still less a fellowship of the community's dead, or even a memorial of a dead teacher, but was a *koinonia* in the resurrection power of Jesus.

149. It is in the light of this complex literature, extending from Paul to Tertullian, that one must assess, for example, the appearance on a Christian sarcophagus, side by side, of scenes depicting the resurrection of Lazarus, baptism of Jesus by John, the Jonah cycle, the *sol invictus*, and finally, the shared meal. Does the literature I have surveyed provide the appropriate code for this combination of iconographic symbols or not? My argument is that, overwhelmingly, it does.

EPILOGUE

The chapters in this book have advanced three arguments, two of them explicit, one implicit. The first and most obvious argument is made by the three case studies of baptism, glossolalia, and meals. By coming at all-too-familiar topics from a slightly different angle, these studies show that there is still much to be learned about early Christianity as a religion. Each study skims the surface, but each also suggests depths of further research and investigation that might fruitfully be engaged. Not only is there more to be learned about each of these subjects, but other religious aspects of early Christianity also invite the same sort of investigation. Before the theoretical argument extended itself so lengthily, I had intended to treat the subject of healing. With this subject, again, everything has been said at one level (the form-critical and comparative analysis of healing stories) and almost nothing at another level (the phenomenology of healing as a religious practice). The topic of healing would have been particularly attractive because it would have brought into consideration texts other than the predictably Pauline, namely, the Letter of James and the Apocryphal Acts. As with healing, so with other specific topics (the phenomenology of prayer and of visions comes to mind). Just as important, the links between topics, such as the connection in early Christianity between the experience of power and the form of the new life generated by that experience (or, to put it another way, the connection between the experiential and the moral) can come to light. In these forays, we have caught glimpses, but there is more to do.

The second line of argument was explicitly stated in the first two chapters and was implicit in the case studies. To get at the specifically religious dimension of these ancient texts, an approach other than the narrowly historical or theological is necessary. As I have suggested, the historical-critical paradigm — in its older and newer forms — is not only impatient with the category of experience. It does not know what to do with it, almost inevitably shifting away from attention to the particular toward some sort of developmental scheme. The same is true of so-called New Testament Theology, which maintains its precarious existence precisely by suppressing the specificity of the texts and their capacity to surprise. Both the historical and theological paradigms — at least as usually practiced — tend toward the general and the abstract, whereas this religious language remains specific and concrete.

My call for a phenomenological approach is not the advancement of a new "method" but the invitation to a way of seeing, a way that begins with the assumption that religious language and religious experience are actually about something and deserving of attention in their own right. It then seeks ways of getting at that register of the texts more adequately. While history and theology might be forgiven for their disinterest or inability here, religious studies cannot. It is one of the most disappointing — even disturbing — paradoxes, that academic centers founded precisely for the purpose of carrying out such investigation into the religious dimensions of human experience have in some cases become the main despisers of the enterprise. The present tendency to dismiss phenomenologists of religion as crypto-theologians and to elevate social-scientific methods as the only intellectually legitimate way to study religion leaves what is most interesting about religion unexamined.

It is in this context that my frequent engagement in these essays with Jonathan Z. Smith should be placed. When I began reading for this project, I was aware of Smith's substantial reputation in the field of religious studies and had read a handful of his classic studies. I was determined to read as much of him as I could get hands on, because I wanted him to represent the best in another and equally valid approach to ancient religions. I wanted to be able to say, "That's one way of doing it, here's another."

The more I read, however, the more problematic his work appeared, for two reasons. First, I became increasingly aware of the way in which his undoubted brilliance and skill sometimes substituted for solid and sustained argumentation. Smith's penchant for the obscure *exemplum* is extraordinarily effective in deflecting criticism: if he can cite these obscure authorities, we assume, then he obviously must control all other authorities equally well. But I began to see that this is a false assumption, that in fact Smith's work (while in many respects useful precisely because of his many stunning insights into broad patterns) was not undeserving of close criticism. Second, I grew increasingly convinced that Smith's own approach was as aggressively hegemonic as theology had ever been. I may be willing to grant Smith's reductionistic readings as having a certain validity, but I now doubt that Smith is willing to grant validity to anything else than his reductionistic readings.

The case studies carried out here should demonstrate, however, that a phenomenological approach to earliest Christianity is not a surreptitious form of theology. Indeed, it makes as vigorous a use of historical, sociological, psychological, and anthropological perspectives as any reductionistic approach. The difference is that the phenomenon is not itself eliminated in the process but remains the steady focus of attention. This is also what distinguishes the rich use of ancient comparative materials from Greco-Roman and Jewish cultures. Since the issues are not those of dependence or development, comparison can be engaged freely and without prejudice. And oddly enough, precisely such patient attention given to particular phenomena in the ancient world enables them to be used for discussion of "broader patterns" in the field of religious studies.

The third argument carried by these essays has been largely implicit, but was expressed by the title of the original lectures, namely, "the power of the resurrection." Against that tendency in contemporary scholarship that reduces all language about power to the level of political positioning, I argue that serious engagement with earliest Christianity demands recognition that its adherents had quite another view: they considered themselves caught up by, defined by, a power not in their control but rather controlling them, a power that derived from the crucified and raised Messiah Jesus. Indeed, I am convinced that any effort to interpret the writings of early Christianity (and here I am thinking of noncanonical as well as canonical literature) that does not proceed on this assumption is fated to fall short of a satisfying interpretation.

Against that tendency in contemporary scholarship, finally, that seeks to fragment early Christianity into as many segments as there are separable strands of tradition, and insists that only some few of these strands had any such conviction concerning the power of the resurrection, I submit that the overwhelming amount of evidence — including the evidence of these case studies, above all that dealing with meals — argues precisely the other way. Despite the diversity within earliest Christianity, a diversity so obvious that it scarcely needs underscoring, the evidence also suggests that from the beginning a certain unity of experience and conviction was sufficient to distinguish this collection of people from others in the Mediterranean world and to provide the basis for its life, movement, change, and growth. This implicit — yet no less real — unity of experience and conviction centered on the presence of transforming power among them because of the resurrection of Jesus.

There exists, in fact, no positive evidence for a movement in the decades after Jesus' death that was not shaped by belief in his resurrection. If there had been such a movement, it was short-lived and has left no traces in the literature, even the earliest of which is marked by the conviction that the one who was crucified is now more powerfully alive. Christianity came to birth because certain people were convinced that they had experienced God's transforming power through the resurrection of Jesus. A scholarship based not on this fact but on its denial may be a study of something or other in antiquity but it certainly is not the study of early Christianity.

INDEX OF
BIBLICAL REFERENCES

INDEX OF
PERSONS AND SUBJECTS